Butterflies

OF **MICHIGAN**

FIELD GUIDE

by Jaret C. Daniels

Adventure Publications
Cambridge, Minnesota

ACKNOWLEDGEMENTS:

I would like to thank my wife, Stephanie, for her unending patience dealing with the countless number of caterpillars, butterflies and associated plant material that happens to always find a way into our home. Thanks to my parents for encouraging my early interest in biology.

Photo credits by photographer and page number:
Cover photos: Eastern Tiger Swallowtail by Jaret C. Daniels; Bog Copper by Jay Cossey
Thomas J. Allen: 42 (larva), 44 (larva), 48 (ventral, larva), 70 (larva), 72 (larva), 76 (larva), 78 (larva), 84 (larva), 94 (larva), 96 (larva), 98 (larva), 104 (larva), 108 (larva), 114 (larva), 120 (larva), 124 (larva), 126 (larva), 132 (larva), 134 (larva), 136 (larva), 138 (larva), 140 (larva), 142 (larva), 144 (larva), 150 (larva), 152 (larva), 154 (larva), 156 (larva), 158 (larva), 160 (larva), 162 (larva), 164 (larva), 166 (larva), 176 (larva), 178 (larva), 182 (larva), 184 (larva), 186 (larva), 192 (larva), 198 (larva), 200 (larva), 202 (larva), 208 (larva), 212 (larva), 220 (larva), 226 (larva), 228 (larva), 230 (larva), 232 (larva), 238 (larva), 242 (larva), 244 (larva), 246 (larva), 252 (larva), 254 (larva), 256 (larva), 260 (larva), 270 (larva), 272 (larva), 274 (larva), 278 (larva), 280 (larva), 284 (larva), 288 (larva), 290 (larva), 292 (larva), 306 (ventral), 310 (larva), 314 (larva), 322 (larva), 324 (larva), 326 (larva), 332 (larva), 344 (larva), 352 (larva) **ATL (Elton Woodbury Collection):** 90 (both), 104 (ventral), 112 (larva), 118 (ventral), 130 (ventral), 174 (larva), 202 (ventral), 284 (dorsal), 286 (ventral), 306 (dorsal), 308 (larva) **Susan Borkin:** 128 (larva), 234 (all) **Bill Bouton:** 92 (F dorsal), 102 (M dorsal, ventral) **Rick & Nora Bowers:** 42 (dorsal), 44 (dorsal, ventral), 68 (M dorsal), 70 (M dorsal, ventral), 86 (F dorsal), 98 (M dorsal), 110 (ventral), 146 (M dorsal), 152 (M dorsal, F dorsal, ventral), 164 (dorsal, ventral), 170 (all), 178 (ventral), 184 (dorsal), 196 (dorsal, ventral), 204 (dorsal), 240 (dorsal), 246 (F dorsal), 250 (ventral, larva), 254 (M dorsal, F dorsal, ventral), 258 (M ventral), 294 (ventral), 304 (all), 326 (F dorsal, ventral) **Jim P. Brock/ Bowers Photo:** 110 (dorsal), 276 (larva), 338 (ventral, larva) **Will Cook:** 226 (larva) **Jay Cossey:** 64 (ventral), 74 (M dorsal), 82 (M dorsal), 88 (M dorsal, F dorsal, ventral), 96 (ventral), 116 (F dorsal), 200 (dorsal), 230 (dorsal), 262 (F dorsal), 332 (dorsal), 334 (dorsal), 340 (dorsal, summer ventral) **Robert P. Dana:** 100 (F dorsal), 168 (M dorsal, F dorsal, larva), 266 (M dorsal, F dorsal, larva) **Randy Emmitt:** 42 (ventral), 48 (dorsal), 58 (dorsal), 66 (F ventral), 72 (ventral), 76 (ventral), 78 (M dorsal, ventral), 80 (M dorsal, ventral), 108 (ventral), 112 (M ventral, F ventral), 120 (ventral), 122 (ventral), 124 (M dorsal, F dorsal, ventral), 134 (dorsal), 138 (F dorsal, F ventral, M dorsal), 140 (dorsal), 142 (dorsal), 144 (M dorsal, ventral), 148 (ventral), 156 (dorsal, ventral), 160 (dorsal), 162 (M dorsal), 166 (M dorsal), 174 (M dorsal, F dorsal, ventral), 176 (F dorsal), 178 (M dorsal, F dorsal), 180 (ventral), 182 (dorsal, ventral), 186 (M dorsal, ventral), 202 (dorsal), 208 (ventral), 216 (dorsal), 224 (dorsal), 230 (ventral), 238 (M dorsal, F dorsal), 248 (M ventral), 250 (dorsal), 256 (F dorsal, ventral), 260 (M dorsal, ventral), 270 (ventral), 272 (M dorsal, F dorsal), 280 (M dorsal, F dorsal, ventral), 284 (ventral), 290 (M dorsal, ventral), 308 (summer dorsal, winter dorsal), 314 (ventral), 332 (larva), 352 (ventral) **Jeff M. Fengler:** 88 (larva), 158 (dorsal) **David Hanson:** 252 (dorsal), 360 (ventral) **Paul A. Opler:** 168 (M ventral), 264 (dorsal), 266 (male ventral), 294 (dorsal), 338 (M dorsal) **David K. Parshall:** 102 (F dorsal), 114 (M dorsal), 136 (M dorsal), 154 (M dorsal), 158 (ventral), 188 (ventral), 264 (ventral), 276 (dorsal, ventral) **Jeff Pippen:** 76 (M dorsal), 82 (F dorsal, ventral), 162 (F dorsal), 212 (M dorsal "alope", ventral "alope"), 244 (dorsal), 260 (F dorsal) **Mike Reese:** 128 (dorsal, ventral), 154 (ventral, F dorsal) **Jane Ruffin:** 136 (M dorsal, M ventral, F variant), 236 (M dorsal) **Judy Semroc:** 252 (ventral) **Jeremy Tatum:** 340 (larva) **John & Gloria Tveten:** 50 (all), 52 (all), 62 (larva), 66 (dark-form F ventral), 68 (larva), 72 (M dorsal), 74 (F dorsal), 80 (larva), 94 (ventral), 106 (green larva, red larva), 108 (dorsal), 118 (larvae), 130 (M dorsal), 134 (ventral), 146 (larva), 150 (larva), 172 (F ventral, larva), 176 (M dorsal, "pocahontas" ventral), 190 (all), 192 (dorsal, ventral), 198 (dorsal, ventral), 208 (dorsal), 216 (ventral, larva), 228 (dorsal), 232 (dorsal, ventral), 238 (M ventral), 242 (dorsal), 246 (M dorsal), 268 (M dorsal, ventral), 274 (dorsal, ventral), 278 (ventral), 282 (M dorsal), 286 (M dorsal, ventral), 288 (M dorsal, M ventral), 292 (dorsal, ventral), 298 (M dorsal, F dorsal, larva), 314 (dorsal), 316 (larva), 318 (larva), 322 (dorsal), 334 (ventral, larva), 340 (spring ventral), 342 (M dorsal), 348 (dorsal), 350 (M dorsal), 354 (M dorsal), 356 (M dorsal), 358 (F dorsal), 360 (dorsal, larva) **John & Gloria Tveten/KAC Productions:** 142 (ventral) **Jaret C. Daniels:** all other photos. To the best of the publisher's knowledge, all photos except those of the Macoun's Arctic are of live larvae and butterflies.

Book and Cover Design by Jonathan Norberg
Illustrations by Julie Martinez
Range Maps and Phenograms by Anthony Hertzel

10 9 8 7 6 5
Butterflies of Michigan Field Guide
Copyright © 2005 by Jaret C. Daniels
Published by Adventure Publications, an imprint of AdventureKEEN
310 Garfield Street South
Cambridge, Minnesota 55008
(800) 678-7006
All rights reserved
Printed in China
ISBN 978-1-59193-098-3 (pbk.)

TABLE OF CONTENTS

Introduction

WATCHING BUTTERFLIES IN MICHIGAN

People are rapidly discovering the joy of butterfly gardening and watching. Both are simple, fun and rewarding ways to explore the natural world and bring the beauty of nature closer. Few other forms of wildlife are more attractive or as easily observed as butterflies. Butterflies occur just about everywhere, from suburban gardens and urban parks to rural meadows and remote natural areas. Regardless of where you may live, there are a variety of butterflies to be seen. *Butterflies of Michigan* is for those who wish to identify and learn more about the butterflies found in this wonderful Great Lake state.

There are more than 725 species of butterflies in North America north of Mexico. While the majority of these are regular breeding residents, others show up from time to time as rare tropical strays. In Michigan, over 150 different butterflies have been recorded. Within this mix, there are some that occur commonly over a large portion of the continent and others that are rare or limited to only a few areas, including two federally endangered species. Although such numbers pale in comparison to many tropical countries, Michigan boasts a rich and diverse butterfly fauna—a unique bounty that is just waiting to be enjoyed! To aid in that exploration, this field guide covers all resident and stray species recorded within the state.

In total area (land and water), Michigan covers some 96,805 square miles, making it the largest state east of the Mississippi River and the eleventh largest overall. The state's total land area encompasses approximately 37 million acres or 56,804 square miles, and includes 3,288 miles of Great Lakes shoreline and numerous islands. The state also boasts more than 11,000 inland lakes and 36,000 miles of rivers and streams. Elevations within Michigan range from 572 feet in the southeastern corner of the Lower Peninsula near the shore of Lake Erie to 1,979 feet at the peak of Mount Arvon in the western Upper Peninsula.

Michigan is literally a state divided. Its two separate and unique peninsulas are surrounded by four of the five Great Lakes and connected by the five-mile-long Mackinac

Bridge. The elongated Upper Peninsula is bordered to the north by Lake Superior and to the south and east by Lake Michigan and Lake Huron. Two major physiographic regions—the eastern lowlands and crystalline uplands—characterize the Upper Peninsula. The eastern lowlands are relatively flat with scattered rolling hills. To the west, the crystalline uplands represent one of the most scenic regions in the entire state, with resistant, igneous rock areas that have been sculpted by continental glaciation. Here, the Porcupine and Huron mountains provide rugged, hilly terrain, prominent rock formations and the highest point in the state at Mount Arvon.

The mitten-shaped Lower Peninsula is surrounded on three sides by Lake Michigan, Lake Heron and Lake Erie. Along the western shore are extensive beaches and pristine dunes that have built up over time as a result of the prevailing westerly winds. Further inland, the southern half of the Lower Peninsula consists of glacial moraines and dissected plateaus that are characterized by broadleaf forests, oak savannahs and a variety of prairie communities. Here, the topography is relatively flat with low rolling hills. Northward, the terrain becomes dominated by more massive moraines and higher-elevation, hilly landscapes.

Michigan extends over 400 miles from top to bottom and transects a broad latitudinal gradient. As a result, the state's climate varies considerably, with the mean annual temperatures of northern and southern counties differing by almost 10 degrees F. Michigan's climate, location, topography and past geological activity influence the number and diversity of botanical communities present. The end result is a broad array of habitats from pine forests and tallgrass prairie to acid bogs and beach dunes that support an equally diverse array of butterflies, including some that are extremely localized and habitat restricted.

Michigan is at the crossroads of a wonderful mix of species' ranges, hosting those with true northern affinities and occasionally welcoming others with more southern tastes. As a butterfly enthusiast, it's hard to ask for much more. Get outside and enjoy Michigan's natural riches!

WHAT ARE BUTTERFLIES?

Butterflies are insects. Along with moths, they comprise the Order Lepidoptera, a combination of Greek words meaning scale-winged, and can be differentiated from all other insects on that basis. Their four wings, as well as body, are typically almost entirely covered with numerous tiny scales. Overlapping like shingles on a roof, they make up the color and pattern of a butterfly's wings. Although generally wide and flat, some scales may be modified in shape, depending on the species and body location.

Butterflies and moths are closely related and often difficult to quickly tell apart. Nonetheless, there are some basic differences that are easy to identify even in the field. Generally, butterflies fly during the day, have large colorful wings that are held vertically together over the back when at rest, and bear distinctly clubbed antennae. In contrast, most moths are nocturnal. They are usually overall drabber in color and may often resemble dirty, hairy butterflies. At rest, they tend to hold their wings to the sides, and have feathery or threadlike antennae.

The following illustration points out the basic parts of a butterfly.

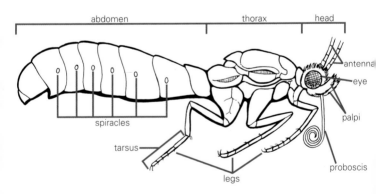

BUTTERFLY BASICS

Adult butterflies share several common characteristics, including six jointed legs, two compound eyes, two antennae, a hard exoskeleton and three main body segments: the head, thorax and abdomen.

Head

The head has two large compound eyes, two long clubbed antennae, a proboscis and two labial palpi. The rounded compound eyes are composed of hundreds of tiny individually lensed eyes. Together, they render a single, somewhat pixelated color image. Adult butterflies have good vision and are able to distinguish light in both the visible and ultraviolet range. Above the eyes are two long and slender antennae that are clubbed at the tip. They bear various sensory structures that help with orientation and smell. At the front of the head, below the eyes, are two protruding, hairy, brush-like structures called labial palpi. They serve to house and protect the proboscis, or tongue. The proboscis is a long, flexible, straw-like structure used for drinking fluids. It can be tightly coiled below the head or extended when feeding. The length of a butterfly's proboscis determines the types of flowers and other foods from which it may feed.

Thorax

Directly behind the head is the thorax. It is a large muscular portion divided into three segments that bear six legs and four wings. Each leg is jointed and contains five separate sections, the last of which is the tarsus (pl. tarsi) or foot, which bears a tiny, hooked claw at the end. In addition to enabling the butterfly to securely grasp leaves, branches or other objects, the tarsi have sensory structures that are used to taste. Adult females scratch a leaf surface with their front tarsi to release the leaf's chemicals and taste whether they have found the correct host plant. Above the legs are two pairs of wings. Made up of two thin membranes supported by rigid veins, the generally large, colorful wings are covered with millions of tiny scales that overlap like shingles on a roof. The wings serve a variety of critical functions, including flight, thermoregulation, sex recognition, camouflage, mimicry and predator deflection.

Abdomen

The last section of a butterfly's body is the long, slender abdomen. It is comprised of ten segments and contains the reproductive, digestive and excretory systems along with a series of small lateral holes, called spiracles, for air exchange. The reproductive organs or genitalia are located at the end of the abdomen. Male butterflies have two modified structures called claspers that are used to grasp the female during copulation. Females possess a genital opening for mating and a second opening for egg laying. While these structures are often difficult to see in certain species, females generally have a much larger, "fatter-looking" abdomen because they carry a large complement of eggs.

THE BUTTERFLY LIFE CYCLE

All butterflies pass through a life cycle consisting of four developmental stages: egg, larva, pupa and adult. Regardless of adult size, they begin life as a small egg. A female butterfly may lay her eggs singly, in small clusters or in large groupings on or near the appropriate host plant. Once an egg hatches, the tiny larva begins feeding almost immediately. Butterfly larvae are herbivores—with the exception of Harvester larvae, which eat aphids—and they essentially live to eat. As a result, they can grow at an astonishing rate. All insects including butterflies have an external skeleton. In order to grow, a developing caterpillar (or larva) must shed its skin, or molt, several times during its life. Each time the larva does, it discards its old, tight skin to make room for the new, roomier and often different-looking skin underneath. These different stages in a caterpillar's growth are called instars. Once fully grown, the larva stops eating and seeks a safe place to pupate. It usually attaches itself to a branch, twig or other surface with silk and molts for the last time to reveal the pupa (or chrysalis). Inside, the larval structures are broken down and reorganized into the form of an adult butterfly. At the appropriate time, the pupa splits open and a beautiful new butterfly emerges. The adult hangs quietly and begins to expand its crumpled wings by slowly forcing blood through the veins. After a few hours, its wings are fully hardened and the butterfly is ready to fly.

BUTTERFLY FAMILIES

Butterflies can be divided into five major families: Hesperiidae, Lycaenidae, Nymphalidae, Papilionidae and Pieridae. The members of each family have certain basic characteristics and behaviors that can be useful for identification. Keep in mind that the features listed are only generalities, and that there may be individual exceptions.

Hesperiidae: Skippers

Skippers are small- to medium-sized butterflies with robust, hairy bodies and relatively compact wings. They are generally brown, orange or white and their antennae bear short, distinct hooks at the tip. Adults have a quick and erratic flight, usually low to the ground. There are four main subfamilies: banded skippers, intermediate skipper, giant-skippers and spread-wing skippers.

Banded skippers (Subfamily Hesperiinae) are small brown or orange butterflies with somewhat pointed forewings. Many have dark markings or distinct black forewing stigmas. They readily visit flowers and hold their wings together over the back while feeding. Adults often perch or rest in a characteristic posture with forewings held partially open and hindwings separated and lowered further.

Intermediate Skippers (Subfamily Heteropterinae) are small, brown and orange butterflies. Many have distinctive spot patterns and lack the short extension at the tip of the antennae (called the apiculus) that characterize other skippers. The adults have a relatively low, weak flight and bask with wings partially open. The Arctic Skipper is Michigan's only representative of this small subfamily.

As their name suggests, *giant-skippers* (Subfamily Megathyminae) dwarf most other members of the family. They are medium-sized brown butterflies with yellow markings and thick, robust bodies. The adults have a fast and rapid flight. Males establish territories and generally perch on low vegetation. Adults do not visit flowers.

Spread-wing skippers (Subfamily Pyrginae) are generally dark, dull-colored butterflies with wide wings. Most have small, light spots on the forewings. Some species have hindwing tails. The adults often feed, rest and perch with their wings outstretched. They readily visit flowers.

Lycaenidae: Gossamer Wings

This diverse family includes coppers, harvesters, blues, hairstreaks and metalmarks. The adults are small and often brilliantly colored but easily overlooked. Throughout the state, blues and hairstreaks predominate, with only one harvester, one metalmark and five coppers.

Coppers (Subfamily Lycaeninae) are small, sexually dimorphic butterflies. The upper wing surfaces of most species are ornately colored with metallic reddish orange or purple. Many eastern species are associated with bogs, wet meadows and marshes. Populations are often quite localized but may be numerous when encountered. Adults typically scurry close to the ground with a quick flight and frequently visit available flowers or perch on low-growing vegetation with their wings held partially open.

The *harvester* (Subfamily Miletinae) is the only North American member of this unique, primarily Old World, subfamily. It is our only butterfly with carnivorous larvae. Instead of feeding on plants, the larvae devour woolly aphids. The adults do not visit flowers, but sip honeydew, a sugary secretion produced by their host aphids.

Aptly named, *blues* (Subfamily Polyommatinae) are generally bright blue on the wings above. The sexes differ and females may be brown or dark gray. The wings beneath are typically whitish gray with dark markings and distinct hindwing eyespots. The eyes are wrapped around the base of the antennae. The palpi are reduced and close to the head. Adults have a moderately quick and erratic flight, usually low to the ground. At rest, they hold their wings together over the back. Males frequently puddle at damp ground. Most blues are fond of open, disturbed sites with weedy vegetation.

Metalmarks (Subfamily Riodininae) are characterized by metallic flecks of color or even overall metallic-looking wings. They have eyes entirely separate from the antennal bases, and the palpi are quite prominent. Metalmarks reach tremendous diversity of colors and patterns in the tropics. Most U.S. species are small rust, gray or brownish butterflies. They characteristically perch with their wings outstretched and may often land on the underside of leaves, especially if disturbed. Adults have a low, scurrying flight. Several species are of conservation concern.

Hairstreaks (Subfamily Theclinae) tend to be larger than blues. The wings below are often intricately patterned and bear colorful eyespots adjacent to one or two small, distinct, hair-like tails on each hindwing. The adults have a quick, erratic flight and can be a challenge to follow. They regularly visit flowers and hold their wings together over the back while feeding and at rest. Additionally, they have a unique behavior of moving their hindwings up and down when perched. The sexes regularly differ. Hairstreaks can be found in a wide range of habitats. Many species have a single spring generation.

Nymphalidae: Brush-Foots

Brush-foots are the largest and most diverse family of butterflies. In all members, the first pair of legs is significantly reduced and modified into small brush-like structures, giving the family its name and the appearance of only having four legs.

Emperors (Subfamily Apaturinae) are medium-sized and brownish with short, stubby bodies and a robust thorax. Their wings typically have dark markings and small dark eyespots. The adults are strong and rapid fliers. Males establish territories and perch on tree trunks or overhanging branches. At rest, they hold their wings together over the back. They feed on dung, carrion, rotting fruit or tree sap and do not visit flowers. Emperors inhabit rich woodlands and rarely venture far into open areas. They are nervous butterflies and difficult to closely approach.

Leafwings (Subfamily Charaxinae) are medium-sized butterflies with irregular wing margins. They are bright tawny orange above, but mottled gray to brown below and resemble a dead leaf when resting with their wings closed. The adults have a strong, rapid and erratic flight. They are nervous butterflies and difficult to closely approach. Males establish territories and perch on tree trunks or overhanging branches. Individuals also often land on the ground. They feed on dung, carrion, rotting fruit or tree sap and do not visit flowers.

Milkweed butterflies (Subfamily Danainae) are large butterflies with boldly marked black and orange wings. Their flight is strong and swift with periods of gliding. Adults are strongly attracted to flowers and feed with their wings folded tightly over the back. Males have noticeable black scent patches in the middle of each hindwing. This subfamily includes the Monarch, which undergoes massive, long-distance migrations.

Longwing butterflies (Subfamily Heliconiinae) are colorful, medium-sized butterflies. They have narrow, elongated wings, slender bodies, long antennae and large eyes. Their flight tends to be slow and fluttering. The adults readily visit flowers and nectar with their wings open. Most tend to be long-lived. Within the group are fritillaries. They are small- to medium-sized orange and black butterflies of open, sunny habitats. Those in the genus *Speyeria* have boldly patterned ventral hindwings with conspicuous metallic silver spots.

Snouts (Subfamily Libytheinae) are medium-sized, generally drab brown butterflies representing about ten species worldwide with only one found in the U.S. They have extremely elongated labial palpi and cryptically colored ventral hindwings. They rest with their wings tightly closed and resemble dead leaves.

Admirals (Subfamily Limenitidinae) are medium- to large-sized butterflies with broad, colorful wings. The adults fly with a series of quick wing beats followed by a brief period of gliding. They are typically associated with immature, secondary-growth woodlands or semi-open shrubby sites. Males perch on sunlit leaves or branches and make periodic exploratory flights. They will feed at flowers as well as rotting fruit, dung, carrion and tree sap.

True brush-foots (Subfamily Nymphalinae) are colorful, small- to medium-sized butterflies with no overall common wing shape. Most have stubby, compact bodies and a robust thorax. The adults have a strong, quick flight, usually low to the ground. Most are nervous and often difficult to approach. At rest, they hold their wings together over the back. Many are attracted to flowers while others feed on dung, carrion, rotting fruit or tree sap.

Satyrs and ***wood-nymphs*** (Subfamily Satyrinae) are small- to medium-sized drab brown butterflies. Their wings are marked with dark stripes and prominent eyespots. The adults have a slow, somewhat bobbing flight usually low to the ground. They inhabit shady woodlands and adjacent open, grassy areas. The adults rarely visit flowers. They are instead attracted to dung, carrion, rotting fruit or tree sap. At rest, they hold their wings together over the back and are generally easy to closely approach. They regularly land on the ground.

Papilionidae: Swallowtails

Swallowtails are easily recognized by their large size and noticeably long hindwing tails. They are generally dark with bold markings. The adults have a swift and powerful flight, usually several meters off the ground, and regularly visit flowers. Most swallowtails continuously flutter their wings while feeding. Males often puddle at damp ground. They generally are found in and along woodland areas and adjacent open sites.

Pieridae: Sulphurs and Whites

Members of the family are small- to medium-sized butterflies, typically some shade of white or yellow. Many have dark markings. Most species are sexually dimorphic and seasonally variable. The adults have a moderately quick and erratic flight, usually low to the ground. They are fond of flowers and hold their wings together over the back while feeding. Males often puddle at damp ground.

Sulphurs (Subfamily Coliadinae) and ***whites*** (Subfamily Pierinae) are common butterflies of open, disturbed sites where their weedy larval host plants abound.

OBSERVING BUTTERFLIES IN THE FIELD

While butterflies are entertaining and beautiful to watch, correctly identifying them can often be a challenge. But it's generally not as difficult as it might seem. With a little practice and some basic guidelines, you can quickly learn to peg that unknown butterfly.

One of the first and most obvious things to note when you spot a butterfly is its size. You will discover that butterflies generally come in one of three basic dimensions: small, medium and large. This system may sound ridiculously arbitrary at first, but when you begin to regularly observe several different butterflies together in the field, these categories quickly start to make sense. For a starting point, follow this simple strategy: the next time you see a Monarch butterfly, pay close attention to its size. You may wish to use your hand as a reference. Most Monarchs have a wingspan close to the length of your palm (about four inches) as measured from the base of your fingers to the start of your wrist. This is considered a large butterfly. From here it's basically a matter of fractions. A medium-sized butterfly by comparison would have a wingspan of generally about half that size (about two inches). Finally, a butterfly would be considered small if it had a wingspan one quarter that of a Monarch (around one inch).

Next, pay close attention to color and pattern of the wings. This field guide is organized by color, and you can quickly navigate to the appropriate section. First, start by noting the overall ground color. Is it, for example, primarily black, yellow, orange or white? Then try to identify any major pattern elements such as distinct stripes, bands or spots. Depending on the behavior of the butterfly in the wild, keep in mind that the most visible portion of a butterfly may either be the upper surface of the wings (dorsal surface) or the underside (ventral surface). If you have a particularly cooperative subject, you may be able to closely observe both sides. Finally, carefully note the color and position of any major markings. For example, if the butterfly has a wide yellow band on the forewing, is it positioned in the middle of the wing or along the outer edge? Lepidopterists have a detailed vocabulary for wing pattern positions. The following illustrations of general wing features and wing areas should help you become familiar with some terminology.

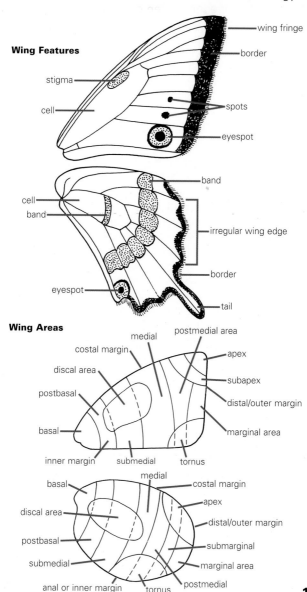

Wing Features

stigma

cell

wing fringe

border

spots

eyespot

band

cell

band

irregular wing edge

eyespot

border

tail

Wing Areas

medial

postmedial area

costal margin

discal area

postbasal

basal

inner margin

submedial

tornus

apex

subapex

distal/outer margin

marginal area

basal

medial

costal margin

discal area

apex

postbasal

distal/outer margin

submedial

submarginal

anal or inner margin

tornus

postmedial

marginal area

15

Next, note the shape of the butterfly's wings, particularly the forewings. Are they generally long and narrow, rounded, broad, pointed or angled? Butterflies such as the Meadow Fritillary have somewhat elongated wings. Others, like the Little Wood-Satyr and Eastern Tailed-Blue, have short, generally rounded wings. Next, do the wings have any unique features? Many swallowtails and hairstreaks have distinct hindwing tails, while Question Marks and Eastern Commas have visibly irregular wing margins. Clues like this can help you quickly narrow the butterfly down to a particular family or distinguish it from a similarly colored species.

The way a butterfly flies may also be useful for identification. While it is generally difficult to easily pick up particular features or color patterns when a butterfly is moving, its flight pattern can often be very distinctive. Carefully follow the butterfly as it flies and watch how it behaves in the air. Is it soaring above your head or scurrying rapidly along the ground? Is it moving fast and erratically, or fluttering slowly about? Monarchs, for instance, have a very unique flight pattern. They flap their wings quickly several times, glide for bit, and then quickly flap their wings again. Other butterflies, such as most wood-nymphs and satyrs, have a characteristic low, bobbing flight.

Sometimes you can gain important clues about a butterfly by the way it behaves when feeding. Next time you see a butterfly feeding, watch its wings. Does it hold them tightly closed, spread them wide open, or flutter them? Most swallowtails continuously flutter their wings. This behavior is a quick and reliable diagnostic that can be seen from a fair distance.

Note the habitat in which the butterfly occurs. Is it darting between branches along a shady and moist woodland path? Perched on the top of a grass blade in a saltwater marsh? Bobbing among low grasses in a wet prairie? Fluttering from one flower to the next in a fallow agricultural field? Many butterflies have strong habitat preferences. Some are restricted to a single particular habitat while others may occur in a wide range of habitats.

Sometimes even the date can offer a useful hint. Many hairstreaks are univoltine, meaning they produce just one generation. As a result, the adults occur only during a narrow window of time each spring. Similarly, several butterflies overwinter as adults. They may be active at times when few other species are around.

Butterfly observation and identification are skills, and it takes time and practice to master them. To speed up the learning curve, you may also wish to join a local butterfly gardening or watching club or society. The members can help give advice, accompany you in the field, or share directions to great butterfly watching spots.

DETERMINING A BUTTERFLY'S COLOR

To help make butterfly field identification fun and easy, this guide is organized by color, allowing you to quickly navigate to the appropriate section. In addition, smaller butterflies are always toward the beginning of each section, and the largest are toward the back. Butterflies are not static subjects, so determining their color can be a bit tricky. Several factors such as age, seasonal variation and complex wing and color patterns may affect your perception of a butterfly's color.

Age

Adult age can influence a butterfly's color. While butterflies don't get wrinkles or gray hairs, they do continue to lose wing scales during their life. This type of normal wing wear combined with more significant wing damage can cause once vibrant colors or iridescence to fade and pattern elements to become less distinct. As a result, the bright tawny orange wings of a freshly emerged Great Spangled Fritillary may appear dull orange or almost yellowish in an old, worn individual.

Seasonal Variation

Time of year can play a role as well. Some butterflies produce distinct seasonal forms that may vary significantly in color and to a lesser extent in wing shape or overall size. For the Sleepy Orange, the change is dramatic. Individuals produced during the summer are bright butter yellow on the wings below. Winter-forms, by contrast, have dark rust-colored ventral hindwings perfect for blending into a predominantly brown fall and winter landscape. For species that display extensive seasonal variation, the differences are discussed and every attempt is made to include an image of both forms. Since you'll probably be looking for butterflies in the warmer months, pictures of winter-forms are insets and not main images.

Complex Wing and Color Patterns

For many butterflies, wing color and pattern can vary tremendously between the dorsal and ventral surface. The wings of a White M Hairstreak are brilliant iridescent blue above and brownish gray below. The bright dorsal coloration is readily visible during flight but concealed at rest when the hairstreak holds its wings firmly closed. As a result, the butterfly may appear either blue or black depending on your perspective and the butterfly's activity.

Most hairstreaks (subfamily Theclinae) and sulphurs (subfamily Coliadinae) typically feed and rest with their wings closed. As a result, very few photographs of the dorsal wing surface of free-flying butterflies in these groups exist. Similarly, most blues (subfamily Polyommatinae) perch and feed with their wings closed or hold them only partially open when basking. Many of these same butterflies are also two-toned (blue on the dorsal surface, but whitish to grubby gray below; or orange on the dorsal surface, but much yellower below). But because a large number of these butterflies are so small, chances are that you'll notice them first when they fly and reveal their brighter dorsal coloration. Two-toned butterflies such as these have been placed in the color section that reflects the brighter coloration that you're most likely to notice first.

For example, if you're looking in the white section for a small butterfly with lots of bands and spots on the ventral surface, but can't find it, try the blue section. You might be looking at a perched Spring Azure, which is bright blue above but a rather nondescript brownish gray white below.

Color can vary slightly even among butterflies of the same

species. If you see a butterfly that appears to be tawny colored, but you can't find it in the orange section, try the brown section. You might be looking at a Tawny Emperor, which can be perceived as orange or brown, depending on the individual.

Finally, females are generally more drab than males of the same species. They can have less iridescent color, fewer or darker markings, and can appear overall darker or paler. For some species, such as the Eastern Tiger Swallowtail and Eastern Tailed-Blue, the females and males look very different and are pictured in separate color sections.

COLOR SECTION TROUBLESHOOTING

With all the variables that can impact the perception of a butterfly's color, identifying these creatures may seem daunting. Taking the time to check a color section or two is worth being able to positively identify a mystery butterfly.

Can't find it in...   Try looking in...

Black   **Brown**

In certain conditions, some of the dark brown butterflies, especially swallowtails and skippers, might appear black

Blue   **Blue or Black**

Blues (subfamily Polyommatinae) often rest or feed with their wings closed, so the blue dorsal coloration is visible primarily during flight or when the individual is basking. Check the illustration and description for field marks. Some black butterflies have varying amounts of iridescent blue scales; they may look blue in certain conditions.

Brown   **Orange**

Many butterflies described as tawny can be perceived as either brown or orange.

Gray   **Brown**

Many of the Hairstreaks (subfamily Theclinae) have light colored ventral wings that can vary in the amount of gray or brown they show.

Green   **White**

Some of the female Sulphurs (subfamily Coliadinae) have a common white form that may appear to be greenish.

Orange   Brown

Many of the skippers are brown but have bright orange field
marks. Other butterflies are tawny colored, so could be perceived as either brown or orange.

White   Blue

Blues (subfamily Polyommatinae) perch with their wings
closed, so appear to be white butterflies.

Yellow   Orange

Some of the Sulphurs (subfamily Coliadinae) have bright
orange dorsal wings.

BUTTERFLY GARDENING

One of the easiest ways to observe local butterflies is to
plant a butterfly garden. Even a small area can attract a
great variety of species directly to your yard. For best
results, include both adult nectar sources and larval host
plants. Most adult butterflies are generalists and will visit
a broad range of colorful flowers in search of nectar.
Developing larvae, on the other hand, typically have very
discriminating tastes and often rely on only a few very specific plant species for food. For assistance with starting a
butterfly garden, seek the guidance of local nursery profes-
sionals. They can help you determine which plants will
grow well in your area. This field guide provides a list of larval host plants for each species, as well as a listing of good
nectar plants. These lists begin on page 368.

BUTTERFLY Q & A:
What's the difference between a butterfly and a moth?

While there is no one simple answer to this question, butterflies and moths generally differ based on their overall habits and structure. Butterflies are typically active during the day (diurnal), while moths predominantly fly at night (nocturnal). Butterflies possess slender antennae that are clubbed at the end. Those of moths vary from long narrow filaments to broad fern-like structures. At rest, butterflies tend to hold their wings together vertically over the back. Moths rest with their wings extended flat out to the sides or folded alongside the body. Butterflies generally have long, smooth and slender bodies. The bodies of moths are often robust and hairy. Finally, most butterflies are typically brightly colored, while most moths tend to be dark and somewhat drab.

What can butterflies see?

Butterflies are believed to have very good vision and to see a single color image. Compared to humans, they have an expanded range of sensitivity and are able to distinguish wavelengths of light into the ultraviolet range.

Do butterflies look the same year-round?

Many butterflies produce distinct seasonal forms that differ markedly in color, size, reproductive activity and behavior. Good examples within Michigan include the Common Buckeye and Sleepy Orange. The seasonal forms are determined by the environmental cues (temperature, rainfall, day length) that immature stages experience during development. Warm summer temperatures and long days forecast conditions that are highly favorable for continued development and reproduction. Summer-form individuals are generally lighter in color, short-lived, and reproductively active. As fall approaches, cooler temperatures and shortening day lengths mean future conditions may be unfavorable for continued development and reproduction. Winter-form adults display increased pattern elements, are generally darker, larger, longer lived, and survive the winter months in a state of reproductive diapause.

Do caterpillars have eyes?

Yes, caterpillars or larvae generally have six pairs of simple eyes called ocelli. They are able to distinguish basic changes in light intensity but are believed to be incapable of forming an image.

How do caterpillars defend themselves?

Caterpillars or larvae are generally plump, slow moving creatures that represent an inviting meal for many predators. To protect themselves, caterpillars employ a variety of different strategies. Many, like the Monarch or Pipevine Swallowtail, sequester specific chemicals from their host plants that render them highly distasteful or toxic. These caterpillars are generally brightly colored to advertise their unpalatability. Others rely on deception or camouflage to avoid being eaten. White Admiral larvae are mottled green, brown and cream, a color pattern that helps them resemble a bird dropping. By contrast, larvae of the Northern Pearly-Eye are solid green and extremely well camouflaged against the green leaves of their host. Some larvae conceal their whereabouts by constructing shelters. American Lady larvae weave leaves and flowerheads together with silk and rest safely inside when not actively feeding. Still others have formidable spines and hairs or produce irritating or foul-smelling chemicals to deter persistent predators.

Do butterfly caterpillars make silk?

Yes, butterfly larvae produce silk. While they don't typically spin an elaborate cocoon around their pupa like moths, they use silk for a variety of purposes, including the construction of shelters, anchoring or attaching their chrysalid, and to gain secure footing on leaves and branches.

What happens when a butterfly's scales rub off?

Contrary to the old wives' tale, if you touch a butterfly's wing and remove scales in the process it is still capable of flying. In fact, a butterfly typically continuously loses scales during its life from normal wing wear. Scales serve a variety of purposes, from thermoregulation and camouflage to pheromone dispersal and species or sex recognition, but are not critical for flight. Once gone, the scales are permanently lost and will not grow back.

Why do butterflies gather at mud puddles?

Adult butterflies are often attracted to damp or moist ground and may congregate at such areas in large numbers. In most cases, these groupings, or "puddle clubs," are made up entirely of males. They drink from the moisture to gain water and salts (sodium ions) that happen to come into solution. This behavior helps males replenish the sodium ions lost when they pass a packet of sperm and accessory gland secretions to the female during copulation. The transferred nutrients have been shown to play a significant role in egg production and, thus, female reproductive output.

How long do butterflies live?

In general, most butterflies are extremely short-lived and survive in the wild for an average of about two weeks. There are, of course, numerous exceptions to this rule. The Mourning Cloak is a perfect example. Adults may survive for 4–6 months. Still others, particularly species that migrate long distances and/or overwinter as adults, are capable of surviving for extended periods of time.

Where do butterflies go at night?
Where do they go during a rainstorm?

In the evening or during periods of inclement weather, most butterflies seek shelter under the leaves of growing plants or among vegetation.

Do all butterflies visit flowers?

All butterflies are fluid feeders. While a large percentage of them rely on sugar-rich nectar as the primary energy source for flight, reproduction and general maintenance, many species also feed on, or exclusively utilize, the liquids and dissolved nutrients produced by other food resources such as dung, carrion, rotting fruit or vegetation, sap and bird droppings.

Do butterflies grow?

No. An adult butterfly is fully grown upon emergence from its chrysalis.

How do caterpillars grow?

A caterpillar's job in life is to eat and grow. But larvae, like all other insects, have an external skeleton. Therefore, in order to increase in size, they must shed their skin, or molt, several times during development. Essentially, their skin is like a trash bag. It is packed full of food until there is no more room. Once full, it is discarded for a larger, baggier one underneath and the process continues.

What eats butterflies?

Butterflies face an uphill battle for survival. Out of every one hundred eggs produced by a female butterfly, approximately only one percent survive to become an adult. And as an adult, the odds don't get much better. Various birds, small mammals, lizards, frogs, toads, spiders and other insects all prey on butterflies.

What's the difference between a chrysalis and a cocoon?

Once fully grown, both moth and butterfly caterpillars molt a final time to form a pupa. Most moths surround their pupae with a constructed silken case called a cocoon. By contrast, a butterfly pupa, frequently termed a chrysalis, is generally naked. In most cases, butterfly chrysalid are attached to a leaf, twig or other surface with silk. In some instances, they may be unattached or surrounded by a loose silken cocoon.

Are all butterfly scales the same?

No. The scales on a butterfly's wings and body come in a variety of different sizes and shapes. Some may be extremely elongated and resemble hairs while others are highly modified for the release of pheromones during courtship. Those responsible for making up wing color and pattern are generally wide and flat. They are attached at the base and overlap like shingles on a roof. The colors we see are the result of either pigments contained in the scales or the diffraction of light caused by scale structure. Iridescent colors such as blue, green, purple and silver usually result from scale structure. While pigmented scales are the norm, many species have a combination of both types on their wings.

Why do butterflies often sit in the bright sun?

Unlike mammals and birds, butterflies are poikilothermic or "cold blooded" organisms. They do not have an internal mechanism to regulate body temperature, so must instead rely on a variety of behaviors for thermoregulation. Basking in the warm sunlight is one of the most obvious and is typically witnessed on cool days or during the morning hours. The butterfly positions its wings at an appropriate angle to capture and transport the sun's heat to the thoracic flight muscles, thereby slowly raising the body temperature to the level needed for flight.

Why are butterflies important?

Butterflies play a number of important roles in the environment. Like bees or wasps, butterflies are pollinators helping to facilitate plant reproduction. They also provide a wealth of food resources for other organisms. Birds, lizards, frogs, spiders, small mammals and various predaceous insects may all feed on butterflies in one life stage or another. Additionally, as butterflies and other insects are able to produce a large number of generations in a relatively short time, they tend to react to changes in the environment much more quickly than birds or mammals. Therefore, they are indicator species that help act like a barometer of ecological health. Due to their tremendous nationwide popularity, butterflies often act as flagship species helping to rally support for various conservation efforts such as habitat protection. Finally, butterflies are colorful and graceful creatures that help promote exploration of the outdoors.

BUTTERFLY QUICK-COMPARE

Common Sootywing pg. 43 	**Grizzled Skipper** pg. 45 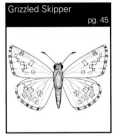	**Red Admiral** pg. 47 
Baltimore Checkerspot pg. 49 	**Milbert's Tortoiseshell** pg. 51 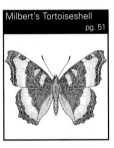	**White Admiral** pg. 53 
Red-spotted Purple pg. 55 	**Zebra Swallowtail** pg. 57 	**Black Swallowtail** pg. 59 
Pipevine Swallowtail pg. 61 	**Mourning Cloak** pg. 63 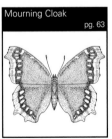	**Spicebush Swallowtail** pg. 65 

Eastern Tiger Swallowtail
pg. 67

Eastern Tailed-Blue
pg. 69

Western Tailed-Blue
pg. 71

Spring Azure
pg. 73

Summer Azure
pg. 75

Northern Blue
pg. 77

Greenish Blue
pg. 79

Silvery Blue
pg. 81

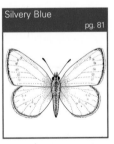

Karner Blue
pg. 83

White M Hairstreak
pg. 85

Eastern Tailed-Blue
pg. 87

Bog Copper
pg. 89

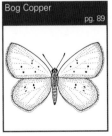

Frosted Elfin
pg. 91

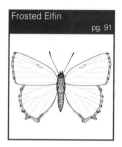

Western Tailed-Blue
pg. 93

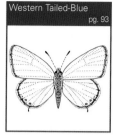

Brown Elfin
pg. 95

Hoary Elfin
pg. 97

Tawny-edged Skipper
pg. 99

Northern Blue
pg. 101

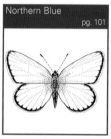

Dorcas Copper
pg. 103

Eastern Pine Elfin
pg. 105

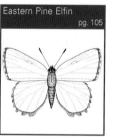

Henry's Elfin
pg. 107

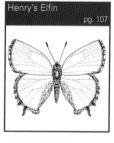

Pepper and Salt Skipper
pg. 109

Western Pine Elfin
pg. 111

Coral Hairstreak
pg. 113

Purplish Copper
pg. 115

Greenish Blue
pg. 117

Banded Hairstreak
pg. 119

Edwards' Hairstreak
pg. 121

Hickory Hairstreak
pg. 123

Crossline Skipper
pg. 125

Peck's Skipper
pg. 127

Poweshiek Skipperling
pg. 129

Northern Oak Hairstreak
pg. 131

Striped Hairstreak
pg. 133

Common Roadside-Skipper
pg. 135

Mulberry Wing
pg. 137

Zabulon Skipper
pg. 139

Northern Broken-Dash
pg. 141

Little Glassywing
pg. 143

Cobweb Skipper
pg. 145

Dun Skipper
pg. 147

Acadian Hairstreak
pg. 149

Dreamy Duskywing
pg. 151

Common Branded Skipper
pg. 153

Two-spotted Skipper
pg. 155

Southern Cloudywing
pg. 157

Columbine Duskywing
pg. 159

Mottled Duskywing
pg. 161

Black Dash
pg. 163

Northern Cloudywing
pg. 165

Bronze Copper
pg. 167

Ottoe Skipper
pg. 169

Persius Duskywing
pg. 171

Horace's Duskywing
pg. 173

Wild Indigo Duskywing
pg. 175

Hobomok Skipper
pg. 177

Sleepy Duskywing
pg. 179

Mitchell's Satyr
pg. 181

Dusted Skipper
pg. 183

Hoary Edge
pg. 185

Leonard's Skipper pg. 187	Red-disked Alpine pg. 189	Juvenal's Duskywing pg. 191

Little Wood-Satyr pg. 193	American Snout pg. 195	Chryxus Arctic pg. 197
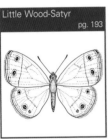		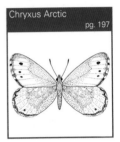
Jutta Arctic pg. 199	Eyed Brown pg. 201	Appalachian Brown pg. 203

Silver-spotted Skipper pg. 205	Common Buckeye pg. 207	Northern Pearly-Eye pg. 209
		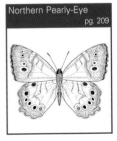

Hackberry Emperor
pg. 211

Common Wood-Nymph
pg. 213

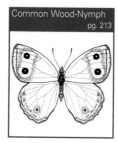

Tawny Emperor
pg. 215

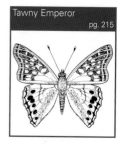

Compton Tortoiseshell
pg. 217

Giant Swallowtail
pg. 219

Red-banded Hairstreak
pg. 221

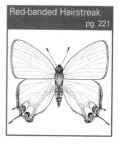

Gray Hairstreak
pg. 223

Acadian Hairstreak
pg. 225

Early Hairstreak
pg. 227

Least Skipper
pg. 229

European Skipper
pg. 231

Arctic Skipper
pg. 233

Swamp Metalmark
pg. 235

Purplish Copper
pg. 237

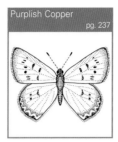

Long Dash
pg. 239

Fiery Skipper
pg. 241

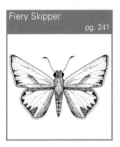

American Copper
pg. 243

Harvester
pg. 245

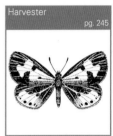

Delaware Skipper
pg. 247

Zabulon Skipper
pg. 249

Gorgone Checkerspot
pg. 251

Common Ringlet
pg. 253

Common Branded Skipper
pg. 255

Indian Skipper
pg. 257

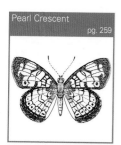

Pearl Crescent
pg. 259

Black Dash
pg. 261

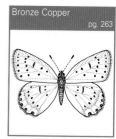

Bronze Copper
pg. 263

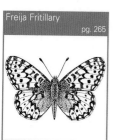

Freija Fritillary
pg. 265

Ottoe Skipper
pg. 267

Hobomok Skipper
pg. 269

Tawny Crescent
pg. 271

Dion Skipper
pg. 273

Bog Fritillary
pg. 275

Frigga Fritillary
pg. 277

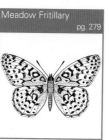

Meadow Fritillary
pg. 279

Dukes's Skipper
pg. 281

Sleepy Orange
pg. 283

Harris's Checkerspot
pg. 285

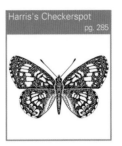

Silvery Checkerspot
pg. 287

Northern Crescent
pg. 289

Broad-winged Skipper
pg. 291

Silver-bordered Fritillary
pg. 293

Hoary Comma
pg. 295

Variegated Fritillary
pg. 297

Orange Sulphur
pg. 299

American Lady
pg. 301

Painted Lady
pg. 303

Satyr Comma
pg. 305

Green Comma
pg. 307

Eastern Comma
pg. 309

Gray Comma
pg. 311

Macoun's Arctic
pg. 313

Atlantis Fritillary
pg. 315

Goatweed Leafwing
pg. 317

Question Mark
pg. 319

Viceroy
pg. 321

Aphrodite Fritillary
pg. 323

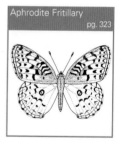

Great Spangled Fritillary
pg. 325

Regal Fritillary
pg. 327

Monarch
pg. 329

Common Checkered-Skipper pg. 331	West Virginia White pg. 333	Olympia Marble pg. 335

 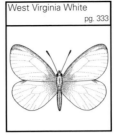 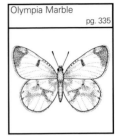

Checkered White pg. 337	Large Marble pg. 339	Mustard White pg. 341

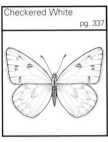 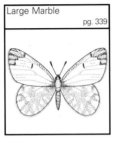 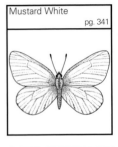

Cabbage White pg. 343	Clouded Sulphur pg. 345	Zebra Swallowtail pg. 347

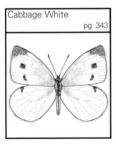 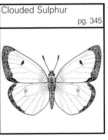 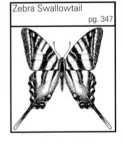

Dainty Sulphur pg. 349	Little Yellow pg. 351	Pink-edged Sulphur pg. 353

38

Southern Dogface
pg. 355

Clouded Sulphur
pg. 357

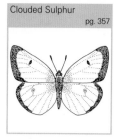

Cloudless Sulphur
pg. 359

Canadian Tiger Swallowtail
pg. 361

Eastern Tiger Swallowtail
pg. 363

Common Name
Scientific Name

color section indicators →

Family/Subfamily: tells which family and subfamily the butterfly belongs to (see p. 9–13 for descriptions)

Wingspan: gives minimum and maximum wing spans, from one forewing tip to the other

Above: description of upper, or dorsal, surface of wings

Below: description of lower, or ventral, surface of wings

Sexes: describes differences in appearance between male and female

Egg: description of eggs and where they are deposited

Larva: description of the butterfly's larva, or caterpillar

Larval Host Plants: lists plants that eggs and larva are likely to be found on

Habitat: describes where you're likely to find the butterflies

Broods: lists number of broods, or generations, hatched in a span of one year

Abundance: when the butterflies are flying, this tells you how often you're likely to encounter them

Compare: describes differences among similar-looking species

range map shows where in Michigan this butterfly is present

Resident: predictably present
Visitor: occasionally present
Stray: rarely present

Resident Visitor Stray

phenogram: shows population flux throughout the year

| Jan. | Feb. | Mar. | Apr. | May | June | July | Aug. | Sept. | Oct. | Nov. | Dec. |

Dorsal (above)

Ventral (below)

silhouette behind Comments section shows actual average size of butterfly

illustration shows field marks and features to look for

41

Ventral

Larva

Comments: The Common Sootywing indeed looks as if it fell into a pail of ashes. The silky blackish brown wings of fresh individuals are particularly lovely when seen in full sun. Tolerant of human disturbance, it is at home in a variety of open, weedy sites that support its weedy hosts. The butterfly is avidly drawn to available flowers as well as damp soil. Adults have a low, erratic flight and frequently perch on low vegetation or bare soil with their wings spread. The larvae construct individual shelters on the host by folding over part of a leaf with silk.

Common Sootywing
Pholisora catullus

Family/Subfamily: Skippers (Hesperiidae)/
Spread-wing Skippers (Pyrginae)

Wingspan: 0.90–1.25" (2.3–3.2 cm)

Above: shiny dark brown to black with a variable number
of small white spots on the forewing and a few on top
of the head

Below: as above but paler brown

Sexes: similar, although female often has larger white
forewing spots

Egg: reddish pink, laid singly on upperside of host leaves

Larva: pale gray-green with a narrow dorsal stripe, pale
green lateral stripes, a black collar and black head;
body is covered with numerous tiny yellow-white dots,
each bearing a short hair

Larval Host Plants: primarily Lamb's Quarters; pigweed may also be used

Habitat: open, disturbed sites including roadsides, old
fields, utility easements and fallow agricultural land

Broods: two generations

Abundance: occasional to common

Compare: unique

Resident Stray

| Jan. | Feb. | Mar. | Apr. | May | June | July | Aug. | Sept. | Oct. | Nov. | Dec. |

male

Dorsal (above)
small white spots
otherwise black

white spots on head

occasionally has a row
of small white spots
on hindwing

Ventral (below)
blackish brown

43

Ventral Larva

Comments: This primarily Canadian butterfly is found in portions of the central Appalachians and the Upper Midwest, where it is considered rare and declining. Within Michigan, the Grizzled Skipper is a species of conservation concern as colonies tend to be extremely local and primarily restricted to openings in oak wood-lands. Superficially similar to the more widespread and abundant Common Checkered-Skipper, the Grizzled Skipper appears noticeably darker. Adults scurry with a very quick, somewhat bouncing flight close to the ground. They periodically perch low on vegetation or in sunlit patches of bare earth with wings outstretched.

Grizzled Skipper
Pyrgus centaureae

Family/Subfamily: Skippers (Hesperiidae)/
Spread-wing Skippers (Pyrginae)

Wingspan: 1.1–1.3" (2.8–3.3 cm)

Above: dark gray to black with scattered small, white spots and black-and-white checkered fringes; forewing has scattered white spots; central band is missing a white spot below cell-end bar

Below: white with irregular olive gray bands and spots

Sexes: similar

Egg: pale green, laid singly on the underside of host leaves

Larva: gray green with a black head; larva overwinters

Larval Host Plants: Virginia Strawberry

Habitat: open woodlands, barrens, forest clearings and margins, utility easements and adjacent disturbed sites and meadows

Broods: single generation

Abundance: rare to uncommon; localized

Compare: Common Checkered-Skipper (pg. 331) is larger and has more extensive white spotting.

Resident

| Jan. | Feb. | Mar. | Apr. | May | June | July | Aug. | Sept. | Oct. | Nov. | Dec. |

Dorsal (above)
scattered small white spots

missing white spot below cell

checkered fringes

Ventral (below)
irregular bands and spots

45

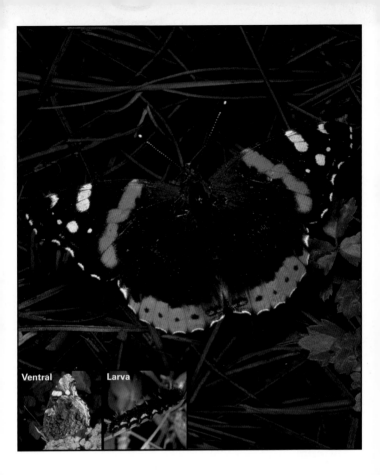

Ventral

Larva

Comments: The Red Admiral is quickly distinguished
from all other butterflies by its distinctive reddish
orange forewing band. Typically unable to survive
harsh winter temperatures, the species is a regular
seasonal colonist of Michigan. As a result, its abundance often fluctuates considerably from year to year
and may occasionally experience tremendous population outbreaks. Males frequently perch on low
vegetation or on the ground in sunlit locations and
aggressively defend established territories. Adults
occasionally nectar at flowers but more frequently visit
sap flows, dung or fermenting fruit.

Red Admiral
Vanessa atalanta

Family/Subfamily: Brush-foots (Nymphalidae)/
True Brush-foots (Nymphalinae)

Wingspan: 1.75–2.50" (4.4–6.4 cm)

Above: dark brownish black with reddish orange hind-wing border and distinct, reddish orange median forewing band; forewing has small white spots near apex

Below: forewing as above with blue scaling and paler markings; hindwing ornately mottled with dark brown, blue and cream in bark-like pattern

Sexes: similar

Egg: small green eggs laid singly on host leaves

Larva: variable; pinkish gray to charcoal with lateral row of cream crescent-shaped spots and numerous branched spines. Larvae construct individual shelters on the host by folding together one or more leaves with silk.

Larval Host Plants: False Nettle, Pellitory and nettles

Habitat: moist woodlands, forest edges, roadside ditches, canals and pond margins, wetlands, parks, meadows and gardens

Broods: two or more generations

Abundance: occasional to common; locally abundant

Compare: unique

Resident

Jan. Feb. Mar. Apr. May June July Aug. Sept. Oct. Nov. Dec.

Dorsal (above)
forewing apex squared off
white spots
reddish orange bands

Ventral (below)
pale apex
reddish orange band

47

Ventral

Larva

Comments: With its outrageous color and pattern, the Baltimore is truly a must-see butterfly! Unfortunately, like many other wetland species, it continues to decline as a result of habitat loss or alteration. It primarily occurs in habitat-restricted populations that tend to be highly fragmented and localized, but nonetheless can often be quite abundant. Females lay their eggs on Turtlehead. Upon hatching, the young larvae construct a communal silken web on the plant and feed gregariously inside until the end of summer. The partially grown larvae overwinter and resume development the following spring on a variety of alternate hosts.

Baltimore Checkerspot
Euphydryas phaeton

Family/Subfamily: Brush-foots (Nymphalidae)/
True Brush-foots (Nymphalinae)

Wingspan: 1.75–2.50" (4.4–6.6 cm)

Above: black with reddish orange spots along the outer
wing margins and several rows of cream white spots

Below: marked as above with several large reddish
orange basal spots on both wings

Sexes: similar

Egg: yellow, soon turning reddish, laid in large clusters of
several hundred on the underside of host leaves

Larva: tawny orange with black transverse stripe and
several rows of black, branched spines; front and rear
end segments are black

Larval Host Plants: Turtlehead is the primary host;
secondary hosts include a wider range of plants such
as false foxglove, Narrowleaf Plantain, ash, Canadian
Lousewort and Southern Arrowwood

Habitat: wet meadows, fens, bogs, stream margins,
marshes and moist fields; occasionally in barrens

Broods: single generation

Abundance: uncommon to common; local

Compare: unique

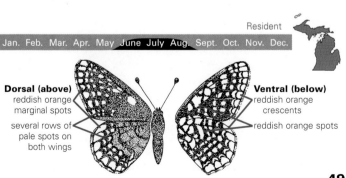

Resident

Jan. Feb. Mar. Apr. May June July Aug. Sept. Oct. Nov. Dec.

Dorsal (above)
reddish orange
marginal spots

several rows of
pale spots on
both wings

Ventral (below)
reddish orange
crescents

reddish orange spots

Ventral

Larva

Comments: This small but electric tortoiseshell has to
be seen in person to be truly appreciated. Particularly
common in the Upper Midwest, Milbert's Tortoiseshell
is a regularly seen resident of Michigan. Unlike other
anglewings, the species regularly visits a variety of
flowers for nectar in addition to feeding at fermenting
fruit, dung, carrion and sap flows. Males frequently
perch on fallen logs or bare earth to await passing
females. They tend to be quite wary and dart off with
a rapid, low flight if disturbed. Young larvae feed gregariously within a communal nest on the host; older
larvae become more solitary.

Milbert's Tortoiseshell
Nymphalis milberti

Family/Subfamily: Brush-foots (Nymphalidae)/
True Brush-foots (Nymphalinae)

Wingspan: 1.9–2.4" (4.8–6.1 cm)

Above: two-toned; basal portion is velvety chocolate
brown with reddish orange bars in the forewing cell,
outer portion has dark wing margins bordered inwardly
with a wide yellow orange band; hindwing border
encloses a row of small blue spots; forewing apex is
extended and squared off; hindwing bears a stubby tail

Below: strongly two-toned; basal half dark blackish
brown and outer portion grayish brown with fine striations and a dark border; resembles tree bark

Sexes: similar

Egg: green, laid in clusters on host leaves

Larva: black with two pale lateral bands, white speckling
and several rows of branched, black spines; the ventral
surface is gray green

Larval Host Plants: Stinging Nettle

Habitat: wet meadows, stream margins, pastures and
other open areas near moist woodlands

Broods: two generations

Abundance: occasional to common

Compare: unique; California Tortoiseshell (*Nymphalis californica*) is a very rare vagrant to Michigan.

Resident

| Jan. | Feb. | Mar. | Apr. | May | June | July | Aug. | Sept. | Oct. | Nov. | Dec. |

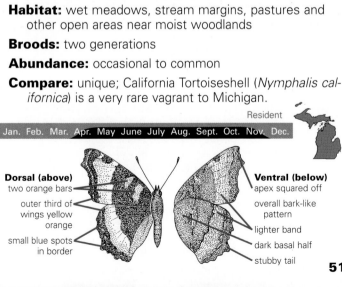

Dorsal (above)
two orange bars

outer third of
wings yellow
orange

small blue spots
in border

Ventral (below)
apex squared off

overall bark-like
pattern

lighter band

dark basal half

stubby tail

51

Ventral   Larva

Comments: This distinctive butterfly of northern forests essentially replaces the Red-spotted Purple throughout much of the Upper Midwest, Northeast and Canada. The two hybridize in areas where their ranges overlap. Numerous intergradations may be encountered in central Michigan. Adults have a strong, gliding flight and are often quite wary. Males regularly perch on sunlit leaves or on gravel roads and make periodic exploratory flights. Both sexes will visit flowers but prefer rotting fruit, dung, carrion or tree sap. Freshly emerged individuals are absolutely electric when seen in sunlight and represent a strong candidate for our most beautiful species.

White Admiral
Limenitis arthemis arthemis

Family/Subfamily: Brush-foots (Nymphalidae)/ Admirals (Limenitidinae)

Wingspan: 3.0–3.5" (7.6–8.9 cm)

Above: dark velvety bluish black with a broad white band across both wings; hindwing has a submarginal row of orange spots and iridescent blue dashes along the margin

Below: brownish black with a broad white band, reddish orange basal spots and a row of reddish orange spots along the outer portion of both wings

Sexes: similar

Egg: gray-green, laid singly on host leaves

Larva: mottled green, brown and cream with two long, knobby horns on the thorax; resembles a bird dropping. Young larvae eat the tip of the leaf to the mid-vein and rest on the end of the vein when not actively feeding.

Larval Host Plants: birches, poplars and aspens

Habitat: open woodlands, forest clearings, wooded roadsides and adjacent open areas

Broods: two generations

Abundance: occasional to common

Compare: Red-spotted Purple (pg. 55) lacks the broad white bands.

Resident

| Jan. | Feb. | Mar. | Apr. | May | June | July | Aug. | Sept. | Oct. | Nov. | Dec. |

Dorsal (above)
wide, white postmedian band
submarginal blue spot band
red spot band

Ventral (below)
wide, white postmedian band
reddish brown

Ventral

Larva

Comments: The Red-spotted Purple is one of four
Michigan butterflies that mimic the toxic Pipevine
Swallowtail to gain protection from predators such as
birds. It is a common butterfly of immature woodlands
throughout southern Michigan, but is rarely encountered in large numbers. Adults have a strong, gliding
flight and are often quite wary. Males perch on sunlit
leaves along trails or forest margins and make periodic
exploratory flights. Adults occasionally visit flowers but
often prefer rotting fruit, dung, carrion or tree sap. It
readily hybridizes with the more northern White
Admiral in areas where their ranges overlap.

Red-Spotted Purple
Limenitis arthemis astyanax

Family/Subfamily: Brush-foots (Nymphalidae)/ Admirals (Limenitidinae)

Wingspan: 3.0–3.5" (7.6–8.9 cm)

Above: dark velvety bluish black with iridescent blue scaling on hindwing and small orange and white spots near forewing apex

Below: brownish black with an iridescent blue sheen and basal red-orange spots; hindwings have a row of red-orange spots toward the outer margin

Sexes: similar

Egg: gray-green, laid singly on the tips of host leaves

Larva: mottled green, brown and cream with two long, knobby horns on thorax; resembles a bird dropping

Larval Host Plants: Black Cherry, Wild Cherry and willow

Habitat: open deciduous woodlands, forest edges and adjacent open areas

Broods: two generations

Abundance: occasional to common

Compare: Pipevine Swallowtail (pg. 61) has hindwing tail and a low, rapid flight; continually flutters wings when nectaring. White Admiral (pg. 53) has distinctive broad white median bands on the wings above.

Resident

Jan. Feb. Mar. Apr. May June July Aug. Sept. Oct. Nov. Dec.

Dorsal (above)
iridescent blue

hindwing is squared off

Ventral (below)
pale forewing apex

red-orange spots

55

Ventral

Larva

Comments: The long-tailed black-and-white-striped Zebra Swallowtail can be confused with no other resident butterfly. It is an uncommon species in Michigan, typically found only in the southernmost counties. Adults have a low, rapid flight and adeptly maneuver through the understory or among shrubby vegetation. Seldom found far from stands of its larval host, it is unlikely to be encountered in highly developed areas but may occasionally wander into nearby home gardens in search of nectar. It has a proportionately short proboscis and cannot feed at many long, tubular flowers. It prefers composites, and is attracted to white flowers.

Zebra Swallowtail
Eurytides marcellus

Family/Subfamily: Swallowtails (Papilionidae)/
Swallowtails (Papilioninae)

Wingspan: 2.5–4.0" (6.4–10.2 cm)

Above: white with black stripes and long, slender tails; hindwings bear a bright red patch above the eyespot; spring-forms are smaller, lighter and have shorter tails

Below: as above, but with a red stripe through hindwing

Sexes: similar

Egg: light green, laid singly on host leaves or budding branches

Larva: several color forms; may be green, green with light blue and yellow stripes or charcoal with white and yellow stripes

Larval Host Plants: pawpaw

Habitat: moist deciduous woodlands, forest openings, stream corridors, forest edges and adjacent clearings and roadsides; occasionally gardens

Broods: two generations

Abundance: rare to occasional

Compare: unique

Visitor

Jan. Feb. Mar. Apr. May June July Aug. Sept. Oct. Nov. Dec.

male

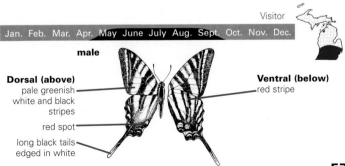

Dorsal (above)
pale greenish white and black stripes

red spot

long black tails edged in white

Ventral (below)
red stripe

57

Male

Female   Ventral   Larva

Comments: The Black Swallowtail is one of our most
common garden butterflies. Its plump, green larvae,
often referred to as "parsley worms," feed on many
cultivated herbs and may occasionally become minor
nuisance pests. It is equally at home in undisturbed
wetlands and rural meadows as in suburban yards and
urban parks. Males have a strong, rapid flight and frequently perch on vegetation or actively patrol open
areas for females. Both sexes are exceedingly fond of
flowers and stop to nectar at available blossoms.
Females mimic the toxic Pipevine Swallowtail to gain
protection from predators.

Black Swallowtail
Papilio polyxenes

Family/Subfamily: Swallowtails (Papilionidae)/ Swallowtails (Papilioninae)

Wingspan: 2.5–4.2" (6.4–10.7 cm)

Above: male is black with a broad, postmedian yellow band and a row of marginal yellow spots; female is mostly black with increased blue hindwing scaling and marginal yellow spots, the yellow postmedian band is reduced; both sexes have a red hindwing eyespot with a central black pupil, and a yellow-spotted abdomen

Below: hindwing has orange-tinted yellow spot bands

Sexes: dissimilar; female has reduced yellow postmedian band and increased blue hindwing scaling above

Egg: yellow, laid singly on host leaves

Larva: green with black bands and yellow-orange spots

Larval Host Plants: wild and cultivated members of the carrot family including Queen Anne's Lace, angelica, Wild Parsnip, dill, fennel and parsley

Habitat: old fields, roadsides, pastures, weedy sites, suburban gardens, marshes, agricultural land, vacant lots, prairies, open woodlands and utility corridors

Broods: two generations

Abundance: occasional to common

Compare: Spicebush Swallowtail (pg. 65) is larger and has green-blue submarginal spots.

Resident

Jan. Feb. Mar. Apr. May June July Aug. Sept. Oct. Nov. Dec.

male

Dorsal (above)
yellow bands
blue scaling
black "pupil" in center of spot
tail

Ventral (below)
yellow-orange bands
faint yellow-orange cell spot

Male

Ventral

Larva

Comments: The larvae of the Pipevine Swallowtail
sequester toxins from their hosts, rendering them and
the resulting adults highly distasteful to predators such
as birds. The butterfly's black wings and orange ventral
markings help advertise its unpalatability. Four other
Michigan butterflies mimic this color pattern to help
gain protection. Rare and sporadic in occurrence from
year to year, this swallowtail is limited to the southernmost counties of the state. Adults have a rapid, low
flight but are fond of colorful flowers and readily stop
to nectar. They rarely linger at one blossom for long,
tending to be wary and nervous of close approach.

Pipevine Swallowtail
Battus philenor

Family/Subfamily: Swallowtails (Papilionidae)/ Swallowtails (Papilioninae)

Wingspan: 2.75–4.00" (7.0–10.2 cm)

Above: overall black; male has iridescent greenish blue hindwings; female is duller black with a single row of white marginal spots

Below: hindwings are iridescent blue with a row of prominent orange spots

Sexes: dissimilar; female is dull black with a more prominent row of white spots

Egg: brownish orange, laid singly or in small clusters

Larva: velvety black with orange spots and numerous fleshy tubercles

Larval Host Plants: Virginia Snakeroot; various ornamental pipevine species

Habitat: fields, pastures, roadsides, open woodlands, stream corridors, suburban gardens

Broods: two generations

Abundance: rare to uncommon

Compare: Spicebush Swallowtail (pg. 65) is larger with prominent crescent-shaped marginal spots. Red-Spotted Purple (pg. 55) lacks hindwing tails. Female Black Swallowtail (pg. 59) is larger with an orange hindwing eyespot.

Visitor

| Jan. | Feb. | Mar. | Apr. | May | June | July | Aug. | Sept. | Oct. | Nov. | Dec. |

male

Dorsal (above)
black forewings
iridescent green-blue
row of pale spots

Ventral (below)
large orange spots
iridescent blue

Ventral

Larva

Comments: This lovely butterfly with the morbid name is often the first harbinger of spring. Hibernating adults occasionally venture from log piles or other protected sites on warm winter days and fly about even with patches of snow still on the ground. Adults from the single generation emerge in early summer, aestivate until fall, and become active again to feed and build up fat reserves before seeking protected sites to overwinter. Although widespread and often fairly common, it is typically encountered in very small numbers or as solitary individuals. Seldom visit flowers, but frequents rotting fruit or sap flows.

Mourning Cloak
Nymphalis antiopa

Family/Subfamily: Brush-foots (Nymphalidae)/
True Brush-foots (Nymphalinae)

Wingspan: 3.0–4.0" (7.6–10.2 cm)

Above: velvety black, often appearing iridescent, with
broad irregular yellow border and a row of bright purple blue spots; forewing apex is extended and squared
off; hindwing bears a single short, stubby tail

Below: silky black with pale wing border, heavily striated
and bark-like in appearance

Sexes: similar

Egg: light brown, laid in clusters on host leaves or twigs

Larva: black with a dorsal row of crimson patches, fine
white speckling and several rows of black, branched
spines

Larval Host Plants: birch, willow, aspen, elm and hackberry

Habitat: deciduous forests, clearings, riparian woodlands, woodland roads, forest edges, wetland and
watercourse margins, and adjacent open areas including suburban yards, parks and golf courses

Broods: single generation

Abundance: uncommon to common

Compare: unique

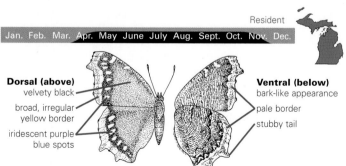

Resident

Jan. Feb. Mar. Apr. May June July Aug. Sept. Oct. Nov. Dec.

Dorsal (above)
velvety black
broad, irregular yellow border
iridescent purple blue spots

Ventral (below)
bark-like appearance
pale border
stubby tail

63

Male

Ventral

Larva

Comments: The lovely Spicebush Swallowtail is one of four Michigan butterflies that mimic the unpalatable Pipevine Swallowtail. Adults are strong, agile fliers that rarely stray far from their preferred habitats and are unlikely to be found in highly urban areas. Although recorded from several northern counties, the species is considerably more common in southern Michigan. A true lover of flowers, the adults avidly pause to feed at blossoms and may frequently wander into nearby gardens. The larvae construct individual shelters on their host by curling up both edges of a leaf with silk. They rest safely inside when not actively feeding.

Spicebush Swallowtail
Papilio troilus

Family/Subfamily: Swallowtails (Papilionidae)/ Swallowtails (Papilioninae)

Wingspan: 3.5–5.0" (8.9–12.7 cm)

Above: black with a row of large, pale greenish blue spots along the margin; hindwings have greenish blue scaling and a single, orange eyespot

Below: black with postmedian band of blue scaling bordered by row of yellow-orange spots on each side; abdomen black with longitudinal rows of light spots

Sexes: similar, female has duller hindwing scaling

Egg: cream, laid singly on the underside of host leaves

Larva: green above, reddish below with enlarged thorax, two false eyespots and several longitudinal rows of blue spots

Larval Host Plants: Sassafras and Spicebush

Habitat: deciduous and mixed forests, barrens, woodland margins and adjacent pastures, old fields, roadsides and gardens

Broods: two generations

Abundance: occasional to common

Compare: Pipevine Swallowtail (pg. 61), female Black Swallowtail (pg. 59) and dark-form female Eastern Tiger Swallowtail (pg. 67) all lack greenish blue submarginal spots.

Resident

| Jan. | Feb. | Mar. | Apr. | May | June | July | Aug. | Sept. | Oct. | Nov. | Dec. |

Dorsal (above)
orange spot
large pale green spots
iridescent green-blue patch
spoon-shaped tails

Ventral (below)
yellow-orange spots
blue scaling

Dark-form female

Dark-form female

Female

Male pg. 363

Female

Larva

Comments: Living up to its name, the majestic Eastern Tiger Swallowtail is easily recognized by its bold, black stripes and bright yellow wings. Adults have a strong, agile flight and often soar high in the treetops. Although fond of woodlands and waterways, it is equally at home in more urban areas and is a conspicuous garden visitor. Unlike many other swallowtails, the adults seldom flutter their wings while feeding. They instead rest on the blossom with their colorful wings outstretched. Dark-form females mimic the toxic Pipevine Swallowtail to gain protection from predators. Males often congregate at moist earth or animal dung.

Eastern Tiger Swallowtail
Papilio glaucus

Family/Subfamily: Swallowtails (Papilionidae)/ Swallowtails (Papilioninae)

Wingspan: 3.5–5.5" (8.9–14.0 cm)

Above: yellow with black forewing stripes and broad black wing margins; single row of yellow spots along outer edge of each wing

Below: yellow with black stripes and black wing margins; abdomen yellow with black stripes; forewing has sub-marginal band broken into spots

Sexes: dissimilar; male always yellow but females have two color forms; yellow female has increased blue scaling in black hindwing border; dark-form female is mostly black with extensive blue hindwing markings

Egg: green, laid singly on upper surface of host leaves

Larva: green; enlarged thorax and two small false eyespots

Larval Host Plants: Wild Cherry, Hop Tree, ash and Tulip Tree

Habitat: deciduous forests, woodland margins, gardens, parks, old fields, pastures and roadsides

Broods: two or more generations

Abundance: occasional to common

Compare: Canadian Tiger Swallowtail (pg. 361) is smaller; black morph female is rare. Spicebush Swallowtail (pg. 65) has greenish blue spots on hind-wing margin.

Resident

| Jan. | Feb. | Mar. | Apr. | May | June | July | Aug. | Sept. | Oct. | Nov. | Dec. |

male

Dorsal (above)
yellow with black stripes

wide black border

yellow spots

long tail

Ventral (below)
band of yellow spots

yellow-orange spots

blue scaling

67

Male

Female pg. 87 | Ventral | Larva

Comments: Widespread and common throughout much of the eastern U.S., the Eastern Tailed-Blue is one of our most abundant butterflies. Named for its distinctive hindwing tail, it is one of two blues in Michigan with this characteristic. Don't rely solely on the presence of tails for identification, as they are fragile and often lost with normal wing wear. Adults have a weak, dancing flight. Both sexes are extremely fond of flowers and are easily attracted to the garden. Males often gather in small puddle clubs at damp sand or gravel. It typically rests and feeds with its wings closed; blue color is seen primarily in flight or while basking.

Eastern Tailed-Blue
Everes comyntas

Family/Subfamily: Gossamer Wings (Lycaenidae)/ Blues (Polyommatinae)

Wingspan: 0.75–1.00" (1.9–2.5 cm)

Above: male is blue with brown border; female is brownish gray; both sexes have one or two small orange and black hindwing spots above single tail

Below: silvery gray with numerous dark spots and bands; hindwing has two small orange-capped black spots above tail

Sexes: dissimilar; female is primarily brownish gray

Egg: pale green, laid singly on flowers or young leaves of host

Larva: variable, typically green with dark dorsal stripe and light lateral stripes

Larval Host Plants: wide variety of herbaceous Fabaceae including clover, bush clover, Alfalfa, sweet clover and beggarweeds

Habitat: open, disturbed sites including roadsides, vacant lots, old fields, utility easements, fallow agricultural land, pastures, prairies and home gardens

Broods: multiple generations

Abundance: occasional to common

Compare: Summer Azure (pg. 75) lacks tails and orange spot along hindwing margin.

Resident

Jan. Feb. Mar. Apr. May June July Aug. Sept. Oct. Nov. Dec.

male

Dorsal (above)
bright blue
one or two orange-capped black spots
tail

Ventral (below)
black spots and bars outlined in white
two orange-capped black spots

Male

Female pg. 93   Ventral   Larva

Comments: Widespread and abundant throughout the western U.S., the Western Tailed-Blue becomes scarcer and more localized eastward. In Michigan, it is an uncommon and seldom seen butterfly with records limited exclusively to the Upper Peninsula. Although easily confused with the Eastern Tailed-Blue, this slightly larger species prefers forest clearings and associated margins over open, disturbed landscapes. Adults scurry about with a somewhat weak flight and regularly visit available flowers. It typically rests and feeds with its wings closed; blue color is seen primarily in flight or while the butterfly is basking.

Western Tailed-Blue
Everes amynthula

Family/Subfamily: Gossamer Wings (Lycaenidae)/ Blues (Polyommatinae)

Wingspan: 0.8–1.1" (2.0–2.8 cm)

Above: male is blue with brown border; female is brownish gray with faint blue scaling near wing bases; both sexes have white wing fringes; hindwing has a single tail

Below: silvery white with numerous tiny faint dark spots; hindwing has a faint, small orange-capped black spot near tail

Sexes: dissimilar; female is primarily brownish gray

Egg: pale green, laid singly on flowers or developing seedpods of host

Larva: variable; typically green with dark dorsal stripe and light lateral stripes

Larval Host Plants: wide variety of herbaceous Fabaceae including Cream Pea and milkvetch

Habitat: forest edges, clearings and nearby shrubby areas

Broods: single generation

Abundance: rare to occasional

Compare: Eastern Tailed-Blue (pg. 69) has larger, more distinct dark markings beneath, more orange near the tail and favors open, disturbed habitats.

Visitor

Jan. Feb. Mar. Apr. May June July Aug. Sept. Oct. Nov. Dec.

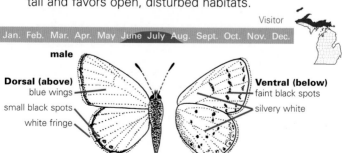

male

Dorsal (above)
blue wings
small black spots
white fringe

Ventral (below)
faint black spots
silvery white

Male

Larva

Comments: The Spring Azure is by far the most abundant and noticeable early-season blue in Michigan, often seen even before many of the colorful spring flowering trees and shrubs are in full bloom. A butterfly of deciduous forests and associated trails or margins, it may occasionally wander into nearby open areas including suburban yards. Adults have a moderately slow flight and erratically scurry from ground level to canopy height, moving just over the surface of the vegetation. They are extremely fond of flowers and often congregate at damp ground. Rests and feeds with wings closed, so blue color shows in flight or while basking.

Spring Azure
Celastrina ladon

Family/Subfamily: Gossamer Wings (Lycaenidae)/ Blues (Polyommatinae)

Wingspan: 0.75–1.25" (2.0–3.2 cm)

Above: male is pale blue with narrow, faint dark forewing border; lacks white scaling on wings; female has broad, dark forewing border and a narrow, dark hindwing border

Below: somewhat variable; dusky gray with black spots and dark scaling along hindwing margin (form marginata) and often a dark patch in the center of the hindwing (form lucia)

Sexes: dissimilar; female has a broader dorsal borders

Egg: whitish green; laid singly on flower buds of host

Larva: variable; green to pinkish green to whitish with dark dorsal stripe and cream bands

Larval Host Plants: flowers of various trees and shrubs including Black Cherry, blueberry, Flowering Dogwood, Gray Dogwood and viburnum

Habitat: open, deciduous woodlands, forest edges, utility easements, wooded swamps and yards

Broods: single generation

Abundance: occasional to common

Compare: Summer Azure (pg. 75) is lighter beneath with reduced dark markings and scaling; wings above with increased white scaling.

Resident

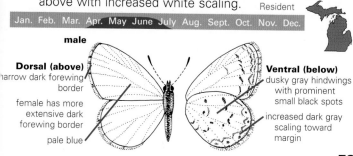

Jan. Feb. Mar. Apr. May June July Aug. Sept. Oct. Nov. Dec.

male

Dorsal (above)
narrow dark forewing border

female has more extensive dark forewing border

pale blue

Ventral (below)
dusky gray hindwings with prominent small black spots

increased dark gray scaling toward margin

73

Male

Female

Larva

Comments: Although now viewed as a distinct species, the Summer Azure was previously considered a lighter, second generation form of the similar, early-season Spring Azure. Adults of this small dusty blue butterfly are found in and along woodlands but readily venture out into nearby open areas in search of nectar and may frequently wander into suburban yards and gardens. They have a moderately slow, dancing flight and unlike most other blues are often encountered fluttering high among the branches of trees and shrubs. Males often congregate at damp ground. Blue color shows in flight or while basking.

Summer Azure

Celastrina neglecta (listed as *Celastrina ladon neglecta* by some authors)

Family/Subfamily: Gossamer Wings (Lycaenidae)/ Blues (Polyommatinae)

Wingspan: 0.80–1.25" (2.0–3.2 cm)

Above: male is light blue with narrow, faint dark border on forewing and increased white scaling on hindwing; female blue with heavy white scaling and broad, dark forewing borders

Below: chalky white with small dark spots and bands

Sexes: dissimilar, female has increased white scaling above and broad, dark forewing borders

Egg: whitish green, laid singly on flower buds of host

Larva: variable; green to pinkish green with dark dorsal stripe and cream bands

Larval Host Plants: flowers of various trees and shrubs (occasionally herbaceous plants) including New Jersey Tea, meadowsweet, Wing-stem, holly and sumac

Habitat: open, deciduous woodlands, forest edges and trails, stream margins, roadsides, brushy fields, utility easements, wooded swamps and gardens

Broods: two or more generations

Abundance: occasional to common

Compare: Spring Azure (pg. 73) is duskier gray and more heavily marked below; lacks dorsal white scaling. Eastern Tailed-Blue (pg. 69) has small orange spots near hindwing tail

Resident

Jan. Feb. Mar. Apr. May June July Aug. Sept. Oct. Nov. Dec.

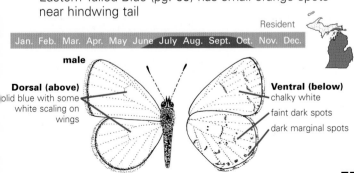

male

Dorsal (above)
solid blue with some white scaling on wings

Ventral (below)
chalky white

faint dark spots

dark marginal spots

75

Male | Female pg. 101 | Larva

Comments: The Northern Blue is primarily a Canadian species. It extends southward into the Upper Great Lakes where it tends to be quite local and uncommon. Within Michigan, it has only been recorded from a few counties in the Upper Peninsula. As a result, the butterfly is listed as threatened by the Michigan Department of Natural Resources. It remains a poorly known species with many aspects of its life history, ecology and behavior requiring further study. It typically rests and feeds with its wings closed; blue color is seen primarily in flight or while the butterfly is basking.

Northern Blue
Lycaeides idas nabokovi

Family/Subfamily: Gossamer Wings (Lycaenidae)/ Blues (Polyommatinae)

Wingspan: 0.85–1.20" (2.2–3.0 cm)

Above: male is bright blue to violet blue with narrow black wing borders and a white wing fringe; female is brown with blue scaling restricted to wing bases

Below: grayish white with white-rimmed round black spots and a submarginal row of orange- and black-capped silvery spots

Sexes: dissimilar; female is brown with reduced blue scaling

Egg: pale blue-green, laid singly on young shoots, new leaves or flower buds of host; eggs overwinter

Larva: poorly known; green

Larval Host Plants: Dwarf Bilberry; possibly also Bog Labrador Tea and Sheep Laurel

Habitat: openings in mixed forests

Broods: single generation

Abundance: rare to occasional; localized

Compare: Karner Blue (pg. 83) is restricted to the Lower Peninsula.

· Resident

Jan. Feb. Mar. Apr. May June July Aug. Sept. Oct. Nov. Dec.

male

Dorsal (above)
white fringe
blue wings
narrow black margin

Ventral (below)
grayish white with black spots
orange-capped silvery spots

Male

Female pg. 117

Larva

Comments: Named for its iridescent greenish blue
wings, this abundant western species knifes eastward
across southern Canada and the northern Great Lakes.
Although generally local in occurrence, it can at times
be rather common in northern Michigan. A butterfly of
open areas, the Greenish Blue has likely benefitted
from human land use practices that provide a wealth
of disturbed landscapes to support its fabaceous
hosts. Males patrol low to the ground near patches of
host plants for females and often congregate at moist
earth. It typically rests and feeds with its wings closed;
blue color is seen primarily in flight or while basking.

Greenish Blue
Plebejus saepiolus

Family/Subfamily: Gossamer Wings (Lycaenidae)/ Blues (Polyommatinae)

Wingspan: 1.00–1.25" (2.5–3.2 cm)

Above: male is light metallic blue to greenish blue with a narrow black border and white wing fringe; female is brown with blue scaling limited to wing bases; hindwing has a marginal row of faint orange-capped black spots

Below: whitish gray with numerous small, white-rimmed black spots and bluish scaling at wing bases

Sexes: dissimilar; female is brown with blue scaling limited to wing bases

Egg: light greenish, laid singly on flowers of host

Larva: green to reddish brown; partially grown larvae overwinter and complete development the following spring

Larval Host Plants: Alsike Clover; White Clover may also be used

Habitat: woodland openings, clearings, moist meadows, bog margins, fields and roadsides

Broods: single generation

Abundance: occasional, local

Compare: Northern Blue (pg. 77) has a submarginal row of orange- and black-capped silvery spots on the ventral hindwing.

Resident

Jan. Feb. Mar. Apr. May June July Aug. Sept. Oct. Nov. Dec.

male

Dorsal (above)
iridescent greenish blue

black border

Ventral (below)
faint blue scaling

small black spots

Male

Larva

Comments: Aptly named, the Silvery Blue's brilliant
metallic blue wings help make it one of our most beautiful spring butterflies. It is often encountered
alongside several of the early-season azures. It typically
occurs in isolated but often good-sized colonies, seldom far from stands of its larval hosts. Adults have a
low, quick and often directed flight but frequently stop
to nectar at small spring flowers and are particularly
fond of their host blossoms. Males often gather at
mud puddles to imbibe moisture. It typically rests and
feeds with its wings closed; blue color is seen primarily in flight or while the butterfly is basking.

Silvery Blue
Glaucopsyche lygdamus

Family/Subfamily: Gossamer Wings (Lycaenidae)/ Blues (Polyommatinae)

Wingspan: 1.00–1.25" (2.5–3.2 cm)

Above: male is uniform bright metallic silvery blue with narrow black wing borders; female somewhat duller blue with broader dark wing borders

Below: light brownish gray with a prominent row of white-rimmed round black spots; spot size somewhat variable (often larger in southern portions of Michigan)

Sexes: dissimilar; female is duller blue with broader and more diffuse dark wing borders

Egg: pale blue-green, laid singly young shoots, new leaves or flower buds of host

Larva: variable; purplish to gray-green with a dark green dorsal stripe and white, oblique dashes

Larval Host Plants: various Fabaceae including vetch, Alfalfa, White Sweet Clover, pea and milkvetch

Habitat: open woodlands, utility corridors, forested roads, brushy fields, meadows and occasionally more disturbed open sites

Broods: single generation

Abundance: occasional to common; local

Compare: Northern Blue (pg. 77) is whitish gray beneath and lacks the uniform row of white-rimmed black spots on the ventral forewing.   Resident

Jan. Feb. Mar. Apr. May June July Aug. Sept. Oct. Nov. Dec.

male

Dorsal (above)
bright blue

narrow black border

female is grayer

Ventral (below)
dull gray

row of round white-rimmed black spots

81

Male

Female

Comments: Once found from New Hampshire to Minnesota, the Karner Blue's range and population have been severely reduced due to urban and agricultural development and fire suppression. Today, the butterfly is critically imperiled, restricted to isolated pockets of remnant habitat; it is state-threatened and federally endangered. Despite this, Michigan boasts one of the largest remaining populations with the butterfly still locally common in certain southwestern counties. It typically rests and feeds with wings closed; blue color shows in flight or while basking.

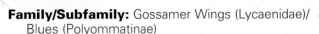

Karner Blue
Lycaeides melissa samuelis

Family/Subfamily: Gossamer Wings (Lycaenidae)/ Blues (Polyommatinae)

Wingspan: 1.00–1.35" (2.5–3.4 cm)

Above: male is bright blue with a narrow black border and white wing fringe; female has reduced blue scaling and broad brown margins; hindwing has a marginal row of small, orange-capped black spots

Below: whitish gray with numerous small, white-rimmed black spots and a distinctive orange submarginal spot band

Sexes: dissimilar; female has reduced blue scaling and marginal row of orange-capped black spots on the hindwing

Egg: light greenish, laid singly on or near the host

Larva: light green; tended by ants

Larval Host Plants: Wild Lupine

Habitat: openings in oak savannas or barrens

Broods: two generations

Abundance: rare to common; local

Compare: Northern Blue (pg. 77) is restricted to the Upper Peninsula.

Resident

| Jan. | Feb. | Mar. | Apr. | May | June | July | Aug. | Sept. | Oct. | Nov. | Dec. |

male

Dorsal (above)
continuous black line

bright blue

Ventral (below)
red-orange submarginal band outlined by black spots

Female
Larva

Comments: A large butterfly compared to most members of the family, the White M Hairstreak is named for the narrow white band on the ventral hindwing that forms a distinct M or W, depending on your perspective. The true beauty of this diminutive species can be seen mainly during flight, when the bright iridescent blue scaling of the upper wing surfaces flashes in the sunlight. Although widespread throughout much of the Southeast, it is a rare vagrant north into Michigan. At home along oak woodlands and moist forest borders, adults explore adjacent open areas for flowers. Adults have a quick, erratic flight and can be difficult to follow.

White M Hairstreak
Parrhasius m-album

Family/Subfamily: Gossamer Wings (Lycaenidae)/ Hairstreaks (Theclinae)

Wingspan: 1.0–1.5" (2.5–3.8 cm)

Above: male is bright iridescent blue with broad, black margins and two hindwing tails; female is dull black with blue scaling limited to wing bases

Below: brownish gray; hindwing has a single red eyespot above tail, white spot along leading margin, and a narrow white line forming a distinct M in middle of wing

Sexes: dissimilar; female duller with blue basal scaling

Egg: whitish, laid singly on twigs or buds of host

Larva: variable, dark green to mauve

Larval Host Plants: various oaks

Habitat: open woodlands, forest margins and adjacent, roadsides, utility easements, and old fields

Broods: potentially one or more generations

Abundance: rare

Compare: Northern Oak Hairstreak (pg. 131) lacks the prominent single red spot inward from the tails and the white spot along the leading margin of the ventral hindwing; wings above are brown.

Stray

| Jan. | Feb. | Mar. | Apr. | May | June | July | Aug. | Sept. | Oct. | Nov. | Dec. |

male

Dorsal (above)
iridescent blue
wide black borders

Ventral (below)
white spot
white M
red spot
blue patch

85

Female

Male pg. 69   Ventral   Larva

Comments: Widespread and common throughout much of the eastern U.S., the Eastern Tailed-Blue is one of our most abundant butterflies. Named for its distinctive hindwing tail, it is one of two blues in Michigan with this characteristic. Don't rely solely on the presence of tails for identification, as they are fragile and often lost with normal wing wear. Adults have a weak, dancing flight. Both sexes are extremely fond of flowers and are easily attracted to the garden. Males often gather in small puddle clubs at damp sand or gravel.

Eastern Tailed-Blue
Everes comyntas

Family/Subfamily: Gossamer Wings (Lycaenidae)/ Blues (Polyommatinae)

Wingspan: 0.75–1.00" (1.9–2.5 cm)

Above: male is blue with brown border; female is brownish gray; both sexes have one or two small orange and black hindwing spots above single tail

Below: silvery gray with numerous dark spots and bands; hindwing has two small orange-capped black spots above tail

Sexes: dissimilar; female is primarily brownish gray

Egg: pale green, laid singly on flowers or young leaves of host

Larva: variable, typically green with dark dorsal stripe and light lateral stripes

Larval Host Plants: A wide variety of herbaceous Fabaceae including clover, bush clover, Alfalfa, sweet clover and beggarweeds

Habitat: open, disturbed sites including roadsides, vacant lots, old fields, utility easements, fallow agricultural land, pastures, prairies and home gardens

Broods: multiple generations

Abundance: occasional to common

Compare: Summer Azure (pg. 75) lacks tails and orange spot along hindwing margin.

Resident

Jan. Feb. Mar. Apr. May June July Aug. Sept. Oct. Nov. Dec.

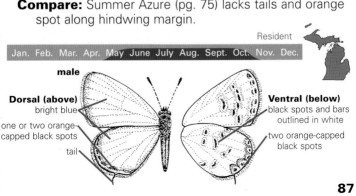

male

Dorsal (above)
bright blue

one or two orange-capped black spots

tail

Ventral (below)
black spots and bars outlined in white

two orange-capped black spots

87

Male

Female　Ventral　Larva

Comments: Our most diminutive copper is entirely restricted to acid bogs with an abundance of cranberries. As a result, colonies tend to be extremely localized. Adults maneuver close to the ground with a relatively weak flight and often alight on low-growing vegetation. They regularly seek nectar from the blossoms of their larval hosts. Three distinct subspecies are recognized throughout northeastern North America, with the ventral hindwing color varying from light gray in to yellowish tan. Subspecies michiganensis and epixanthe intersect in southeastern Quebec but display no signs of hybridization.

Bog Copper
Lycaena epixanthe michiganensis

Family/Subfamily: Gossamer Wings (Lycaenidae)/ Coppers (Lycaeninae)

Wingspan: 0.75–1.00" (1.9–2.5 cm)

Above: male is brown with a purplish iridescence and a prominent black cell-end spot on the forewing; female is brown with numerous black spots on both wings; hindwing of both sexes have a short and narrow orange submarginal band

Below: light gray with scattered white-rimmed black spots on both wings; hindwing has a narrow zigzag orange submarginal band

Sexes: dissimilar; female is duller brown with an increased number of black spots

Egg: whitish, laid singly on host leaves or stems

Larva: blue-green with a darker green dorsal stripe, light lateral stripe and numerous short whitish hairs

Larval Host Plants: Cranberry and Small Cranberry

Habitat: acid bogs

Broods: single generation

Abundance: uncommon to locally common

Compare: Dorcas Copper (pg. 103) is larger, has orange-brown ventral hindwings, and more extensive black dorsal spotting. Purplish Copper (pg. 115) is larger and has orange-tan ventral hindwings; female has more extensive orange ventral scaling. Resident

| Jan. | Feb. | Mar. | Apr. | May | June | July | Aug. | Sept. | Oct. | Nov. | Dec. |

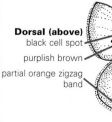

Dorsal (above)
black cell spot
purplish brown
partial orange zigzag band

Ventral (below)
light gray with faint black spots
narrow orange zigzag band

89

Larva

Comments: Living up to its name, the Frosted Elfin has extensive whitish gray scaling along the outer portion of its ventral hindwing, making it appear as if it were dusted lightly with powdered sugar. This uncommon and localized butterfly is closely associated with openings in oak savannas or other dry, sandy sites that support lupine, its sole larval host. Such habitat areas also harbor populations of the federally endangered Karner Blue butterfly and require periodic fire or other disturbance to prevent overgrowth and maintain a relatively open canopy. As a result, the species is currently listed by the Michigan DNR as threatened.

Frosted Elfin
Callophrys irus

Family/Subfamily: Gossamer Wings (Lycaenidae)/ Hairstreaks (Theclinae)

Wingspan: 0.8–1.0" (2.0–2.5 cm)

Above: unmarked dark brown; male has dark forewing stigma; female often has some reddish brown scaling above

Below: forewing brown; hindwing dark brown at wing base, outer portion somewhat lighter with extensive gray frosting along outer margin; hindwing bears short, stubby tail

Sexes: similar, although female lacks forewing stigma

Egg: whitish, laid singly host flower buds

Larva: blue-green with pale white oblique dorsal dashes and a pale white lateral stripe

Larval Host Plants: Wild Lupine

Habitat: openings in oak savannas, barrens and forest margins

Broods: single generation

Abundance: rare; localized

Compare: Hoary Elfin (pg. 97) is smaller and lacks both the short hindwing tail-like projection as well as the distinct small black spot near the tail. Henry's Elfin (pg. 107) lacks black spot near short, stubby tail. Brown Elfin (pg. 95) lacks hindwing frosting and a short, stubby tail.

Resident

Jan.	Feb.	Mar.	Apr.	May	June	July	Aug.	Sept.	Oct.	Nov.	Dec.

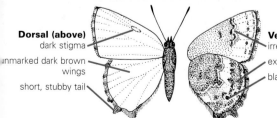

Dorsal (above)
dark stigma

unmarked dark brown wings

short, stubby tail

Ventral (below)
irregular white line

extensive gray frosting

black spot above tail

91

Female

Male pg. 71   Ventral   Larva

Comments: Widespread and abundant throughout the western U.S., the Western Tailed-Blue becomes scarcer and more localized eastward. In Michigan, it is an uncommon and seldom seen butterfly with records limited exclusively to the Upper Peninsula. Although easily confused with the Eastern Tailed-Blue, this slightly larger species prefers forest clearings and associated margins over open, disturbed landscapes. Adults scurry about with a somewhat weak flight and regularly visit available flowers.

Western Tailed-Blue
Everes amynthula

Family/Subfamily: Gossamer Wings (Lycaenidae)/
Blues (Polyommatinae)

Wingspan: 0.8–1.1" (2.0–2.8 cm)

Above: male is blue with brown border; female is
brownish gray with faint blue scaling near wing bases;
both sexes have white wing fringes; hindwing has a
single tail

Below: silvery white with numerous tiny faint dark spots;
hindwing has a faint, small orange-capped black spot
near tail

Sexes: dissimilar; female is primarily brownish gray

Egg: pale green, laid singly on flowers or developing
seedpods of host

Larva: variable; typically green with dark dorsal stripe and
light lateral stripes

Larval Host Plants: wide variety of herbaceous
Fabaceae including Cream Pea and milkvetch

Habitat: forest edges, clearings and nearby shrubby
areas

Broods: single generation

Abundance: rare to occasional

Compare: Eastern Tailed-Blue (pg. 87) has larger, more
distinct dark markings beneath, more orange near the
tail and favors open, disturbed habitats.

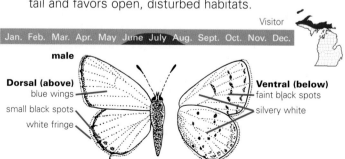

Visitor

| Jan. | Feb. | Mar. | Apr. | May | June | July | Aug. | Sept. | Oct. | Nov. | Dec. |

male

Dorsal (above)
blue wings
small black spots
white fringe

Ventral (below)
faint black spots
silvery white

Larva

Comments: The Brown Elfin is a delicate, tailless early-season species. Although widespread throughout Michigan and found in a variety of different habitats, it is seldom encountered in large numbers. The butterfly's small size and dull brown color make individuals easy to overlook. The adults generally remain close to the ground, often pausing to perch on the ends of bare twigs, low vegetation or on bare soil. If disturbed, they rapidly dart off but travel only a short distance before alighting once more. They seek nectar from a variety of early-season flowers.

Brown Elfin
Callophrys augustinus

Family/Subfamily: Gossamer Wings (Lycaenidae)/
Hairstreaks (Theclinae)

Wingspan: 0.8–1.1" (2.0–2.8 cm)

Above: dark brown; male has dark forewing stigma

Below: forewing brown; hindwing dark brown at base
with outer portion lighter reddish brown to mahogany

Sexes: similar

Egg: whitish, laid singly host flower buds

Larva: yellow green with pale yellow oblique dorsal
dashes and a yellow lateral stripe

Larval Host Plants: primarily plants in the heath family
including blueberries, Bog Laurel, Bearberry, Bog
Labrador Tea and Leatherleaf

Habitat: open woodlands, pine barrens, forest margins,
wooded roadsides, utility easements and bogs

Broods: single generation

Abundance: occasional; localized

Compare: Eastern Pine Elfin (pg. 105) has strongly patterned hindwings with numerous dark bands outlined
in white. Frosted Elfin's (pg. 91) hindwing has extensive frosting and a short, stubby tail. Henry's Elfin (pg.
107) has some white on outer portion of dark basal
hindwing patch, frosting along margin of hindwing and
a short, stubby tail.

Resident

Jan. Feb. Mar. Apr. May June July Aug. Sept. Oct. Nov. Dec.

Dorsal (above)
brown wings

lobed anal angle
of hindwing

Ventral (below)
hindwing much darker
at base

reddish brown toward
outer margin

95

Larva

Comments: The diminutive Hoary Elfin is named for the heavy gray scaling along the outer portion of the wings beneath that gives it a frosted appearance, particularly evident in fresh individuals. Primarily limited to northern counties, colonies of this uncommon spring butterfly tend to be small and isolated. As a result, it may be best sought by first locating patches of its larval host and then searching the surrounding area. Adults scurry low to the ground and regularly perch on vegetation or seek nectar at a variety of spring blooms.

Hoary Elfin
Callophrys polios

Family/Subfamily: Gossamer Wings (Lycaenidae)/ Hairstreaks (Theclinae)

Wingspan: 0.8–1.1" (2.0–2.8 cm)

Above: unmarked dark brown; male has gray forewing stigma

Below: forewing and hindwing dark brown at base with extensive violet gray frosting along outer margin; hindwing has dark postmedian band lacking or with limited white at the ends; hindwing lacks tail

Sexes: similar, although female lacks forewing stigma

Egg: whitish, laid singly on host leaves and flower buds

Larva: bright green with faint lighter green lines

Larval Host Plants: Bearberry; Trailing Arbutus may occasionally be used

Habitat: forest margins, barrens and dunes

Broods: single generation

Abundance: rare to uncommon; localized

Compare: Henry's Elfin (pg. 107) has a short, stubby tail. Brown Elfin (pg. 95) is larger and lacks frosting on the wings beneath. Frosted Elfin (pg. 91) is larger and has more extensive violet gray frosting on the wings beneath; hindwing has small black spot near short, tail-like projection.

Resident

Jan. Feb. Mar. Apr. May June July Aug. Sept. Oct. Nov. Dec.

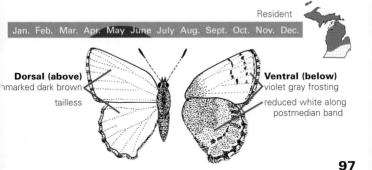

Dorsal (above)
unmarked dark brown
tailless

Ventral (below)
violet gray frosting
reduced white along postmedian band

97

Male

Male   Larva

Comments: As its name suggests, the Tawny-edged
Skipper has prominent bright orange scaling along the
costal margin of the forewing that is visible from both
the dorsal and ventral surfaces. Superficially quite similar to the somewhat larger Crossline Skipper, close
observation is often required for a definitive field identification. The species prefers open grassy areas and is
readily drawn to available wildflowers. Adults have a
low, rapid flight and often alight on bare soil or low
vegetation.

Tawny-edged Skipper
Polites themistocles

Family/Subfamily: Skippers (Hesperiidae)/
Banded Skippers (Hesperiinae)

Wingspan: 0.8–1.2" (2.0–3.0 cm)

Above: male is dark brown; forewing has a prominent
black stigma and tawny orange scaling along costal
margin; female forewing is dark brown with small yellow spots and reduced orange along costal margin

Below: hindwing light brown to olive brown; forewing
has distinct contrasting orange scaling along costal
margin

Sexes: dissimilar; female darker with reduced orange coloration; forewing lack black stigma

Egg: greenish white, laid singly on host leaves

Larva: reddish brown with dark dorsal stripe and black
head

Larval Host Plants: various grasses including panic
grass, Slender Crabgrass, mannagrass and bluegrass

Habitat: stream corridors, wet meadows, old fields, pastures, prairies, roadsides and suburban yards

Broods: two generations

Abundance: occasional to abundant

Compare: Crossline Skipper (pg. 125) is larger and usually has a faint band of small, pale spots through the
center of the hindwing beneath. Tolerates
drier habitats.   Resident

Jan. Feb. Mar. Apr. May June July Aug. Sept. Oct. Nov. Dec.

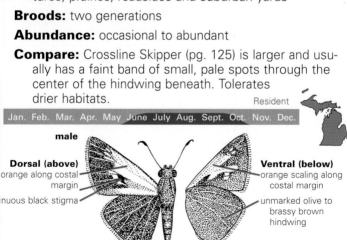

male

Dorsal (above)
orange along costal
margin

nuous black stigma

Ventral (below)
orange scaling along
costal margin

unmarked olive to
brassy brown
hindwing

Female   Male pg. 77   Larva

Comments: The Northern Blue is primarily a Canadian species. It extends southward into the Upper Great Lakes where it tends to be quite local and uncommon. Within Michigan, it has only been recorded from a few counties in the Upper Peninsula. As a result, the butterfly is listed as threatened by the Michigan Department of Natural Resources. It remains a poorly known species with many aspects of its life history, ecology and behavior requiring further study.

Northern Blue
Lycaeides idas nabokovi

Family/Subfamily: Gossamer Wings (Lycaenidae)/ Blues (Polyommatinae)

Wingspan: 0.85–1.20" (2.2–3.0 cm)

Above: male is bright blue to violet blue with narrow black wing borders and a white wing fringe; female is brown with blue scaling restricted to wing bases

Below: grayish white with white-rimmed round black spots and a submarginal row of orange- and black-capped silvery spots

Sexes: dissimilar; female is brown with reduced blue scaling

Egg: pale blue-green, laid singly on young shoots, new leaves or flower buds of host; eggs overwinter

Larva: poorly known; green

Larval Host Plants: Dwarf Bilberry; possibly also Bog Labrador Tea and Sheep Laurel

Habitat: openings in mixed forests

Broods: single generation

Abundance: rare to occasional; localized

Compare: Karner Blue (pg. 83) is restricted to the Lower Peninsula

Resident

Jan. Feb. Mar. Apr. May June July Aug. Sept. Oct. Nov. Dec.

male

Dorsal (above)
white fringe
blue wings
narrow black margin

Ventral (below)
grayish white with black spots
orange-capped silvery spots

101

Male

Female

Ventral

Comments: This primarily boreal species essentially replaces the Purplish Copper northward into Canada. A butterfly of wet, often shrubby habitats, it is intensely localized but often common when encountered. Adults seldom venture far from patches of their larval host. They have a relatively weak flight and frequently alight on low-growing vegetation with their wings partially open. Both sexes are fond of flowers and may be closely observed at available blossoms.

Dorcas Copper
Lycaena dorcas

Family/Subfamily: Gossamer Wings (Lycaenidae)/ Coppers (Lycaeninae)

Wingspan: 0.85–1.20" (2.2–3.0 cm)

Above: male is brown with a purplish iridescence and several small scattered black spots on both wings; female is brown (occasionally with a hint of orange) with several scattered black spots on both wings

Below: forewing yellow-orange with an orange-brown apex and scattered small black spots; hindwing orange-brown with very small scattered black spots and a narrow zigzag orange submarginal band

Sexes: dissimilar; female is dull brown with a small amount of orange scaling

Egg: whitish, laid singly on host leaves

Larva: light green with a darker green dorsal stripe and pale oblique dashes

Larval Host Plants: Shrubby Cinquefoil

Habitat: meadows, bogs, seeps, stream margins, fens and wet roadsides

Broods: single generation

Abundance: uncommon to locally common

Compare: Purplish Copper (pg. 115) is larger and has orange submarginal line on the dorsal hindwing; females have more extensive orange dorsal scaling.

Resident

Jan. Feb. Mar. Apr. May June July Aug. Sept. Oct. Nov. Dec.

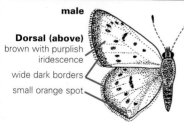

male

Dorsal (above)
brown with purplish iridescence

wide dark borders

small orange spot

Ventral (below)
orange-brown hindwing

narrow red submarginal line

103

Larva

Comments: With its boldly patterned hindwings, this beautiful little early-season species is one of our most distinctive elfins. The butterfly is frequently encountered in pine barrens and other open woodland areas with appropriate host pines, where it tends to be in close association with younger trees. Adults spend much of their time perched on sunlit host branches, often high above the ground, but frequently venture down to nectar at nearby blossoms. Males are often encountered sipping moisture at damp soil.

Eastern Pine Elfin
Callophrys niphon

Family/Subfamily: Gossamer Wings (Lycaenidae)/ Hairstreaks (Theclinae)

Wingspan: 0.80–1.25" (2.0–3.2 cm)

Above: male unmarked dark brown with pale gray forewing stigma; female brown with increased orange-brown scaling; hindwing lacks tail

Below: brown, strongly banded with blackish brown, reddish brown and gray; hindwing has distinct gray marginal band

Sexes: similar, although female is tawnier above and lacks pale forewing stigma

Egg: pale green, laid singly at the base of host needles

Larva: bright green with cream longitudinal stripes

Larval Host Plants: various pines including Eastern White Pine and Jack Pine

Habitat: pine barrens, woodland clearings, brushy fields, roadsides and utility easements

Broods: single generation

Abundance: occasional to common

Compare: Western Pine Elfin (pg. 111) appears overall darker beneath and ventral hindwing lacks a distinct gray marginal band. Often difficult to quickly separate in the field in areas where the ranges of both species overlap.

Resident

| Jan. | Feb. | Mar. | Apr. | May | June | July | Aug. | Sept. | Oct. | Nov. | Dec. |

male

Dorsal (above)
pale gray stigma

tailless

Ventral (below)
banded with black, reddish brown and gray

gray marginal band

105

Larva (green)

Larva (red)

Comments: This lovely but reclusive tailed elfin is found in a variety of open wooded areas or along forest margins in close association with stands of its larval host. Generally an uncommon butterfly, colonies tend to be spotty and highly local in occurrence. Adults have a quick, erratic flight and regularly perch on the tips of small tree branches or on low, shrubby vegetation. They may also be encountered at nearby spring blossoms or sipping moisture at damp earth.

Henry's Elfin
Callophrys henrici

Family/Subfamily: Gossamer Wings (Lycaenidae)/ Hairstreaks (Theclinae)

Wingspan: 0.9–1.2" (2.3–3.0 cm)

Above: brown with amber-orange scaling along hindwing margin; hindwing has short, stubby tail; males lack a forewing stigma

Below: brown; hindwing distinctly two-toned with dark brown basal half and light brown outer half; gray frosting along outer margin

Sexes: similar

Egg: whitish, laid singly on host twigs or flower buds

Larva: variable; green to reddish with oblique white dorsal markings

Larval Host Plants: Mapleleaf Viburnum is the primary host; Redbud, holly, huckleberry and blueberry are utilized in other states and may occasionally be used

Habitat: deciduous woodlands, barrens, forest edges and clearings, shrubby areas, old fields and roadsides

Broods: single spring generation

Abundance: occasional; localized

Compare: Hoary Elfin (pg. 97) is smaller, has more violet gray frosting beneath and lacks a hindwing tail. Frosted Elfin (pg. 91) has more frosting on hindwing beneath and a small dark spot near tail. Brown Elfin (pg. 95) lacks a hindwing tail.

Resident

Jan. Feb. Mar. Apr. May June July Aug. Sept. Oct. Nov. Dec.

Dorsal (above)
dull brown
amber scaling
stubby tail

Ventral (below)
two-toned pattern
white at upper and lower ends of dark patch
gray frosting

107

Dorsal

Larva

Comments: Well named, this distinctive skipper does indeed look as if it were sprinkled with salt and pepper. Although widespread throughout the East, it tends to be a universally uncommon butterfly. It is most often encountered individually or in small numbers darting in and out of sunlit woodland openings or along forested roadways. The small adults speed along near the ground with a rapid and somewhat erratic flight. Males often imbibe moisture and other nutrients at damp earth.

Pepper and Salt Skipper
Amblyscirtes hegon

Family/Subfamily: Skippers (Hesperiidae)/
Banded Skippers (Hesperiinae)

Wingspan: 0.9–1.2" (2.3–3.0 cm)

Above: dark brown with checkered fringes and a band of
small white spots on the forewing

Below: variable; hindwing is greenish gray with cream
spot band; wing fringes are strongly checkered

Sexes: similar, female has more rounded forewing apex

Egg: light green, laid singly on host leaves

Larva: whitish green with a dark green dorsal line, a
paler green subdorsal line and a reddish brown head
with a pale brown crescent on each side

Larval Host Plants: various grasses including Fowl
Mannagrass, Indian Grass, Kentucky Bluegrass and
Indian Woodoats

Habitat: sunlit forest clearings, woodland margins,
glades, stream corridors and adjacent fields

Broods: single generation

Abundance: rare to uncommon; localized

Compare: Common Roadside-Skipper (pg. 135) lacks the
heavy gray overscaling and cream postmedian spot
band on the ventral hindwing.

Resident

Jan.	Feb.	Mar.	Apr.	May	June	July	Aug.	Sept.	Oct.	Nov.	Dec.

Dorsal (above)
white spots

brown

Ventral (below)
cream spot band

hindwing frosted with
light greenish gray

strongly checkered
fringes

Larva

Comments: Despite its name, the Western Pine Elfin
ranges far eastward in patchy, isolated populations. It
often flies with the very similar-looking Eastern Pine
Elfin in the Upper Peninsula making reliable identification somewhat tricky. An uncommon butterfly,
colonies tend to be quite local and found in close association with stands of Eastern White Pine. Adults
perch on the needles of sunlit host branches and occasionally venture down to nectar at nearby blossoms.

Western Pine Elfin
Callophrys eryphon

Family/Subfamily: Gossamer Wings (Lycaenidae)/ Hairstreaks (Theclinae)

Wingspan: 0.85–1.30" (2.2–3.3 cm)

Above: male unmarked dark brown with pale gray forewing stigma; female brown with increased amber scaling; hindwing lacks tail

Below: brown, strongly banded with black, reddish brown and gray; hindwing has sharply jagged dark sub-marginal band

Sexes: similar, although female is tawnier above and lacks pale forewing stigma

Egg: pale green, laid singly at the base of young host needles

Larva: bright green with cream longitudinal stripes

Larval Host Plants: various pines including Eastern White Pine and Jack Pine

Habitat: pine woodlands and associated clearings, margins, roadsides and utility easements

Abundance: rare to occasional; local

Compare: Eastern Pine Elfin (pg. 105) appears overall lighter beneath and the ventral hindwing has a distinct gray marginal band. Often difficult to quickly separate in the field in areas where the ranges of both species overlap.

Resident

| Jan. | Feb. | Mar. | Apr. | May | June | July | Aug. | Sept. | Oct. | Nov. | Dec. |

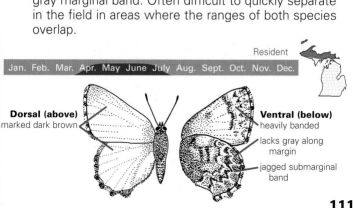

Dorsal (above)
marked dark brown

Ventral (below)
heavily banded

lacks gray along margin

jagged submarginal band

Male

Female

Larva

Comments: This distinctive tailless hairstreak is unlikely
to be confused with any other small butterfly on
Michigan. The Coral Hairstreak frequents a variety of
semi-open, brushy habitats in close association with its
somewhat aggressive, thicket-forming hosts. Adults
have a quick, erratic flight and readily perch on the top
of small trees or shrubs. Both sexes avidly visit flowers and are exceedingly fond of milkweed blossoms
where they are often observed feeding alongside various other hairstreaks.

Coral Hairstreak
Satyrium titus

Family/Subfamily: Gossamer Wings (Lycaenidae)/ Hairstreaks (Theclinae)

Wingspan: 0.90–1.25" (2.3–3.2 cm)

Above: unmarked brown; male has a small gray forewing stigma and somewhat triangular wings

Below: light gray brown with a row of small, white-rimmed black spots across both wings and a second row of larger bright coral spots along the hindwing margin; tailless

Sexes: similar, although female has more rounded wings and lacks forewing stigma

Egg: cream, laid singly on host twigs, low on the trunks of small host trees or occasionally on leaf litter below the host

Larva: yellow green with pinkish red patches on each end; larvae are associated with ants

Larval Host Plants: Black Cherry, Wild Cherry and American Plum

Habitat: overgrown fields near forest margins, brushy woodland clearings, shrubby roadsides and trails, and unmanaged pastures or fencerows

Broods: single generation

Abundance: occasional to common

Compare: unique

Resident

| Jan. | Feb. | Mar. | Apr. | May | June | July | Aug. | Sept. | Oct. | Nov. | Dec. |

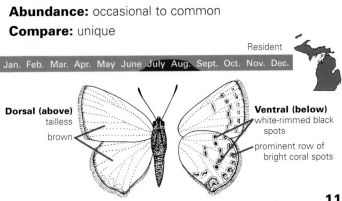

Dorsal (above)
tailless
brown

Ventral (below)
white-rimmed black spots
prominent row of bright coral spots

Male

Female pg. 237

Larva

Comments: Living up to its name, male Purplish Coppers
have an iridescent purple sheen on the wings above
that is stunning when seen in sunlight. Found in a variety of moist areas, colonies tend to be small and
somewhat localized, but can be relatively abundant
when encountered. While it is not as habitat restricted
as many other coppers, expanding agricultural activities,
urban development and habitat degradation nonetheless
continue to restrict the number of suitable wetland
areas available to the butterfly throughout its eastern
range. Males perch low on grasses or other vegetation
with their wings partially open to await passing females.

Purplish Copper
Lycaena helloides

Family/Subfamily: Gossamer Wings (Lycaenidae)/ Coppers (Lycaeninae)

Wingspan: 1.0–1.2" (2.5–3.0 cm)

Above: male is brown with a strong purplish iridescence and scattered black; female is primarily orange with scattered black spots and broad brown borders; hindwing has a broad scalloped orange submarginal band

Below: forewing is orange with scattered black spots and a purplish brown apex and outer margin; hindwing purplish brown with small black spots and a narrow, irregular reddish orange submarginal line

Sexes: dissimilar; female has increased orange scaling on both wings

Egg: greenish white, laid singly on the host

Larva: green with several yellow stripes

Larval Host Plants: knotweed and dock

Habitat: open, moist habitats including wet meadows, stream margins, roadside ditches, pond margins, fallow agricultural land and marshes

Broods: two or more generations

Abundance: occasional to common; localized

Compare: Dorcas Copper (pg. 103) is generally smaller and lacks or has a less extensive orange submarginal band on the dorsal hindwing. Female has less orange dorsal scaling.

Resident

Jan. Feb. Mar. Apr. May June July Aug. Sept. Oct. Nov. Dec.

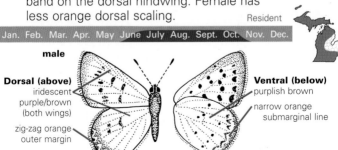

male

Dorsal (above)
iridescent purple/brown (both wings)

zig-zag orange outer margin

Ventral (below)
purplish brown

narrow orange submarginal line

Female | Male pg. 79 | Larva

Comments: Named for its iridescent greenish blue
wings, this abundant western species knifes eastward
across southern Canada and the northern Great Lakes.
Although generally local in occurrence, it can at times
be rather common in northern Michigan. A butterfly of
open areas, the Greenish Blue has likely benefitted
from human land use practices that provide a wealth
of disturbed landscapes to support its fabaceous
hosts. Males patrol low to the ground near patches of
host plants for females and often congregate at moist
earth.

Greenish Blue
Plebejus saepiolus

Family/Subfamily: Gossamer Wings (Lycaenidae)/
Blues (Polyommatinae)

Wingspan: 1.00–1.25" (2.5–3.2 cm)

Above: male is light metallic blue to greenish blue with a
narrow black border and white wing fringe; female is
brown with blue scaling limited to wing bases; hindwing has a marginal row of faint orange-capped black
spots

Below: whitish gray with numerous small, white-rimmed
black spots and bluish scaling at wing bases

Sexes: dissimilar; female is brown with blue scaling limited to wing bases

Egg: light greenish, laid singly on flowers of host

Larva: green to reddish brown; partially grown larvae
overwinter and complete development the following
spring

Larval Host Plants: Alsike Clover; White Clover may
also be used

Habitat: woodland openings, clearings, moist meadows,
bog margins, fields and roadsides

Broods: single generation

Abundance: occasional, local

Compare: Northern Blue (pg. 101) has a submarginal
row of orange- and black-capped silvery
spots on the ventral hindwing.   Resident

Jan. Feb. Mar. Apr. May June July Aug. Sept. Oct. Nov. Dec.

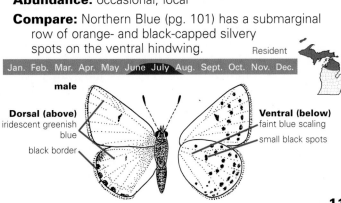

male

Dorsal (above)
iridescent greenish
blue

black border

Ventral (below)
faint blue scaling

small black spots

Larvae

Comments: The Banded Hairstreak is one of Michigan's
most abundant hairstreaks. A small, inconspicuous
butterfly of mixed hardwood forests, it may be found
nectaring at flowers in nearby clearings or along adjacent roadsides. It may even be encountered in more
urban locations if its larval hosts are present. Males
perch on shrubs or low, overhanging limbs and aggressively dart out at other passing individuals. They return
to the same or nearby perch following the short, but
furious whirling interaction.

Banded Hairstreak
Satyrium calanus falacer

Family/Subfamily: Gossamer Wings (Lycaenidae)/ Hairstreaks (Theclinae)

Wingspan: 1.00–1.25" (2.5–3.2 cm)

Above: unmarked dark brown with two hindwing tails

Below: gray-brown; hindwing has an irregular dark post-median spot-band edged outwardly in white, and a red-capped black spot and blue patch near the tails

Sexes: similar

Egg: pinkish brown, laid singly on twigs of host

Larva: variable, green to gray brown; ight lateral stripe

Larval Host Plants: various oaks, hickories and walnuts including White Oak, Northern Red Oak, Pignut Hickory, Shagbark Hickory, Black Walnut and Bitternut

Habitat: mixed deciduous forests, oak woodlands, forest clearing, roadsides, old fields, parks, utility easements and suburban gardens

Broods: single generation

Abundance: occasional to common

Compare: Edwards's Hairstreak (pg. 121) has a row of white-rimmed oval black spots, not dashes, below. Hickory Hairstreak (pg. 123) is extremely similar and may not reliably be separated in the field. Hickory typically has the ventral blue hindwing patch extending further inward and a more offset dark post-median band on the ventral forewing. Resident

Jan. Feb. Mar. Apr. May June July Aug. Sept. Oct. Nov. Dec.

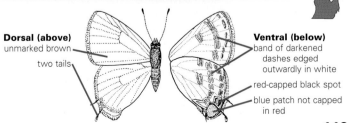

Dorsal (above)
unmarked brown
two tails

Ventral (below)
band of darkened dashes edged outwardly in white

red-capped black spot

blue patch not capped in red

119

Larva

Comments: Edwards's Hairstreak is associated with dry areas dominated by short, scrubby oaks. Its short flight period and resemblance to other, more abundant hairstreaks make it easy to overlook. Despite its overall rarity, it can be locally numerous. The slug-like larvae are regularly tended (and guarded from predators) by ants (*Formica integra*). Older larvae spend the day in ant nests at the base of the host tree and venture out at night to feed. In return for their protection, the ants receive food from the larvae in the form of nutritious sugar-rich secretions. Its reliance on ants may contribute to the butterfly's spotty and localized distribution.

Edwards's Hairstreak
Satyrium edwardsii

Family/Subfamily: Gossamer Wings (Lycaenidae)/
Hairstreaks (Theclinae)

Wingspan: 1.00–1.25" (2.5–3.2 cm)

Above: unmarked brown with a small orange spot near
short tail; male has small dark forewing stigma

Below: light gray brown with a row of small, white-
rimmed black spots; hindwing has a large blue patch
and a series of orange spots near tails

Sexes: similar, although female has slightly more
rounded wings and lacks dark forewing stigma above

Egg: cream pink, laid singly on host twigs near buds;
eggs overwinter

Larva: dark brown with dark dorsal band and a series of
pale oblique dashes along the sides

Larval Host Plants: various oaks including Scarlet Oak,
Black Oak, White Oak and Bur Oak

Habitat: prairie hills, ridges, open oak barrens, forest
margins, roadsides, utility easements and trail margins

Broods: single generation

Abundance: rare to uncommon; localized

Compare: Striped (pg. 133) and Banded (pg. 119)
Hairstreaks have bands of white-edged dashes, not
distinctly separated white-rimmed dark oval spots, on
the wings below. Acadian Hairstreak (pg.
149) is restricted to moist habitats.   Resident

| Jan. | Feb. | Mar. | Apr. | May | June | July | Aug. | Sept. | Oct. | Nov. | Dec. |

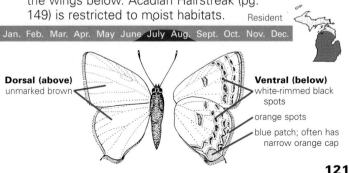

Dorsal (above)
unmarked brown

Ventral (below)
white-rimmed black
spots

orange spots

blue patch; often has
narrow orange cap

121

Comments: The Hickory Hairstreak is an uncommon butterfly of mixed deciduous forests and second growth woodlands. As its name implies, it utilizes a variety of hickories and walnuts as larval hosts. Populations tend to be small and highly localized in occurrence. In addition to its rarity, the species may further be overlooked because of its close resemblance to the more widespread and abundant Banded Hairstreak with which it often flies. The adults often perch high on the branches of their hosts and aggressively dart out at passing butterflies with a fast, erratic flight before alighting again.

Hickory Hairstreak
Satyrium caryaevorum

Family/Subfamily: Gossamer Wings (Lycaenidae)/ Hairstreaks (Theclinae)

Wingspan: 1.00–1.25" (2.5–3.2 cm)

Above: uniform dark brown with a short hindwing tail; male has a gray forewing stigma

Below: brown with a row of fairly wide and somewhat offset dark dashes edged in white across both wings, a large blue hindwing patch and orange-capped black spot near the tail

Sexes: similar, although female lacks forewing stigma

Egg: pinkish brown, laid singly on twigs; eggs overwinter

Larva: yellow green, often with dark green dorsal stripe, yellow lateral stripe and dark dashes edged in white

Larval Host Plants: various hickories, walnuts and oaks including Pignut Hickory, Shagbark Hickory, Bitternut Hickory, Northern Red Oak and Bitternut

Habitat: mixed deciduous forests, forest clearings, old fields and semi-open brushy areas

Broods: single generation

Abundance: rare to occasional; local

Compare: Edwards's Hairstreak (pg. 121) has row of white-rimmed oval black spots, not dashes, below. Banded Hairstreak (pg. 119) is extremely similar, but the blue ventral hindwing patch doesn't extend as far inward.

Resident

Jan. Feb. Mar. Apr. May June July Aug. Sept. Oct. Nov. Dec.

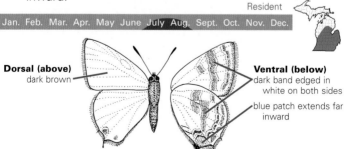

Dorsal (above)
dark brown

Ventral (below)
dark band edged in white on both sides

blue patch extends far inward

Male

Female

Larva

Comments: Although widespread throughout much of the East, this small species is seldom overly abundant in Michigan. Colonies tend to be rather small and often quite local. Easily confused with the similar Tawny-edged Skipper, the two can often be distinguished on the basis of habitat, with the Crossline Skipper preferring drier locations. Adults have a low, rapid flight and often alight on low vegetation. Males may occasionally be encountered sipping moisture at mud puddles.

Crossline Skipper
Polites origenes

Family/Subfamily: Skippers (Hesperiidae)/
  Banded Skippers (Hesperiinae)

Wingspan: 1.00–1.25" (2.5–3.2 cm)

Above: male is dark olive brown; forewing has tawny
  orange scaling along costal margin and yellow orange
  spots along the outer edge of black stigma; female is
  primarily dark brown with a few light forewing spots

Below: hindwing is yellow brown with a faint, straight
  band of small pale spots; forewing has dull tawny
  orange scaling along costal margin, not strongly contrasting with color of hindwing

Sexes: dissimilar; female darker above with cream spots
  on forewing and reduced orange scaling along costal
  margin; forewing lacks black stigma

Egg: greenish, laid singly on host leaves

Larva: dark brown, faint white mottling; round black head

Larval Host Plants: various grasses including Little
  Bluestem, Purpletop Grass, mannagrass and bluegrass

Habitat: dry, grassy areas including old fields, pastures,
  prairies, forest clearings and utility easements

Broods: single generation

Abundance: uncommon to occasional; local

Compare: Tawny-edged Skipper (pg. 99) is smaller,
  prefers wetter habitats and usually has
  unmarked ventral hindwing.   Resident

Jan. Feb. Mar. Apr. May June July Aug. Sept. Oct. Nov. Dec.

male

Dorsal (above)
orange scaling
yellow orange spots
long straight stigma
faint orange scaling

Ventral (below)
dull orange scaling
faint, straight band of
  small pale spots

125

Female

Larva

Comments: What this skipper lacks in size it more than
makes up for in sheer numbers, being one of
Midwest's most abundant species. Primarily a butterfly
of moist meadows and marshes, it tolerates a wide
range of more human-disturbed, grassy areas including
roadsides and suburban lawns. The small adults
maneuver close to the ground with a rapid, darting
flight but regularly alight on low vegetation. Its distinctive yellow ventral hindwing patch is somewhat
variable in appearance and may be continuous or broken into separate spots.

Peck's Skipper
Polites peckius

Family/Subfamily: Skippers (Hesperiidae)/
Banded Skippers (Hesperiinae)

Wingspan: 1.00–1.25" (2.5–3.2 cm)

Above: dark brown; forewing has orange scaling toward
base and a few tiny orange spots near apex; hindwing
has a band of elongated narrow orange spots; male
forewing has sinuous black stigma

Below: somewhat variable; hindwing is dark brown with
a distinctive irregular central golden yellow patch

Sexes: similar, although female lacks black forewing
stigma and has somewhat larger and paler forewing
spots

Egg: whitish green, laid singly on host leaves

Larva: dark maroon brown with short light hairs and a
black head and anal patch

Larval Host Plants: various grasses including Rice
Cutgrass and Kentucky Bluegrass

Habitat: open grassy areas including pastures roadsides, old fields, wet meadows, marshes, utility
easements and lawns

Broods: two or more generations

Abundance: occasional to abundant

Compare: unique

Resident

Jan. Feb. Mar. Apr. May June July Aug. Sept. Oct. Nov. Dec.

Dorsal (above)
orange scaling
dark brown borders

Ventral (below)
variable central golden
yellow patch; often
fused or separated
into component
spots

Dorsal

Larva

Comments: The Powesheik Skipperling is a small but distinctive species. Although once occupying a continuous range from southern Michigan west around the tip of Lake Michigan to western Iowa and the eastern portions of the Dakotas, it has suffered from the continued loss of habitat. In Michigan, it is currently limited to a few southern counties with highly localized and isolated colonies. As a result, the skipper is listed as threatened by the Michigan DNR and populations should be protected wherever found. Adults scurry close to the ground with a rapid, darting flight and frequently alight on low vegetation.

Poweshiek Skipperling
Oarisma poweshiek

Family/Subfamily: Skippers (Hesperiidae)/
Banded Skippers (Hesperiinae)

Wingspan: 1.00–1.25" (2.5–3.2 cm)

Above: dark chocolate brown; forewing has orange scaling along costal margin

Below: hindwing light brown with white-lined veins and a dark brown anal margin

Sexes: similar

Egg: yellow-green, laid singly on host leaves

Larva: green with a dark green dorsal stripe edged in white and white lateral stripes

Larval Host Plants: Elliptic Spikerush

Habitat: tallgrass prairie remnants, prairie fens and moist sedge meadows

Broods: single generation

Abundance: occasional to abundant

Compare: unique

Resident

Jan. Feb. Mar. Apr. May June July Aug. Sept. Oct. Nov. Dec.

Dorsal (above)
orange scaling along leading edge

dark brown

Ventral (below)
veins outlined in white

Larva

Comments: Although previously treated as a separate species (the Northern Hairstreak), populations outside of the Florida peninsula and the extreme southern Atlantic Coast are now recognized to be geographic races (or subspecies) of the same butterfly. The Northern Oak Hairstreak inhabits oak-dominated wood-lands and adjacent open areas. The butterfly is found in Indiana and Ohio but just barely enters the southern fringe of Michigan, where records are scarce. Adults have a quick, erratic flight and frequently perch high on the leaves of surrounding vegetation, regularly venturing down to nectar at a variety of small blossoms.

Northern Oak Hairstreak
Satyrium favonius ontario

Family/Subfamily: Gossamer Wings (Lycaenidae)/ Hairstreaks (Theclinae)

Wingspan: 1.0–1.3" (2.5–3.3 cm)

Above: dark brown with dark forewing stigma and a small orange spot near the tails

Below: gray-brown with a white postmedian line strongly zigzagged toward hindwing tails, a large blue patch often capped lightly in orange, and short row of small orange spots, the largest of which borders a black spot

Sexes: similar

Egg: pinkish brown, laid singly on twigs; eggs overwinter

Larva: yellow-green with a dark green dorsal stripe and covered with tiny yellow dots

Larval Host Plants: various oaks including Black Oak, White Oak and Red Oak

Habitat: woodlands with oaks, and adjacent margins, clearings, roadsides, fields and utility easements

Broods: single generation

Abundance: rare

Compare: White M Hairstreak (pg. 85) has single red ventral hindwing spot. Gray Hairstreak (pg. 223) is light gray below with a less jagged white line.

Stray

Jan. Feb. Mar. Apr. May June July Aug. Sept. Oct. Nov. Dec.

male

Dorsal (above)
all, gray brown wings

Ventral (below)
jagged black-and-white line

blue patch with orange cap

131

Larva

Comments: The Striped Hairstreak's name comes from the numerous white-edged dark dashes that give it an overall striped appearance. Although widespread throughout the state, it is generally uncommon, highly localized and seldom seen in any numbers. Adults are often encountered alongside a variety of other similar hairstreaks at available flowers. Females lay the small, flattened eggs singly on host twigs. The eggs overwinter and the young larvae hatch the following spring to feed on the buds and young leaves.

Striped Hairstreak
Satyrium liparops

Family/Subfamily: Gossamer Wings (Lycaenidae)/ Hairstreaks (Theclinae)

Wingspan: 1.0–1.3" (2.5–3.3 cm)

Above: unmarked dark brown with two hindwing tails

Below: brown to slate gray with numerous wide, dark bands outlined in white; hindwing has an orange-capped blue patch and several red spots near tails

Sexes: similar

Egg: pinkish brown, flattened, laid singly on twigs of host

Larva: bright green with yellow-green oblique stripes and dark dorsal line

Larval Host Plants: various trees and shrubs in the heath and rose families including Highbush Blueberry, Pin Cherry, Black Cherry, Wild Cherry, serviceberry and hawthorn

Habitat: mixed deciduous forests, thickets, forest clearings, woodland edges and adjacent open areas

Broods: single generation

Abundance: rare to occasional; localized

Compare: Banded (pg. 119) and Hickory (pg. 123) Hairstreaks have less extensive, narrower ventral bands and lack orange cap over blue hindwing patch. Edwards's Hairstreak (pg. 121) has white-rimmed dark oval spots, not dashes, on the wings below.

Resident

Jan. Feb. Mar. Apr. May June July Aug. Sept. Oct. Nov. Dec.

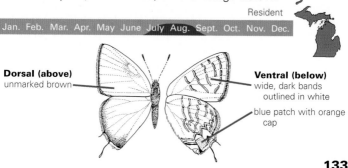

Dorsal (above)
unmarked brown

Ventral (below)
wide, dark bands outlined in white

blue patch with orange cap

133

Dorsal

Larva

Comments: As its name implies, this small drab species is the most widespread and abundant roadside-skipper in Michigan. Nonetheless, it is seldom encountered in large numbers and is often fairly local. Look for the butterfly in forest opening and other sun-dappled wooded sites. Like many small skippers, its flight is quick and low to the ground. Adults are often observed on low perches or nectaring at nearby blossoms, where they tend to be rather wary of close approach. Males often sip moisture at damp earth.

Common Roadside-Skipper
Amblyscirtes vialis

Family/Subfamily: Skippers (Hesperiidae)/ Banded Skippers (Hesperiinae)

Wingspan: 1.0–1.3" (2.5–3.3 cm)

Above: primarily dark blackish brown with a few small white spots near the forewing apex and a checkered wing fringe

Below: dark grayish black with faint gray frosting; forewing has a few small white spots (sometimes fused into a tapering band) near the apex

Sexes: similar, female has a more rounded forewing apex

Egg: pale green, laid singly on host leaves

Larva: pale green with a whitish head marked with reddish brown vertical lines

Larval Host Plants: various grasses including Indian Woodoats, Bermuda Grass and bentgrass

Habitat: sunlit forest clearings, woodland margins, stream corridors, utility easements and adjacent fields

Broods: single generation

Abundance: occasional; local

Compare: Pepper and Salt Skipper (pg. 109) has heavy gray overscaling and a cream postmedian spot band on the hindwing below.

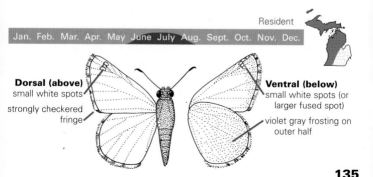

Resident

Jan. Feb. Mar. Apr. May June July Aug. Sept. Oct. Nov. Dec.

Dorsal (above)
small white spots
strongly checkered fringe

Ventral (below)
small white spots (or larger fused spot)
violet gray frosting on outer half

135

Male

Male **Female** **Female variant** **Larva**

Comments: The Mulberry Wing occurs in a limited patchwork range from Massachusetts west to Minnesota. It is a small and extremely distinctive skipper of sedge-dominated wetlands. Restricted by its habitat, it typically occurs in small and very highly localized populations that may be overlooked. As a result, it is poorly known with little detailed information available on its biology and life history. Adults flutter low with a slow, feeble flight somewhat reminiscent of the Least Skipper's. They alight frequently and are most often observed at nearby flowers or when flushed into the air by disturbances in their habitat.

Mulberry Wing
Poanes massasoit

Family/Subfamily: Skippers (Hesperiidae)/
Banded Skippers (Hesperiinae)

Wingspan: 1.0–1.4" (2.5–3.6 cm)

Above: dark blackish brown with a few scattered yellow-orange spots; forewings are noticeably rounded

Below: forewing is unmarked dark blackish brown; hindwing is dark blackish brown with a golden yellow postmedian band intersected by a wide central ray

Sexes: similar, although female has more prominent whitish, not yellow-orange, spots

Egg: white, laid singly on host

Larva: currently undocumented

Larval Host Plants: various sedges including Upright Sedge

Habitat: swamps, marshes, wet grassy meadows, fens, roadside ditches, woodland margins and other open wetland sites

Abundance: rare to occasional; localized

Broods: single generation

Compare: unique

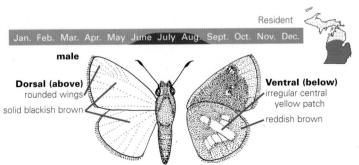

Resident

Jan. Feb. Mar. Apr. May June July Aug. Sept. Oct. Nov. Dec.

male

Dorsal (above)
rounded wings
solid blackish brown

Ventral (below)
irregular central yellow patch
reddish brown

137

Female

Male pg. 249   Female   Male   Larva

Comments: The Zabulon Skipper is strikingly dimorphic with bright orange males and purplish brown females. A denizen of wooded habitats, the butterfly is most often encountered in dappled sunlit patches along forest trails or clearings. Nonetheless, individuals will wander into nearby, more open landscapes in search of available nectar resources. The pugnacious males perch on branches around head-height to await passing mates and aggressively fly out to engage rival males before returning to the same or nearby perch moments later. Females generally prefer to remain within the confines of shadier locales.

Zabulon Skipper
Poanes zabulon

Family/Subfamily: Skippers (Hesperiidae)/
Banded Skippers (Hesperiinae)

Wingspan: 1.0–1.4" (2.5–3.6 cm)

Above: male is golden orange with dark brown borders
and small brown spot near forewing apex; female is
dark brown with band of cream spots across forewing

Below: male hindwing yellow with a brown base enclosing a yellow spot; female forewing is dark brown with
small light subapical spots; hindwing has lavender scaling on wing margins, and white bar along leading
margin of hindwing

Sexes: dissimilar, female brown with little orange color

Egg: pale green, laid singly on host leaves

Larva: tan with dark dorsal stripe, white lateral stripe and
short, light-colored hairs; reddish brown head

Larval Host Plants: various grasses including
Purpletop Grass, Whitegrass and lovegrass

Habitat: open woodlands, forest margins and roadsides,
stream corridors and adjacent open landscapes

Broods: two generations

Abundance: uncommon to occasional

Compare: Female Hobomok Skipper form Pocahontas
(pg. 177) and lacks white bar along leading margin of
ventral hindwing.

Stray

| Jan. | Feb. | Mar. | Apr. | May | June | July | Aug. | Sept. | Oct. | Nov. | Dec. |

male

Dorsal (above)
dark spot
narrow black cell
end bar
golden orange
clear golden
orange

Ventral (below)
dark base encloses
yellow spot
yellow with darker
spots

139

Dorsal

Larva

Comments: This widespread eastern skipper was once considered the same species as the Southern Broken-Dash. Its unique name comes from the dark forewing stigma that is separated or "broken" into two distinct dashes. Encountered in open habitats bordering woodlands, it readily ventures into nearby gardens in search of nectar. Although ranging far to the north, it is actually more common throughout the Southeast. Adults are highly active butterflies but frequently stop to perch or feed where they can be easily and closely observed.

Northern Broken-Dash
Wallengrenia egeremet

Family/Subfamily: Skippers (Hesperiidae)/ Banded Skippers (Hesperiinae)

Wingspan: 1.0–1.5" (2.5–3.8 cm)

Above: dark brown; male forewing has yellow orange scaling along the costal margin, a distinct separated stigma and an elongated bright yellow orange spot extending outward from the tip of the stigma; female forewing dark brown with a few elongated cream yellow spots

Below: hindwing is brown with a purplish sheen and a central band of faint, light spots

Sexes: dissimilar; female is primarily dark brown above with a few elongated cream yellow forewing spots

Egg: green, laid singly on host leaves

Larva: light green with darker green mottling, yellow lateral stripes; dark brown head with faint vertical stripes

Larval Host Plants: various grasses including Hairy Crabgrass and Deertongue

Habitat: open, sunny areas near woodlands including forest clearings and margins, roadsides, fallow agricultural land, pastures, old fields and gardens

Broods: single generation

Abundance: occasional to common

Compare: Little Glassywing (pg. 143) has prominent glassy forewing spots.

Resident

Jan. Feb. Mar. Apr. May June July Aug. Sept. Oct. Nov. Dec.

male

Dorsal (above)
yellow orange spot at end of stigma

"broken" black stigma

Ventral (below)
dull yellow brown

light spot band

Dorsal

Larva

Comments: The Little Glassywing is named for the distinct translucent or "glassy" white spots on its
forewing. It is a small dark butterfly of shaded forest
margins and adjacent, moist habitats or even open
fields, but is not readily encountered in home gardens.
Populations tend to be fairly small and somewhat
local. Adults have a low, quick flight and readily visit
available wildflowers. Males perch on low-growing
vegetation in sunny areas to await passing females.

Little Glassywing
Pompeius verna

Family/Subfamily: Skippers (Hesperiidae)/
Banded Skippers (Hesperiinae)

Wingspan: 1.0–1.5" (2.5–3.8 cm)

Above: male is dark brown with black stigma and several semitransparent spots across forewing; female is dark brown with several semitransparent spots across forewing

Below: dark brown; hindwing purplish brown with band of faint, light spots

Sexes: similar, female darker with more rounded wings and larger forewing spots; forewing lacks black stigma

Egg: white, laid singly on host leaves

Larva: green to greenish brown with dark mottling and stripes; head is reddish brown

Larval Host Plants: grasses including Purpletop Grass

Habitat: moist, open woodlands, forest edges, wetlands, roadsides, pastures, old fields and gardens

Broods: single generation

Abundance: occasional; localized

Compare: Dun Skipper (pg. 147) and Northern Broken-Dash (pg. 141) lack the prominent, somewhat square semitransparent spots on the forewing above. Dun also lacks the discrete central band on the ventral hindwing.

Resident

| Jan. | Feb. | Mar. | Apr. | May | June | July | Aug. | Sept. | Oct. | Nov. | Dec. |

male

Dorsal (above)
semitransparent spots
(central spot
somewhat square)

black stigma

Ventral (below)
purplish brown

faint pale band

143

Male

Larva

Comments: The Cobweb Skipper is named for the distinctively jagged pattern on the hindwing below that resembles a spider's web. On the wing for a single spring flight, look for it in open barrens, prairies or other grassy sites in close association with stands of its larval hosts. Generally uncommon throughout Michigan, colonies tend to be spotty, highly localized and often low density. The adults have a rapid and extremely low flight. It is a wary butterfly but readily perches on or near the ground and visits a variety of low-growing spring flowers.

Cobweb Skipper
Hesperia metea

Family/Subfamily: Skippers (Hesperiidae)/ Banded Skippers (Hesperiinae)

Wingspan: 1.1–1.4" (2.8–3.6 cm)

Above: olive brown; male forewing has tawny orange spots and a narrow black stigma bordered outwardly by orange scaling; hindwing has angled band of yellowish spots; female forewing is olive brown with cream spots

Below: hindwing is olive brown with irregular whitish band and spots; white scaling often extending slightly along veins giving an overall cobweb appearance

Sexes: dissimilar; female is primarily dark brown with a few pale forewing spots; lacks black forewing stigma

Egg: white, laid singly on or near host leaves

Larva: gray brown with a dark dorsal stripe and a round black head; larvae overwinter

Larval Host Plants: various grasses including Little Bluestem and Big Bluestem

Habitat: woodland clearings, pastures, prairie, utility easements, old fields and recently cleared or burned sites

Broods: single generation

Abundance: uncommon to occasional; local

Compare: unique

Resident

Jan. Feb. Mar. Apr. May June July Aug. Sept. Oct. Nov. Dec.

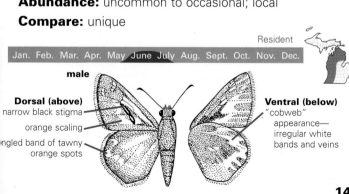

male

Dorsal (above)
narrow black stigma

orange scaling

angled band of tawny orange spots

Ventral (below)
"cobweb" appearance— irregular white bands and veins

145

Male

Larva

Comments: The Dun Skipper is a small, chocolate
brown butterfly with few markings. Although preferring moist, grassy or sedge-dominated areas
associated with deciduous woodlands, it frequently
ventures into surrounding open habitats and is periodically encountered in home gardens. It can occasionally
be exceedingly abundant. Adults have a quick, low
flight and dart around erratically over the vegetation. It
is an avid flower visitor readily drawn to available blossoms. Males occasionally visit damp ground.

Dun Skipper
Euphyes vestris

Family/Subfamily: Skippers (Hesperiidae)/
Banded Skippers (Hesperiinae)

Wingspan: 1.0–1.5" (2.5–3.8 cm)

Above: male is dark chocolate brown with black stigma;
female is dark brown with several whitish forewing
spots

Below: brown; hindwing typically unmarked, but occasionally has faint spot band

Sexes: similar, although female has small, white
forewing spots

Egg: green, laid singly on host leaves

Larva: green with thin white lines; head is brown with
light outer stripes and dark center

Larval Host Plants: various sedges including Upright
Sedge

Habitat: moist areas in or near deciduous woodlands,
wet meadows, marshes, forest margins, stream corridors, roadsides, pastures, prairies, fens, utility
easements and old fields

Broods: single generation

Abundance: occasional to abundant

Compare: Little Glassywing (pg. 143) has distinct glassy
white spots on forewing and defined ventral hindwing
band.

Resident

Jan. Feb. Mar. Apr. May June July Aug. Sept. Oct. Nov. Dec.

male

Dorsal (above)
brown black wings
dark black stigma

Ventral (below)
unmarked or with faint
spot band

147

Comments: This lovely grayish hairstreak is restricted to
wetland habitats or other moist areas that support willows. Although widespread across much of the
Northeast and Great Lakes, the species tends to occur
in relatively small, highly localized colonies but can be
rather common when encountered. Adults have a
quick, erratic flight and are most often observed at
nearby moisture-loving flowers. They are particularly
fond of milkweed blossoms.

Acadian Hairstreak
Satyrium acadica

Family/Subfamily: Gossamer Wings (Lycaenidae)/ Hairstreaks (Theclinae)

Wingspan: 1.10–1.45" (2.8–4.0 cm)

Above: brown with a small orange crescent-shaped hindwing spot above a short tail

Below: uniform gray with a postmedian row of round, white-rimmed black spots; hindwing has a submarginal row of orange crescent-shaped spots and a orange-capped blue patch near the tail

Sexes: similar

Egg: white, laid singly on host twigs; eggs overwinter

Larva: green and white lateral stripe, pale white oblique dashes, and a darker green dorsal stripe edged in white

Larval Host Plants: various willows

Habitat: stream margins, pond edges, marshes, swamps, wet roadside ditches, depressions, bogs and moist meadows

Broods: single generation

Abundance: uncommon to occasional; localized

Compare: Edwards's Hairstreak (pg. 121) has gray-brown ventral wings and is typically found in more xeric (dry) habitats with oaks.

Resident

| Jan. | Feb. | Mar. | Apr. | May | June | July | Aug. | Sept. | Oct. | Nov. | Dec. |

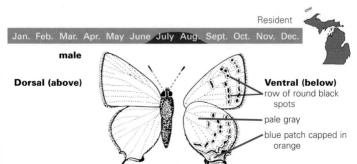

male

Dorsal (above)

Ventral (below)
row of round black spots

pale gray

blue patch capped in orange

149

Male

Larva

Comments: The Dreamy Duskywing is a small, early spring species common throughout much of boreal North America. Both it and the similar but somewhat larger Sleepy Duskywing lack the glassy white forewing spots that characterize all other members of this group. Adults scurry low to the ground along forest trails or margins with a fast, bouncing flight. Males perch low on the ends of bare twigs or in sunlit patches of soil to await passing females and are often encountered puddling at moist areas. Larvae construct individual shelters on the host by tying one or more leaves together with silk.

Dreamy Duskywing
Erynnis icelus

Family/Subfamily: Skippers (Hesperiidae)/
Spread-wing Skippers (Pyrginae)

Wingspan: 1.0–1.6" (2.5–4.1 cm)

Above: dark brown; forewing has extensive gray scaling toward outer margin, two black chain-like bands enclosing a broad gray patch, a dark base, lacks glassy spots; hindwing has two rows of pale spots; labial palpi are noticeably long and project forward

Below: dark brown, hindwing has two rows of pale spots

Sexes: similar, although female is lighter with more heavily patterned forewings

Egg: green turning reddish, laid singly on stems or leaves

Larva: pale green with a dark dorsal stripe, a white lateral stripe, numerous tiny white tubercles, and a black head marked with yellow and red spots

Larval Host Plants: various willow, poplar, aspen and birch

Habitat: open woodlands, forest edges and clearings, roadsides, moist woodland depressions

Broods: single generation

Abundance: occasional to common

Compare: Sleepy Duskywing (pg. 179) flies earlier, is larger with shorter, more rounded forewings, has shorter labial palpi and tends to occur in drier habitats.

Resident

Jan. Feb. Mar. Apr. May June July Aug. Sept. Oct. Nov. Dec.

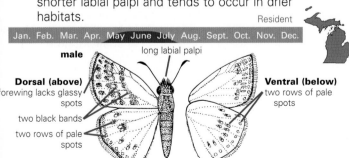

male

long labial palpi

Dorsal (above)
forewing lacks glassy spots

two black bands

two rows of pale spots

Ventral (below)
two rows of pale spots

Male Female Larva

Comments: The Common Branded Skipper is a widespread and highly variable species found throughout
much of the western U.S. and Canada. Our subspecies laurentina occurs across the Great Lakes and
Northeast. As a result, many authors refer to this butterfly as the Laurentian Skipper. Despite a preference
for open grassy landscapes, it is seldom common and
often relatively local. Adults have a quick, darting flight
and may be encountered feeding on a variety of available blooms.

Common Branded Skipper
Hesperia comma laurentina

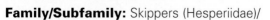

Family/Subfamily: Skippers (Hesperiidae)/
Banded Skippers (Hesperiinae)

Wingspan: 1.1–1.5" (2.8–3.8 cm)

Above: male forewing orange basally with broad, dark
brown margin and a prominent black stigma; hindwing
brown with an irregular orange spot band; female dark
brown with reduced orange markings

Below: hindwing orange with white spots

Sexes: dissimilar; female brown with reduced orange
markings and without black forewing stigma

Egg: whitish green, laid singly on host leaves or stems

Larva: dark greenish brown, often with lighter mottling
and a round black head

Larval Host Plants: various grasses including
bluestem, bluegrass, fescue and brome grass

Habitat: grassy clearings, meadows, old fields and roadsides

Abundance: rare to occasional; local

Compare: Leonard's Skipper (pg. 187) is larger, has a
reddish brown ventral hindwing with a less angled pale
postmedian spot band.

Resident Stray

| Jan. | Feb. | Mar. | Apr. | May | June | July | Aug. | Sept. | Oct. | Nov. | Dec. |

Dorsal (above)
elongated stigma
orange basal scaling
wide brown borders

Ventral (below)
golden orange
small white spots

153

Male

Female

Larva

Comments: The Two-spotted Skipper is a reclusive
species of sedge-dominated wetlands. Considered a
relatively rare butterfly throughout Michigan, populations tend to be small and highly localized in
occurrence. Like many other habitat-restricted species,
it has declined as a result of ever-expanding human
activity and urban development. Despite its distinctive
ventral markings, the species is named for two small
white spots on the upper surface of the forewing in
females. Males perch low of grasses or sedges and
readily fly out to engage rival males before returning to
the same vicinity moments later.

Two-spotted Skipper
Euphyes bimacula

Family/Subfamily: Skippers (Hesperiidae)/
Banded Skippers (Hesperiinae)

Wingspan: 1.25–1.40" (3.2–3.6 cm)

Above: male dark brown with white fringes; forewing has small tawny orange patch and black stigma; female forewing dark brown with two small cream spots in the center

Below: brownish orange with pale veins and a whitish anal hindwing margin

Sexes: dissimilar; female is primarily dark brown with two cream spots in the center of the forewing above

Egg: green, laid singly on host leaves

Larva: pale green with a darker dorsal stripe and numerous tiny wavy white dashes; reddish brown head marked with a black oval ringed in cream on the forehead, and a cream band around the outer margin

Larval Host Plants: various sedges including Upright Sedge

Habitat: wet meadows, fens; sometimes moist roadsides

Broods: single generation

Abundance: rare to uncommon; localized

Compare: Crossline Skipper (pg. 125) lacks the white anal margin and pale veins on the ventral hindwing. Ventral hindwing typically also has faint postmedian band. Resident

Jan. Feb. Mar. Apr. May June July Aug. Sept. Oct. Nov. Dec.

male

Dorsal (above)
tawny orange scaling
white fringe

Ventral (below)
paler veins
white anal margin

155

Ventral

Larva

Comments: Although called the Southern Cloudywing,
the range of this dull brown skipper extends from
Florida to the Canadian border. It is often found alongside the very similar Northern Cloudywing with which
it is easily confused. Worn individuals can present a
challenge even for experienced butterfly watchers.
Adults have a strong, erratic flight but frequently stop
to nectar. Males perch on low vegetation and aggressively dart out to investigate intruders before returning
to the same general location moments later. Adults
rest with their wings partially open but are often rather
nervous and difficult to closely approach.

Southern Cloudywing
Thorybes bathyllus

Family/Subfamily: Skippers (Hesperiidae)/
Spread-wing Skippers (Pyrginae)

Wingspan: 1.2–1.6" (3.0–4.1 cm)

Above: brown with a straight, glassy white spot band
across the forewing; hindwing tapered slightly toward
bottom; antennal club has a white spot at bend; male
lacks forewing costal fold

Below: brown; hindwing darker at base with two dark
brown bands; light face

Sexes: similar

Egg: green, laid singly on the leaves of host

Larva: greenish brown with black head, thin, dark dorsal
stripe and narrow light lateral stripe; body covered
with numerous short, light-colored hairs

Larval Host Plants: various legumes including beggarweeds, bush clover, Hog Peanut and milkvetch

Habitat: brushy fields, utility easements, forest edges,
dry woodlands and adjacent dry, open areas

Broods: single generation

Abundance: occasional to common

Compare: Northern Cloudywing (pg. 165) has noticeably
smaller glassy white dorsal forewing spots; male
Northern has forewing costal fold.

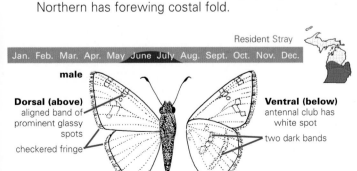

Resident Stray

Jan. Feb. Mar. Apr. May June July Aug. Sept. Oct. Nov. Dec.

male

Dorsal (above)
aligned band of
prominent glassy
spots

checkered fringe

Ventral (below)
antennal club has
white spot

two dark bands

Ventral

Larva

Comments: This is a small duskywing of rich northern woodlands. Found in ravines, clearings and along trails, individuals tend to occur in close proximity with patches of their namesake larval host. Easily confused with several other members of the genus, the Columbine Duskywing is best separated by habitat preference and host association. Adults have a quick, somewhat bouncing flight and maneuver erratically low among understory vegetation. Both sexes readily nectar at a variety of available wildflowers including blossoms of their host. Larvae overwinter in individual leaf shelters and complete development the following spring.

Columbine Duskywing
Erynnis lucilius

Family/Subfamily: Skippers (Hesperiidae)/
Spread-wing Skippers (Pyrginae)

Wingspan: 1.2–1.6" (3.0–4.1 cm)

Above: dark brown with gray scaling; forewing is noticeably darker basally with several small glassy spots
toward the apex and an indistinct brown patch at the
end of the cell; subapical white spots are misaligned

Below: dark brown; hindwing has marginal and submarginal rows of prominent light spots

Sexes: similar, although female is lighter with more heavily patterned wings and larger glassy spots

Egg: green, laid singly on host leaves

Larva: pale green with numerous tiny white tubercles, a
dark green dorsal stripe and a white lateral stripe; dark
brown head. Larvae construct individual shelters on
the host by weaving two or more leaves together with
silk.

Larval Host Plants: Wild Columbine

Habitat: moist woodlands, forest clearings and margins,
ravines and rocky outcrops

Broods: two generations

Abundance: occasional to common

Compare: Wild Indigo Duskywing (pg. 175) is slightly
larger. May not be reliably distinguished in
the field.

Resident Stray

Jan. Feb. Mar. Apr. May June July Aug. Sept. Oct. Nov. Dec.

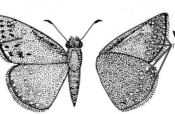

Dorsal (above)
brown patch at
end of cell
indistinct

Ventral (below)
marginal and
submarginal rows
of distinct pale
spots

Larva

Comments: Finally an easy-to-identify duskywing! This small skipper can reliably be told apart from all other members of this complicated genus by its distinctively mottled wings. Restricted by the habitat requirements of its larval hosts, the Mottled Duskywing is typically encountered in dry landscapes where the terrain is somewhat undulating. As a result, colonies tend to occur sporadically and are often highly localized. Males patrol hilltops and other prominences for females. They often puddle at damp ground alongside other duskywings but are rarely the most prevalent species present.

Mottled Duskywing
Erynnis martialis

Family/Subfamily: Skippers (Hesperiidae)/
Spread-wing Skippers (Pyrginae)

Wingspan: 1.2–1.6" (3.0–4.1 cm)

Above: brown and strongly patterned with numerous
dark blotches giving a distinctive mottled appearance;
forewing has several small glassy spots toward the
apex; fresh individuals have a subtle violet sheen

Below: brown with numerous light and dark spots

Sexes: similar, although female is lighter with increased
gray scaling and more heavily patterned wings

Egg: green soon turning pinkish, laid singly on host
leaves

Larva: pale green with numerous tiny white tubercles
and a black head marked with orange spots around the
margin

Larval Host Plants: Redstem Ceanothus, Jersey Tea
and New Jersey Tea

Habitat: open upland woodland, forest edges and clearings, barrens, prairie hills and old fields

Broods: two generations

Abundance: rare to occasional; local

Compare: unique

Resident

Jan. Feb. Mar. Apr. May June July Aug. Sept. Oct. Nov. Dec.

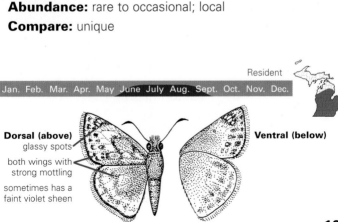

Dorsal (above)
glassy spots

both wings with
strong mottling

sometimes has a
faint violet sheen

Ventral (below)

Male

Female

Larva

Comments: Generally an uncommon butterfly throughout its limited Midwestern range, the Black Dash is
restricted to marshes, wet meadows and other open
wetlands with abundant sedge. As a result, populations tend to be small and highly localized to suitable
habitat areas. The adults are swift on the wing but are
easily observed when feeding at nearby wetland wildflowers. Males perch like sentinels on tall grasses
watching keenly for passing females and readily fly out
to engage intruders.

Black Dash
Euphyes conspicua

Family/Subfamily: Skippers (Hesperiidae)/
Banded Skippers (Hesperiinae)

Wingspan: 1.25–1.60" (3.2–4.1 cm)

Above: male golden-orange with broad, dark brown borders and broad black stigma on forewing; female dark brown with cream-yellow spot band through both wings

Below: hindwing orange-brown with a broad yellow post-median patch

Sexes: dissimilar; female is primarily dark brown above with pale yellow forewing spots

Egg: laid singly on host

Larva: green with fine white mottling; brown head marked with cream lines around the margin and a black oval on the forehead

Larval Host Plants: various sedges including Upright Sedge and Eastern Narrowleaf Sedge

Habitat: marshes, wet grassy meadows, fens, roadside ditches, bogs, woodland margins, other open wetlands

Abundance: uncommon to occasional; localized

Broods: single generation

Compare: Peck's Skipper (pg. 127) is smaller and has yellow basal spots on the hindwing below. Dion Skipper (pg. 273) is larger and has a long pale ray through the hindwing without adjacent postmedian spots.

Resident

Jan.	Feb.	Mar.	Apr.	May	June	July	Aug.	Sept.	Oct.	Nov.	Dec.

male

Dorsal (above)
broad stigma
dark brown borders
orange

Ventral (below)
red-brown hindwing
curved yellow patch

163

Ventral

Larva

Comments: Widespread from the Gulf Coast to central Canada, the Northern Cloudywing essentially replaces the Southern Cloudywing as the only member of the genus in the northern half of Michigan. Where they do fly together, close examination is required to reliably separate the two species. The adults have a low, skipping flight and quickly scurry along trails or clearings, occasionally pausing at a nearby flower to feed. Males perch on the ground or low on vegetation and aggressively dart out to engage rival males or passing females. At rest, they hold their wings in a relaxed, partially open position.

Northern Cloudywing
Thorybes pylades

Family/Subfamily: Skippers (Hesperiidae)/
Spread-wing Skippers (Pyrginae)

Wingspan: 1.2–1.7" (3.0–4.3 cm)

Above: brown with several small, misaligned, subapical glassy white spots on forewing and light, checkered wing fringe; male has a forewing costal fold

Below: brown; hindwing darker at base with two dark brown bands; both wings have slight lavender gray scaling along margin; dark face

Sexes: similar

Egg: pale greenish white, laid singly on leaves of host

Larva: greenish brown with black head, thin, dark dorsal stripe and narrow pinkish brown lateral stripe; body covered with numerous short, light-colored hairs

Larval Host Plants: various legumes including beggar-weeds, Hog Peanut, bush clovers, milkvetch, Alfalfa, Leadplant and clovers

Habitat: open woodlands, forest edges, roadsides, utility easements, brushy fields and other dry, open areas

Broods: single generation

Abundance: occasional to common

Compare: Southern Cloudywing (pg. 157) has larger glassy white forewing spots that form an aligned band. Male Southern lacks forewing costal fold.

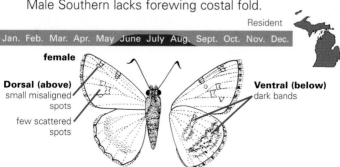

Resident

Jan. Feb. Mar. Apr. May June July Aug. Sept. Oct. Nov. Dec.

female

Dorsal (above)
small misaligned spots

few scattered spots

Ventral (below)
dark bands

Male

Female pg. 263   Ventral   Larva

Comments: This sexually dimorphic species is our largest copper. Although primarily restricted to moist areas where its weedy larval hosts occur, it frequently wanders into nearby drier habitats in search of nectar. The Bronze Copper tends to occur in small, highly localized colonies but can be rather numerous when encountered. Like many other wetland species, it has suffered from the loss or degradation of available habitat. Males perch low on grasses or other vegetation with their wings partially open to await passing females.

Bronze Copper
Lycaena hyllus

Family/Subfamily: Gossamer Wings (Lycaenidae)/
Coppers (Lycaeninae)

Wingspan: 1.25–1.65" (3.2–4.2 cm)

Above: male is brown with a purplish iridescence and a
broad orange submarginal band containing black spots
on the hindwing; female has light orange forewings
with scattered black spots and a broad brown border;
hindwing is purplish brown with a broad orange submarginal band containing black spots

Below: scattered white-rimmed black spots on both
wings; forewing is orange with silvery gray apex and
margin; hindwing is silvery gray with broad orange
submarginal band containing black spots

Sexes: dissimilar; female is larger with rounder wings
and increased orange scaling on the dorsal forewing

Egg: whitish, laid singly on host leaves or stems

Larva: yellow-green with a darker green dorsal stripe

Larval Host Plants: knotweed, Curly Dock, Water Dock

Habitat: open, moist habitats including fens, wet meadows and marshes; also adjacent fields

Broods: two generations

Abundance: uncommon to locally common

Compare: American (pg. 243) and Purplish (pg. 115)
Coppers are smaller and have a narrow, reddish orange
submarginal line on ventral hindwing.   Resident

Jan. Feb. Mar. Apr. May June July Aug. Sept. Oct. Nov. Dec.

male

Dorsal (above)
iridescent
purple/brown
above

orange band

Ventral (below)
pale orange forewing

small spots

silvery white hindwing

wide orange
submarginal band

167

Male Female Larva

Comments: This is a large orange skipper of native tall-grass prairies. Like many other prairie species, the Ottoe Skipper has continued to disappear from many portions of its former range as a result of habitat loss. Within Michigan, it can be found only in a few scattered southern counties. Remaining colonies tend to be uncommon and highly local in occurrence. As a result, it is currently listed as a threatened species by the state. The adults are strong fliers and often wary of close approach but may regularly be spotted at available flowers.

Ottoe Skipper
Hesperia ottoe

Family/Subfamily: Skippers (Hesperiidae)/
Banded Skippers (Hesperiinae)

Wingspan: 1.3–1.6" (3.3–4.1 cm)

Above: male bright orange with broad, dark brown borders and a black forewing stigma; female forewing
brown with reduced orange scaling and a few glassy
cream spots

Below: hindwing clear yellow-orange; often with faint
postmedian spot band in females

Sexes: dissimilar, female brown with pale forewing
spots; lacks black forewing stigma

Egg: whitish, laid singly on host leaves

Larva: light greenish brown with a dark brown head

Larval Host Plants: Fall Witchgrass

Habitat: woodland clearings, tallgrass prairie and adjacent open areas with native grasses

Broods: single generation

Abundance: rare to occasional; localized

Compare: unique

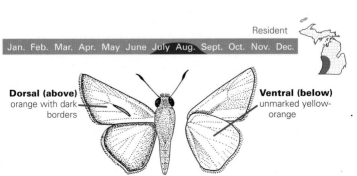

Resident

Jan. Feb. Mar. Apr. May June July Aug. Sept. Oct. Nov. Dec.

Dorsal (above)
orange with dark
borders

Ventral (below)
unmarked yellow-
orange

Female

Ventral

Larva

Comments: A butterfly of oak barrens and adjacent dry
areas, this rare skipper occurs in scattered and often
highly localized populations throughout the Midwest and
Northeast. Listed by the Michigan DNR as threatened,
the Persius Duskywing shares its affinity for this special
habitat with a few other imperiled butterflies including
the Karner Blue and Frosted Elfin. Adults have a quick,
somewhat bouncing flight and maneuver erratically low
among vegetation. Like other members of its genus, it
roosts at night on bare twigs with wings folded down
around the branch. Larvae construct individual shelters
by weaving two or more host leaves together with silk.

Persius Duskywing
Erynnis persius

Family/Subfamily: Skippers (Hesperiidae)/
Spread-wing Skippers (Pyrginae)

Wingspan: 1.25–1.70" (3.2–4.3 cm)

Above: dark brown with noticeable hair-like gray scaling;
forewing is noticeably darker basally with several small
aligned glassy spots toward the apex and a distinctive
gray patch at the end of the cell

Below: dark brown, hindwing has two rows of prominent
light spots

Sexes: similar, although female is lighter with more heavily patterned wings and larger glassy spots

Egg: yellow-green, laid singly on underside of host leaves

Larva: pale green with numerous tiny white tubercles,
dark dorsal stripe and white lateral stripe; dark brown
head marked with pale orange or yellow spots around
the margin. Larvae overwinter in individual leaf shelters.

Larval Host Plants: Wild Lupine

Habitat: oak barrens, dry open woodlands and adjacent
utility easements, margins and fields

Broods: single generation

Abundance: rare to occasional; local

Compare: Wild Indigo (pg. 175), Columbine (pg. 159)
and Horace's Duskywings (pg. 173) lack the prominent
gray hair-like forewing scales and have misaligned subapical forewing spots.

Resident

Jan.	Feb.	Mar.	Apr.	May	June	July	Aug.	Sept.	Oct.	Nov.	Dec.

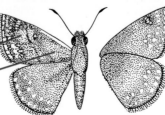

male

Dorsal (above)
grayish patch at
end of cell

numerous raised
white hairs on
upperside

Ventral (below)

Male

Female   Female   Larva

Comments: This widespread eastern skipper extends its range northward only into our southernmost counties. Generally an uncommon butterfly, look for it in oak-dominated woodlands and nearby disturbed sites, especially at available blossoms. The dull brown adults flutter about with quick, somewhat erratic flight usually low to the ground. Males readily perch in sunlit spots on low vegetation or on the tips of bare twigs to await passing females. They may also be encountered at damp sand or gravel.

Horace's Duskywing
Erynnis horatius

Family/Subfamily: Skippers (Hesperiidae)/
Spread-wing Skippers (Pyrginae)

Wingspan: 1.25–1.75" (3.2–4.4 cm)

Above: dark brown overall with gray scaling usually lacking; forewing has cluster of small glassy white spots near apex and one at end of forewing cell; female is lighter with more contrasting pattern; subapical white spots are misaligned

Below: brown with faint rows of light spots along outer edge of hindwing

Sexes: similar, although female is lighter with more heavily patterned forewings and larger forewing spots

Egg: pale yellow green, laid singly on new growth of host

Larva: pale green with tiny white spots; reddish brown head marked with orange spots around the margin

Larval Host Plants: various oaks including Northern Red Oak and Black Oak

Habitat: oak woodlands, forest edges and clearings, roadsides, utility easements and nearby open areas

Broods: two generations

Abundance: uncommon to occasional

Compare: Juvenal's Duskywing (pg. 191) has two light spots along leading margin of ventral hindwing and extensive gray scaling on dorsal forewing.

Resident

Jan. Feb. Mar. Apr. May June July Aug. Sept. Oct. Nov. Dec.

male

Dorsal (above)
glassy spots

glassy spot at end of cell

lacks extensive gray scaling

Ventral (below)
lacks spots along leading margin

Male

Female Ventral Larva

Comments: The Wild Indigo Duskywing is named for one of its preferred larval hosts. Common throughout much of the eastern U.S., it has become more widespread in recent decades as a result of its opportunistic ability to feed on the introduced groundcover Crown Vetch. As a result, it is now often found along highways or other rights-of-way. Within Michigan, the species is primarily restricted to the southernmost counties where it remains local and generally uncommon. Adults have a quick, scurrying flight. Males frequently puddle at damp ground.

Wild Indigo Duskywing
Erynnis baptisiae

Family/Subfamily: Skippers (Hesperiidae)/
Spread-wing Skippers (Pyrginae)

Wingspan: 1.3–1.7" (3.3–4.3 cm)

Above: dark brown with pale spots; forewing has darker base with several small misaligned glassy white spots toward the apex and distinctive reddish brown patch at end of cell; hindwing typically has faint cell-end bar

Below: dark brown, hindwing has two rows of prominent light spots

Sexes: similar, although female is lighter with more heavily pattered wings and larger glassy spots

Egg: green, laid singly on host leaves

Larva: pale green with numerous tiny white tubercles, dark dorsal stripe, white lateral stripe; dark brown head marked with pale orange or yellow around the margin

Larval Host Plants: Wild Indigo, Blue Wild Indigo, White Wild Indigo, Canadian Milkvetch, Wild Lupine and Crown Vetch

Habitat: dry open woodlands, prairies, oak barrens, forest edges and clearings, roadsides, utility easements and old fields

Broods: two generations

Abundance: rare to occasional; local

Compare: Horace's Duskywing (pg. 173) has glassy spot at end of forewing cell.

Stray

Jan. Feb. Mar. Apr. May June July Aug. Sept. Oct. Nov. Dec.

male

Dorsal (above)
red-brown spot at end of cell

typically lacks glassy spot at end of cell

basal half of wing darker

faint cell-end bar

Ventral (below)
two rows of white spots

175

Female "Pocahontas"

Male pg. 269 | Female | Ventral | Larva

Comments: This small woodland skipper has a single spring flight. Males perch on sunlit leaves and aggressively dart out at other passing butterflies. They may also frequently be encountered at wet earth along forested roads or trails. Although preferring shadier conditions, both sexes will venture into nearby open areas to nectar at early-season blossoms. Female Hobomoks produce two distinct forms. The lighter form resembles the male and the darker form "Pocahontas" is superficially similar to Zabulon Skipper females. Larvae construct individual leaf shelters on the host. Larvae overwinter.

Hobomok Skipper
Poanes hobomok

Family/Subfamily: Skippers (Hesperiidae)/
Banded Skippers (Hesperiinae)

Wingspan: 1.4–1.6" (3.6–4.1 cm)

Above: golden orange with irregular dark brown borders
and a narrow black cell-end bar on the forewing

Below: purplish brown with a broad yellow orange patch
through the hindwing

Sexes: dissimilar; female has two forms. Normal form
resembles male but has reduced orange scaling above.
"Pocahontas" form is dark brown above with pale
forewing spots; hindwing is purplish brown below with
faint band and violet gray frosting along outer margin.

Egg: white, laid singly on host leaves

Larva: brown green with numerous short, light-colored
hairs; round, brown head

Larval Host Plants: various grasses including Little
Bluestem, panic grasses, Poverty Oatgrass, bluegrass
and Rice Cutgrass

Habitat: open woodlands, forest edges, clearings and
trails, roadsides and along forested stream margins

Broods: single generation

Abundance: occasional to common

Compare: Female Zabulon Skipper (pg. 139) has a white
bar along leading edge of ventral hindwing.

Resident

| Jan. | Feb. | Mar. | Apr. | May | June | July | Aug. | Sept. | Oct. | Nov. | Dec. |

male

Dorsal (above)
narrow cell-end bar
no stigma
irregular dark brown
borders

Ventral (below)
purplish brown
broad yellow orange
patch

177

Male

Female

Ventral

Larva

Comments: The Sleepy Duskywing typically starts its spring flight earlier than the smaller and similar-looking Dreamy Duskywing. Together, they are the only two members of the genus in the state that lack small glassy forewing spots. As a result, they often present a challenge to reliably separate in the field. Although fairly common statewide, the species occasionally undergoes marked fluctuations in abundance. Adults perch and feed with their mottled gray-brown wings held in an open posture, a common characteristic of all duskywings. Larvae construct individual leaf shelters and overwinter inside, pupating the following spring.

Sleepy Duskywing
Erynnis brizo

Family/Subfamily: Skippers (Hesperiidae)/
Spread-wing Skippers (Pyrginae)

Wingspan: 1.30–1.75" (3.3–4.4 cm)

Above: dark brown; forewing has extensive gray scaling
toward outer margin and two black chain-like bands;
hindwing has two rows of faint pale spots

Below: dark brown, hindwing has two often faint rows
of pale spots

Sexes: similar, female is lighter with more heavily patterned forewing and more prominent hindwing spots

Egg: green, laid singly on host leaves

Larva: pale green with a yellow white lateral stripe and
numerous tiny white tubercles; brown head marked
with six orange spots around the margin

Larval Host Plants: various oaks including Bur Oak and
Black Oak

Habitat: open oak woodlands and scrub, dry forest
edges and clearings, roadsides and adjacent open
sites

Broods: single generation

Abundance: uncommon to common

Compare: Dreamy Duskywing (pg. 151) is smaller, has
longer labial palpi; forewing has darker base and more
distinct gray patch between black bands;
flies later; prefers more moist habitats. Resident

Jan. Feb. Mar. Apr. May June July Aug. Sept. Oct. Nov. Dec.

Dorsal (above)
lacks glassy forewing
spots

stinct black, chainlike
bands

Ventral (below)
faint spots

179

Comments: A butterfly of specialized wetlands called fens, Mitchell's Satyr once occurred in isolated populations from New Jersey and Maryland west to Michigan and northern Indiana but has unfortunately disappeared from many of its former haunts as a result of habitat loss or alteration. Today, it is only reported in southern Michigan and extreme northern Indiana. It remains critically imperiled and is listed as both a state and federal endangered species. The adults have a slow, bobbing flight and maneuver low among the wetland vegetation stopping frequently to perch. Individual colonies tend to be small and are easily overlooked.

Mitchell's Satyr
Neonympha mitchellii

Family/Subfamily: Brush-foots (Nymphalidae)/ Satyrs and Wood-Nymphs (Satyrinae)

Wingspan: 1.3–1.8" (3.3–4.6 cm)

Above: uniform unmarked brown

Below: brown with a submarginal row of rounded yellow-rimmed black eyespots bearing silvery blue highlights; two orange-brown lines across both wings

Sexes: similar, although female is slightly larger

Egg: cream, laid singly on host

Larva: elongate, green with longitudinal white stripes

Larval Host Plants: currently undocumented in the wild, but likely various sedges

Habitat: prairie fens

Broods: single generation

Abundance: rare to occasional; local

Compare: unique

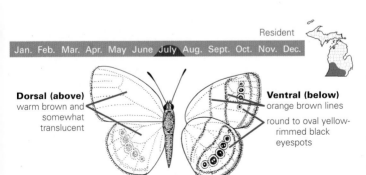

Resident

Jan. Feb. Mar. Apr. May June July Aug. Sept. Oct. Nov. Dec.

Dorsal (above)
warm brown and somewhat translucent

Ventral (below)
orange brown lines

round to oval yellow-rimmed black eyespots

Dorsal

Larva

Comments: The Dusted Skipper is a butterfly of open, dry habitats, preferring areas that have been fire-maintained or subject to some level of disturbance to support its native host grasses. Although widespread throughout much of the East, populations are scarce in Michigan. As a result, it is listed by the Michigan Department of Natural Resources as threatened. Populations tend to be scattered and highly localized but are most definitely worth the effort to locate. Males frequently perch on low vegetation.

Dusted Skipper
Atrytonopsis hianna

Family/Subfamily: Skippers (Hesperiidae)/ Banded Skippers (Hesperiinae)

Wingspan: 1.4–1.7" (3.6–4.3 cm)

Above: dark chocolate brown with small glassy forewing spots

Below: dark brown with gray frosting toward outer margin; forewing has small white forewing spots near apex; hindwing has tiny white spot near base; face is white with black mask

Sexes: similar, although female has larger forewing spots

Egg: yellow, laid singly on host leaves

Larva: gray, pinkish dorsally, with numerous cream hairs, a brown anal segment; reddish purple head

Larval Host Plants: various grasses including Little Bluestem and Big Bluestem

Habitat: dry habitats including barrens, utility easements, brushy fields and prairies

Broods: single generation

Abundance: rare to uncommon; local

Compare: Dun Skipper (pg. 147) has a rounder forewing and lacks the small white basal spot on the hindwing below.

Resident

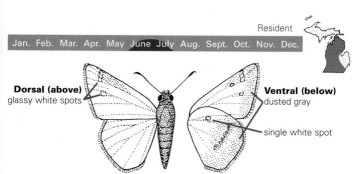

Jan. Feb. Mar. Apr. May June July Aug. Sept. Oct. Nov. Dec.

Dorsal (above)
glassy white spots

Ventral (below)
dusted gray

single white spot

183

Dorsal

Larva

Comments: The Hoary Edge is named for its distinct
frosty white (hoary) patch on the underside of the
hindwing. Primarily a butterfly of dry, brushy sites and
open woodlands, it regularly ventures into nearby disturbed sites and may at times show up in home
gardens. Although widespread throughout much of the
East, it tends to be highly localized and most often
encountered as lone individuals. Adults have a low,
strong flight and can be a challenge to follow. Males
perch on low, protruding vegetation and aggressively
investigate and chase passing insects.

Hoary Edge
Achalarus lyciades

Family/Subfamily: Skippers (Hesperiidae)/
Spread-wing Skippers (Pyrginae)

Wingspan: 1.40–1.75" (3.6–4.4 cm)

Above: brown with a broad band of semitransparent
gold spots across forewing; both wings have a checkered fringe; hindwing slightly tapered

Below: brown; forewing as above but muted; hindwing
mottled dark brown at base with a distinct broad
whitish gray marginal patch

Sexes: similar

Egg: cream, laid singly on host leaves

Larva: dark green with a dark dorsal stripe, numerous
tiny pale yellow dots and a thin, brownish orange lateral stripe; black head

Larval Host Plants: primarily beggarweeds, but other
legumes including bush clovers may occasionally be
used

Habitat: open woodlands, forest edges and adjacent disturbed roadsides and brushy areas

Broods: single generation

Abundance: uncommon to occasional

Compare: Silver-spotted Skipper (pg. 205) is larger, has a
clear white median ventral hindwing patch and a short,
stubby tail.

Resident

Jan. Feb. Mar. Apr. May June July Aug. Sept. Oct. Nov. Dec.

male

Dorsal (above)
gold band

Ventral (below)
pale outer portion

outer half hoary
white

Male   Larva

Comments: Leonard's Skipper is a large, reddish brown skipper with a distinctive pale spot band on the hind-wing below. A late season species, it produces a single generation each year that emerges in July and continues flying well into September or even early October. The distinctive adults have an extremely powerful flight. Although often encountered at available flowers, they tend to be nervous and extremely wary of close approach.

Leonard's Skipper
Hesperia leonardus

Family/Subfamily: Skippers (Hesperiidae)/
Banded Skippers (Hesperiinae)

Wingspan: 1.50–1.75" (3.8–4.4 cm)

Above: male orange with broad dark brown borders,
forewing elongated and pointed with black stigma;
female brown with orange basal scaling and pale yellow spots

Below: hindwing is reddish brown with a distinct row of
cream white spots

Sexes: dissimilar, female is primarily brown with pale
forewing spots; lacks black forewing stigma

Egg: whitish green, laid singly on or near host leaves

Larva: olive green with a black head marked with cream;
partially grown larvae overwinter

Larval Host Plants: a variety of grasses including bentgrass, panic grass and Poverty Oatgrass

Habitat: old fields, roadsides, meadows and woodland
clearings and margins

Broods: single generation

Abundance: occasional to common

Compare: Indian Skipper (pg. 257) has a light orange
hindwing with a pale yellow spot band on the ventral
hindwing; flies earlier in season.

Resident

Jan. Feb. Mar. Apr. May June July Aug. Sept. Oct. Nov. Dec.

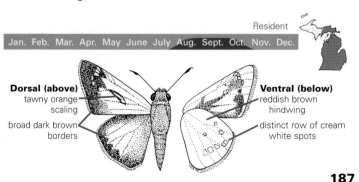

Dorsal (above)
tawny orange
scaling

broad dark brown
borders

Ventral (below)
reddish brown
hindwing

distinct row of cream
white spots

187

Comments: This distinctive but poorly known butterfly
is named for its prominent reddish brown forewing
patch. Restricted to bog margins and moist meadows,
the Red-disked Alpine is an uncommon and highly
localized resident of the Upper Peninsula. Adults have
a low, extremely weak flight and frequently alight on
the ground or within grassy vegetation. As a result,
colonies may be easily overlooked.

Red-disked Alpine
Erebia discoidalis

Family/Subfamily: Brush-foots (Nymphalidae)/
Satyrs and Wood-Nymphs (Satyrinae)

Wingspan: 1.50–1.85" (3.8–4.7 cm)

Above: unmarked dark brown; forewing has a prominent
reddish brown patch in the center

Below: forewing brown with a reddish brown central
patch and gray frosting along the outer margin; hindwing brown with fine striations and gray frosting
toward outer margin

Sexes: similar

Egg: currently undocumented

Larva: poorly known in Michigan

Larval Host Plants: currently undocumented in
Michigan, likely various grasses or sedges

Habitat: bogs and wet meadows

Broods: single generation

Abundance: rare to uncommon; local

Compare: unique

Resident

Jan. Feb. Mar. Apr. May June July Aug. Sept. Oct. Nov. Dec.

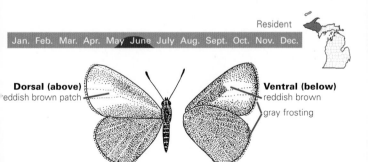

Dorsal (above)
reddish brown patch

Ventral (below)
reddish brown

gray frosting

189

Male

Female   Male   Larva

Comments: Juvenal's Duskywing is a widespread and
common early spring species that can at times be
exceedingly abundant. It is often confused with the
similar Horace's Duskywing with which it often flies.
At home in oak woodlands and other scrubby habitats,
adults dart up and down sunlit trails and explore adjacent open sites with a quick, low flight. They
frequently visit flowers or bask on bare ground with
their wings spread. Males perch on low vegetation and
actively pursue passing butterflies, often creating a
whirl of activity. They frequently puddle at damp sand
or gravel.

Juvenal's Duskywing
Erynnis juvenalis

Family/Subfamily: Skippers (Hesperiidae)/
Spread-wing Skippers (Pyrginae)

Wingspan: 1.5–1.9" (3.8–4.8 cm)

Above: dark brown; forewing has small cluster of tiny
clear spots near wingtip and one at end of cell, and is
heavily patterned with brown, gray, black and tan;
female has increased gray scaling and heavier pattern

Below: brown, lightening toward wing margin; hindwing
has two small, light spots along leading margin

Sexes: similar, although female is lighter and more heavily patterned with larger forewing spots

Egg: pale green, laid singly on host leaves

Larva: pale green with thin, light lateral stripe; reddish
brown head with a row of light orange spots around
the margin; larvae construct individual shelters on the
host by tying one or more leaves together with silk

Larval Host Plants: a wide variety of oaks including
White Oak and Black Oak

Habitat: oak woodlands and scrub, forest margins and
clearings, roadsides and utility easements

Broods: single generation

Abundance: occasional to abundant

Compare: Horace's Duskywing (pg. 173) lacks the two
light spots along leading margin of ventral hindwing.

Resident

| Jan. | Feb. | Mar. | Apr. | May | June | July | Aug. | Sept. | Oct. | Nov. | Dec. |

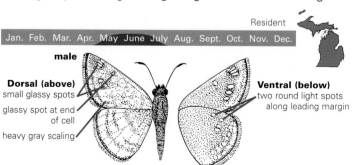

male

Dorsal (above)
small glassy spots
glassy spot at end
of cell
heavy gray scaling

Ventral (below)
two round light spots
along leading margin

191

Ventral

Larva

Comments: The Little Wood-Satyr is one of our most
abundant and commonly encountered satyrs. A butterfly of shady woodlands and associated clearings and
margins, it dances along the forest floor with a relatively slow, bobbing flight but can move rapidly if
disturbed. Adults periodically perch on leaf litter or low
vegetation with their wings partially open. Adults feed
at sap flows, animal dung, rotting fungi and fermenting
fruit and do not visit flowers.

Little Wood-Satyr
Megisto cymela

Family/Subfamily: Brush-foots (Nymphalidae)/ Satyrs and Wood-Nymphs (Satyrinae)

Wingspan: 1.5–1.9" (3.3–4.8 cm)

Above: brown; forewing has two prominent yellow-rimmed eyespots; hindwing has one to three (usually one is quite small) prominent yellow-rimmed eyespots

Below: light brown with two dark brown lines across both wings; each wing has some pearly silver markings between two large, yellow-rimmed eyespots

Sexes: similar, although female has larger eyespots

Egg: green, laid singly on host leaves

Larva: brown with a dark dorsal stripe, brown lateral dashes, two short stubby tails on the rear and two small horns on the head

Larval Host Plants: various grasses including bluegrass and Orchardgrass

Habitat: open woodlands, forest clearings, fens, woodland margins and adjacent brushy areas

Broods: single generation

Abundance: common

Compare: Mitchell's Satyr (pg. 181) lacks eyespots on the wings above and has a row of five yellow-rimmed black eyespots on the ventral hindwing.

Resident

| Jan. | Feb. | Mar. | Apr. | May | June | July | Aug. | Sept. | Oct. | Nov. | Dec. |

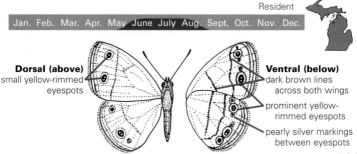

Dorsal (above)
small yellow-rimmed eyespots

Ventral (below)
dark brown lines across both wings

prominent yellow-rimmed eyespots

pearly silver markings between eyespots

193

Dorsal

Larva

Comments: The American Snout gets its odd name from
the long labial palpi that resemble an elongated, beak-
like nose. This unique feature, combined with the cryptic
coloration of the wings beneath enhances the butterfly's
overall "dead leaf" appearance when it is at rest. It is a
permanent resident in the Deep South, but regularly
moves north to temporarily colonize much of the U.S.
each year. The butterfly occasionally ventures into southern portions of the Michigan where it presence is spotty
and unreliable. Adults have a quick, somewhat bouncing
flight and frequently visit available flowers.

American Snout
Libytheana carinenta

Family/Subfamily: Brush-foots (Nymphalidae)/ Snouts (Libytheinae)

Wingspan: 1.6–1.9" (4.1–4.8 cm)

Above: brown with orange patches and white forewing spots; forewing apex is extended and squared off

Below: brown with orange basal forewing scaling and white spots; hindwing variable; plain gray brown or pinkish brown with heavy mottling

Sexes: similar

Egg: tiny white eggs laid in axils of host leaves

Larva: light green with numerous small yellow dots and yellow lateral stripe; rear portion has two small black lateral spots

Larval Host Plants: Common Hackberry and Dwarf Hackberry

Habitat: rich, deciduous woodlands, stream corridors, swamps, forest edges, woodland clearings and adjacent open, brushy areas

Broods: one or more generations

Abundance: rare to occasional

Compare: unique

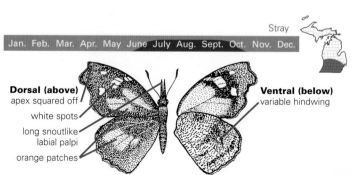

Stray

Jan. Feb. Mar. Apr. May June July Aug. Sept. Oct. Nov. Dec.

Dorsal (above)
apex squared off
white spots
long snoutlike labial palpi
orange patches

Ventral (below)
variable hindwing

195

Dorsal

Comments: This is our most widespread and abundant arctic. Found in dry grassy sites and open woodlands, individuals tend to be rather local but can be rather numerous when encountered. The Chryxus Arctic is a strong flier. The orange-brown adults maneuver quickly over open ground and present a serious challenge to follow. They frequently alight on rocks or bare patches, but tend to be quite wary and difficult to closely approach.

Chryxus Arctic
Oeneis chryxus

Family/Subfamily: Brush-foots (Nymphalidae)/ Satyrs and Wood-Nymphs (Satyrinae)

Wingspan: 1.6–2.1" (4.1–5.3 cm)

Above: orange-brown with darker brown margins; forewing has submarginal row of two to four black eye-spots; male forewing darkened toward base with scent scales; hindwing has small black spot at anal angle

Below: forewing has submarginal row of black eyespots and dark postmedian line bearing a sharp, outward pointing tooth; hindwing mottled brown and gray with fine striations, white veins and a darker median band

Sexes: similar, although female is larger with broader, more rounded wings; forewing lacks dark scent scales

Egg: whitish, laid singly on host leaves

Larva: tan with brown and tan stripes separated by white; covered in short reddish brown hairs

Larval Host Plants: various sedges including Pennsylvania Sedge

Habitat: dry woodland clearings, open pine barrens, forest margins and adjacent grassy landscapes

Broods: single generation

Abundance: occasional to common; local

Compare: Macoun's Arctic (pg. 313) is larger, paler golden brown above and is limited to Isle Royale.

Resident

| Jan. | Feb. | Mar. | Apr. | May | June | July | Aug. | Sept. | Oct. | Nov. | Dec. |

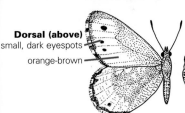

Dorsal (above)
small, dark eyespots
orange-brown

Ventral (below)
white veins
mottled with dark striations

197

Dorsal

Larva

Comments: This distinctive arctic is restricted entirely to black spruce and tamarack bogs, where it is usually encountered near the protected confines of more wooded margins. They seldom venture into open areas of the wetland. Despite its colonial habit, the species can be relatively common in the right location. Adults regularly perch on tree trunks and fly rapidly if disturbed. The Jutta Arctic requires two seasons to produce a single generation, with the resulting adults on the wing only in odd-numbered years in Michigan.

Jutta Arctic
Oeneis jutta

Family/Subfamily: Brush-foots (Nymphalidae)/
Satyrs and Wood-Nymphs (Satyrinae)

Wingspan: 1.7–2.1" (4.3–5.3 cm)

Above: dull gray-brown; forewing has yellow submarginal patches enclosing one to three (typical) black spots; hindwing has yellow submarginal patched and a single black spot at the anal angle

Below: hindwing mottled brown and gray with fine striations and a darker brown median band; median band bordered outwardly by gray; often has a single small black eyespot at the anal angle

Sexes: similar, although female is larger with broader, more rounded wings

Egg: pale yellow, laid singly and haphazardly near host leaves

Larva: green with green and whitish lateral stripes; covered in short, reddish brown hairs

Larval Host Plants: various sedges including Tussock Cottongrass

Habitat: black spruce and tamarack bogs and margins

Broods: biennial; the larvae require two seasons to complete development

Abundance: occasional to common; local

Compare: unique; only arctic with pale patches surrounding black eyespots

Resident

Jan. Feb. Mar. Apr. May June July Aug. Sept. Oct. Nov. Dec.

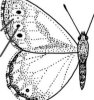

Dorsal (above)
yellow submarginal patches
dark eyespots

Ventral (below)
mottled with fine striations

199

Dorsal

Larva

Comments: The Eyed Brown is a frail butterfly of damp meadows and other sedge-dominated wetlands. Restricted by habitat, colonies tend to be spotty and highly localized. Nonetheless, the butterfly can be quite abundant when encountered. Adults have a slow, bouncing flight and traverse low through wetland vegetation, stopping frequently to perch where they are easily overlooked. They seldom stray far from suitable habitat areas.

Eyed Brown
Satyrodes eurydice

Family/Subfamily: Brush-foots (Nymphalidae)/
Satyrs and Wood-Nymphs (Satyrinae)

Wingspan: 1.60–2.25" (4.1–5.7 cm)

Above: light brown (occasionally darker in the U.P.) with
a submarginal row of small, solid black eyespots

Below: soft brown; forewing has straight, uniform row of
4 double-rimmed black eyespots; hindwing has row of
5 to 6 double-rimmed black eyespots with pale centers, bordered inwardly by dark, jagged postmedian line

Sexes: similar, although female is generally paler brown
with larger eyespots

Egg: greenish white, laid singly on or near host leaves

Larva: light yellow-green with lateral red stripes and two
short tails on the rear; two reddish horns on the head

Larval Host Plants: various sedges including Upright
Sedge and Hairy Sedge

Habitat: marshes, sedge meadows, fens, roadside
ditches and adjacent habitats

Broods: single generation

Abundance: occasional to common; local

Compare: Appalachian Brown (pg. 203) has a smoother,
more sinuous postmedian line on ventral hindwing; the
middle two eyespots on the ventral forewing are generally smaller than the one above or below.

Resident

Jan. Feb. Mar. Apr. May June July Aug. Sept. Oct. Nov. Dec.

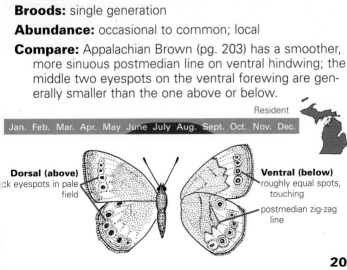

Dorsal (above)
ck eyespots in pale
field

Ventral (below)
roughly equal spots,
touching

postmedian zig-zag
line

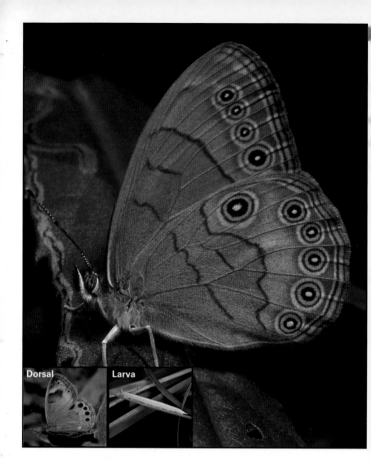

Dorsal

Larva

Comments: Although called the Appalachian Brown, the range of this butterfly winds from northern Florida to southern Canada. In Michigan, it is reclusive, spotty and often highly localized within damp woodlands and shaded swamps. Like other wetland butterflies, it has suffered from continued loss of habitat due to urban development or agriculture. Adults have an erratic, low, bouncing flight and stop frequently to perch. Even when disturbed, they typically fly only a short distance before alighting again. Like most satyrs, the adults feed at sap flows, fermenting fruit, dung or rotting fungi and do not visit flowers.

Appalachian Brown
Satyrodes appalachia

Family/Subfamily: Brush-foots (Nymphalidae)/ Satyrs and Wood-Nymphs (Satyrinae)

Wingspan: 1.90–2.25" (4.8–5.7 cm)

Above: light brown with small, solid black eyespots

Below: soft brown; forewing has a row of 4 double-rimmed black eyespots, the middle two generally smaller than one above or below; hindwing has row of 5 to 6 double-rimmed black eyespots with pale centers bordered inwardly by dark sinuous postmedian line

Sexes: similar, although female is generally paler brown with larger eyespots

Egg: greenish white, laid singly on or near host leaves

Larva: light green with narrow longitudinal yellow stripes, two short tails on the rear and two reddish horns on the head

Larval Host Plants: various grasses and sedges including Hairy Sedge, Upright Sedge and Fowl Mannagrass

Habitat: wooded swamps, moist grassy glades, wet woodlands, stream corridors, fens and forest margins

Broods: single generation

Abundance: occasional to common; local

Compare: Eyed Brown (pg. 201) has a more jagged brown postmedian line on the ventral hindwing and a fairly straight and uniform row of eyespots on the ventral forewing.

Resident

| Jan. | Feb. | Mar. | Apr. | May | June | July | Aug. | Sept. | Oct. | Nov. | Dec. |

Dorsal (above)
warm brown
dark eyespots

Ventral (below)
middle spots usually smaller

dark, smoothly curved postmedian line

Dorsal

Larva

Comments: The Silver-spotted Skipper is a large, robust butterfly named for the distinctive, pure silver-white patch on the hindwing below. Adults have a powerful, darting flight that offers a challenging pursuit. Luckily, they are fond of flowers and readily pause to feed where they can be closely observed. They have a long proboscis and can easily gain access to nectar from a wide variety of blossoms. Males perch on shrubs or overhanging branches and aggressively investigate passing organisms. The colorful larvae construct individual shelters on the host by tying one or more leaves together with silk.

Silver-spotted Skipper
Epargyreus clarus

Family/Subfamily: Skippers (Hesperiidae)/
Spread-wing Skippers (Pyrginae)

Wingspan: 1.75–2.40" (4.4–6.1 cm)

Above: brown with median row of gold spots on
forewing and checkered wing fringe; hindwing is
tapered into small, rounded, lobe-like tail

Below: brown; forewing as above; hindwing has distinct,
elongated clear silver-white patch in center; both
wings have a slightly frosted outer margin

Sexes: similar

Egg: green, laid singly on host leaves

Larva: yellow-green with dark bands and reddish brown
head bearing two orange spots

Larval Host Plants: wide variety of plants in the pea
family (Fabaceae) including Black Locust, wisteria,
bush clover, False Indigo and Honey Locust

Habitat: forest edges, open woodlands, roadsides, utility
easements, brushy fields, parks and gardens

Broods: two or more generations

Abundance: occasional to common

Compare: Hoary Edge (pg. 185) is smaller, lacks the
stubby hindwing tail, and has a marginal white ventral
hindwing patch.

Resident

| Jan. | Feb. | Mar. | Apr. | May | June | July | Aug. | Sept. | Oct. | Nov. | Dec. |

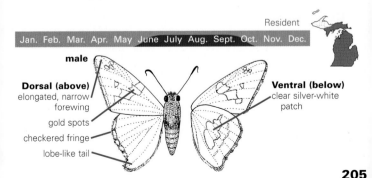

male

Dorsal (above)
elongated, narrow
forewing

gold spots

checkered fringe

lobe-like tail

Ventral (below)
clear silver-white
patch

Female

Ventral   Larva

Comments: The Common Buckeye is one of our most distinctive butterflies. The large eyespots help deflect attack away from the insect's vulnerable body or serve to startle would-be predators. It is fond of most open, sunny locations with low vegetation and may be an occasional garden visitor. Adults frequently alight on bare soil or gravel but are extremely wary and difficult to approach. Males readily establish territories and actively investigate most any passing insect. Flight is rapid and low to the ground. It is a frequent seasonal colonist, particularly in southern Michigan. Fairly common in certain years and rare or absent in others.

Common Buckeye
Junonia coenia

Family/Subfamily: Brush-foots (Nymphalidae)/
True Brush-foots (Nymphalinae)

Wingspan: 1.5–2.7" (3.8–6.9 cm)

Above: brown with prominent eyespots; forewing bears a distinct white patch and two small orange bars

Below: forewing has prominent white band; hindwings seasonally variable in color; summer forms are light brown with numerous pattern elements; cool-season forms are reddish brown with reduced markings

Sexes: similar, although female has broader wings and larger hindwing eyespots

Egg: dark green, laid singly on host leaves

Larva: black with lateral white stripes, orange patches and branched spines

Larval Host Plants: a wide variety of herbaceous plants several families (Acanthaceae, Verbenaceae, Scrophulariaceae, and Plantaginaceae) including toad-flax, false foxglove and plantain

Habitat: fields, pastures, roadsides, fallow agricultural land, gardens, open pineland, disturbed sites

Broods: two or more generations

Abundance: rare to occasional

Compare: unique

Stray

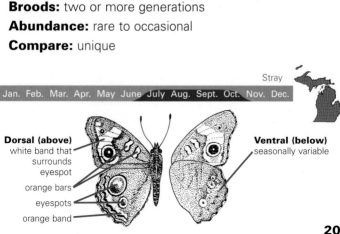

Jan. Feb. Mar. Apr. May June July Aug. Sept. Oct. Nov. Dec.

Dorsal (above)
white band that surrounds eyespot

orange bars

eyespots

orange band

Ventral (below)
seasonally variable

207

Dorsal **Larva**

Comments: This is a large, somewhat reclusive butterfly of moist, shaded woodlands and stream corridors.
Colonies tend to be spotty and found in close association with patches of larval hosts; can be locally
numerous when encountered. Adults have a quick,
bobbing flight and maneuver close to the ground,
often through dense forest undergrowth. They frequently alight on low vegetation, tree trunks or on leaf
litter. They do not visit flowers but instead feed at sap
flows, rotting fruit, decaying vegetation, fungi and
dung. Unlike most butterflies, the adults are active on
overcast days and often fly late into the evening.

Northern Pearly-Eye
Enodia anthedon

Family/Subfamily: Brush-foots (Nymphalidae)/ Satyrs and Wood-Nymphs (Satyrinae)

Wingspan: 1.75–2.60" (4.3–6.6 cm)

Above: light brown with black eyespots in a pale field; hindwing has a slightly scalloped margin; antennal clubs are black at base

Below: brown with a violet cast; forewing has a straight row of four yellow-rimmed dark eyespots; hindwing has a cream band enclosing a row of yellow-rimmed dark eyespots with light highlights

Sexes: similar, although female generally has broader, more rounded wings and larger eyespots

Egg: greenish white, laid singly on host leaves

Larva: yellow green with narrow longitudinal yellow stripes, a dark green dorsal stripe, two short red-tipped tails on the rear and two reddish horns on the head

Larval Host Plants: various grasses including Whitegrass, Indian Woodoats, Tall Fescue, Silver Plumegrass, Bearded Shorthusk and Reed Canarygrss

Habitat: moist, shaded woodlands, stream corridors, marsh edges, fens and semi-open grassy areas along forest margins

Broods: single generation

Abundance: uncommon to common; local

Compare: unique

Resident

Jan. Feb. Mar. Apr. May June July Aug. Sept. Oct. Nov. Dec.

Dorsal (above)
black bases on antennae

Ventral (below)
straight row of four eyespots; bottom two larger

dark, gently curved postmedian line

209

Male

Ventral   Larva

Comments: This lovely brown butterfly is named after its preferred larval host. A denizen of rich, shaded decidu-ous woodlands and wetland margins, it may occasionally show up in suburban yards or parks. Adults have a strong, rapid flight and often perch on sunlit leaves, overhanging branches or tree trunks along for-est trails and woodland edges. They are exceedingly aggressive and inquisitive, and readily dart out investi-gate most any passing object, occasionally even landing on humans. Adults do not visit flowers but are drawn to sap flows or rotting fruit. Although often spotty and localized, it can be quite abundant when encountered.

Hackberry Emperor
Asterocampa celtis

Family/Subfamily: Brush-foots (Nymphalidae)/ Emperors (Apaturinae)

Wingspan: 2.0–2.6" (5.1–6.6 cm)

Above: amber-brown with dark markings and borders; forewing bears several small white spots near the apex and a single submarginal black eyespot; hindwing has a postmedian row of dark spots

Below: as above with muted coloration; hindwing has postmedian row of yellow-rimmed black spots with blue green centers

Sexes: similar, although female has broader wings

Egg: cream-white, laid singly or in small clusters on leaves

Larva: light green with two narrow dorsal yellow stripe; mottled with small yellow spots; dark head bears two stubby, branched horns; rear end has a pair of short tails

Larval Host Plants: Common Hackberry

Habitat: moist, rich woodlands, forest margins and clearings, stream corridors, parks and yards

Broods: two generations

Abundance: occasional to common; local

Compare: Tawny Emperor (pg. 215) is more orange-brown above and lacks white forewing spots and single forewing eyespot.

Resident

Jan. Feb. Mar. Apr. May June July Aug. Sept. Oct. Nov. Dec.

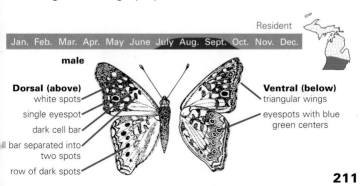

male

Dorsal (above)
white spots
single eyespot
dark cell bar
ll bar separated into two spots
row of dark spots

Ventral (below)
triangular wings
eyespots with blue green centers

211

nephele

Dorsal *alope* • *alope* • Larva

Comments: This is one of our largest and most distinctive wood-nymphs. Adults have a low, relaxed flight and bob erratically among the vegetation, stopping frequently to alight low within the grasses. Unlike most satyrs, it is an opportunistic feeder and frequently visits flowers along with sap flows and fermenting fruit. The Common Wood-Nymph is geographically variable and two forms or subspecies occur within the state. Populations with yellow forewing patches are common in southern regions of Michigan, whereas in more northern counties dark forewings predominate. Numerous intermediate forms can also be found.

Common Wood-Nymph
Cercyonis pegala

Family/Subfamily: Brush-foots (Nymphalidae)/ Satyrs and Wood-Nymphs (Satyrinae)

Wingspan: 1.8–2.8" (4.6–7.1 cm)

Above: brown; subspecies *alope* (southern counties) has two dark eyespots containing white highlights surrounded by a large yellow patch on the forewing; subspecies *nephele* lacks the yellow forewing patch

Below: brown with dark striations; subspecies *alope* has a large yellow patch surrounding two dark eyespots containing white highlights on the forewing; subspecies *nephele* lacks the yellow forewing patch and has two yellow-rimmed two dark eyespots containing white highlights

Sexes: similar, although female is paler and has larger eyespots

Egg: cream, laid singly on host leaves

Larva: green with dark green dorsal stripe and light side stripes

Larval Host Plants: various grasses including bluegrass, Poverty Oatgrass and Purpletop Grass

Habitat: wet meadows, grassy fields, open woodlands, prairie and open, shrubby landscapes

Broods: single generation

Abundance: occasional to common

Compare: unique

Resident

| Jan. | Feb. | Mar. | Apr. | May | June | July | Aug. | Sept. | Oct. | Nov. | Dec. |

form *alope*

Dorsal (above)
two large eyespots
yellow patch

Ventral (below)
geographically variable throughout the U.S.

yellow-rimmed eyespots

brown with black striations

213

Male

Male   Female   Larva

Comments: The Tawny Emperor shares its affinity for rich woodlands with the Hackberry Emperor. The two species are often found together but tend to be localized and seldom found far from stands of larval hosts. Adults are rapid, strong fliers, often difficult to closely approach. Males perch on sunlit leaves or on the sides of large trees along forest edges or clearings. They are pugnacious and inquisitive, and readily dart out to investigate virtually any passing object before returning to the same or nearby perch. The developing larvae remain together and feed communally through the first three instars before becoming more solitary.

Tawny Emperor
Asterocampa clyton

Family/Subfamily: Brush-foots (Nymphalidae)/
Emperors (Apaturinae)

Wingspan: 2.00–2.75" (5.1–7.0 cm)

Above: orange-brown with dark markings and borders;
hindwing has a postmedian row of dark spots

Below: as above with muted gray-brown cast and small,
dark-blue-centered hindwing eyespots

Sexes: similar, although female is much larger with
broader, more rounded wings

Egg: cream-white, laid in large pyramidal clusters on the
underside of host leaves

Larva: light green with broad dorsal yellow stripes, narrow yellow lateral stripes and mottled with small
yellow spots; head is green and bears two stubby,
branched horns; rear end has a pair of short tails

Larval Host Plants: Common Hackberry

Habitat: rich, moist deciduous woodlands, swamp margins, forest clearings and margins, stream corridors,
parks and yards

Broods: single generation

Abundance: uncommon to occasional; locally common

Compare: Hackberry Emperor (pg. 211) is lighter brown
with single forewing black eyespot and white spots
near the apex.

Resident

| Jan. | Feb. | Mar. | Apr. | May | June | July | Aug. | Sept. | Oct. | Nov. | Dec. |

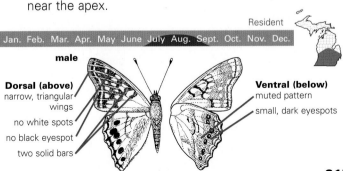

male

Dorsal (above)
narrow, triangular wings
no white spots
no black eyespot
two solid bars

Ventral (below)
muted pattern
small, dark eyespots

215

Ventral

Larva

Comments: This is a large, distinctive butterfly of northern forests. Although generally uncommon in southern counties, it can at times be extremely abundant in the Upper Peninsula. Compton's Tortoiseshell is a long-lived butterfly with the large adults seeking shelter in log piles, tree cavities or manmade structures to pass the harsh winter months. It has a quick, darting flight and is often quite wary of close approach. Adults readily bask with their wings open in sunlit patches on gravel roads or in woodland clearings. They do not visit flowers but instead feed at fermenting fruit, dung, carrion and sap flows.

Compton Tortoiseshell
Nymphalis vaualbum

Family/Subfamily: Brush-foots (Nymphalidae)/
True Brush-foots (Nymphalinae)

Wingspan: 2.5–3.1" (6.4–7.9 cm)

Above: rusty brown with heavy black spots and golden
scaling toward outer margin; each wing bears a bright
white spot just below the apex; forewing apex is
extended and squared off; hindwing bears a single
short, stubby tail

Below: appears bark-like; heavily striated with gray and
brown; outer portion noticeably lighter than basal half

Sexes: similar

Egg: green, laid in clusters on host

Larva: light green with pale mottling and several rows of
lateral cream and dorsal black branched spines

Larval Host Plants: birch, willow and Quaking Aspen

Habitat: deciduous or mixed forest openings, woodland
roads and trails, forest edges and adjacent open areas

Broods: single generation

Abundance: uncommon to occasional; occasionally
abundant

Compare: unique

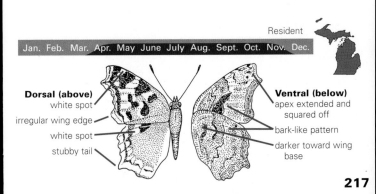

Resident

Jan. Feb. Mar. Apr. May June July Aug. Sept. Oct. Nov. Dec.

Dorsal (above)
white spot
irregular wing edge
white spot
stubby tail

Ventral (below)
apex extended and
squared off
bark-like pattern
darker toward wing
base

Male

Ventral   Larva

Comments: With a wingspan approaching six inches, the Giant Swallowtail is one of the largest butterflies in North America. Restricted to southern Michigan, populations tend to be relatively small and localized in close association with stands of its larval host. It is not tolerant of urban development. Adults are fond of flowers and continuously flutter their wings while feeding. The mottled larvae resemble bird droppings. If disturbed, they extend a red hornlike structure called an osmeterium from behind the head. The defensive gland omits a pungent odor and chemical irritant and is particularly effective against insect predators or parasitoids.

Giant Swallowtail
Papilio cresphontes

Family/Subfamily: Swallowtails (Papilionidae)/
Swallowtails (Papilioninae)

Wingspan: 4.5–5.5" (11.4–14.0 cm)

Above: chocolate brown with broad crossing bands of
yellow spots; characteristic diagonal band extends
from tip of forewing to base of abdomen; hindwing tail
has yellow center

Below: cream yellow with brown markings and blue
median hindwing band

Sexes: similar, although female is generally larger

Egg: amber-brown, laid singly on upperside of host
leaves

Larva: brown with yellow and cream patches; resembles
bird dropping

Larval Host Plants: Prickly Ash

Habitat: open woodlands, pastures, forest margins,
shrubby wetlands and adjacent open areas including
pastures, roadsides, fields and rural gardens

Broods: two generations

Abundance: uncommon to occasional; localized

Compare: unique

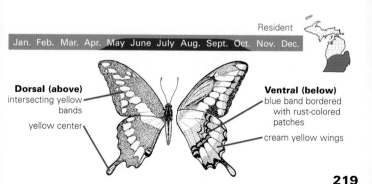

Resident

Jan. Feb. Mar. Apr. May June July Aug. Sept. Oct. Nov. Dec.

Dorsal (above)
intersecting yellow
bands

yellow center

Ventral (below)
blue band bordered
with rust-colored
patches

cream yellow wings

219

Larva

Comments: The Red-banded Hairstreak has a rapid, erratic flight. Males typically perch on the sunlit leaves of small trees and shrubs (often on their hosts) and readily fly out to interact with other individuals, often spiraling high into the air before returning to a nearby perch. Unlike most other butterflies, female Red-banded Hairstreaks do not lay their eggs directly on the larval host. Instead, they land on the ground below appropriate hosts and deposit the small eggs singly on the undersides of dead, fallen leaves or other debris. The larvae feed primarily on this decaying plant material. May infrequently stray into southern Michigan.

Red-banded Hairstreak
Calycopis cecrops

Family/Subfamily: Gossamer Wings (Lycaenidae)/
Hairstreaks (Theclinae)

Wingspan: 0.75–1.00" (1.9–2.5 cm)

Above: male is slate gray above with no markings;
female is slate gray with iridescent blue scaling on
hindwing; hindwing bears two short tails

Below: light gray with broad, red band edged outwardly
by a thin, wavy white line; blue scaling and a black
eyespot near tails

Sexes: similar, although female has blue scaling above

Egg: cream brown, laid on dead leaves below host

Larva: pinkish brown with numerous short hairs

Larval Host Plants: larvae are primarily detritivores,
feeding on dead leaves and other plant material below
certain shrubs or small trees including Winged Sumac
and Staghorn Sumac

Habitat: woodland edges and adjacent disturbed, brushy
areas, suburban gardens

Broods: two or more generations southward; stray individuals could potentially breed in Michigan

Abundance: rare

Compare: Southern Hairstreak (pg. 131) lacks complete
red hindwing band.

Stray

Jan. Feb. Mar. Apr. May June July Aug. Sept. Oct. Nov. Dec.

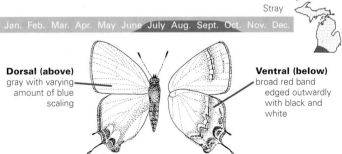

Dorsal (above)
gray with varying
amount of blue
scaling

Ventral (below)
broad red band
edged outwardly
with black and
white

Ventral   Larva

Comments: The Gray Hairstreak may be encountered in
just about any open habitat because it is able to utilize
an enormous variety of plants as larval hosts. Adults
have a quick, erratic flight and are exceedingly fond of
flowers. They regularly perch with their wings partially
open, an unusual behavior for most hairstreaks. The
small tails on the hindwing resemble antennae and pre-
sumably help deflect the attack of would-be predators
away from the vulnerable body. This charade,
employed by many members of the family, is enhanced
by the orange spots and converging lines on the wings
below that draw attention to this false head feature.

Gray Hairstreak
Strymon melinus

Family/Subfamily: Gossamer Wings (Lycaenidae)/ Hairstreaks (Theclinae)

Wingspan: 1.0–1.5" (2.5–3.8 cm)

Above: slate gray with distinct reddish orange-capped black hindwing spot above tail

Below: light gray with black-and-white line across both wings (often with some orange); hindwing has reddish orange-capped black spot and blue scaling above tail

Sexes: similar; female larger with broader wings

Egg: light green, laid singly on flower buds or flowers of host

Larva: highly variable; bright green with lateral cream stripes to pinkish red

Larval Host Plants: wide variety of plants including Partridge Pea, beggarweeds, milk peas, milkvetch, lupine, bush clover, clover, vetch, mallow and Sida

Habitat: open, disturbed sites including roadsides, fallow agricultural land, pastures, old fields, suburban gardens; also woodland margins, prairies and rural meadows

Broods: two or more generations

Abundance: occasional to common

Compare: Southern Hairstreak (pg. 131) is brown on both wing surfaces. White M Hairstreak (pg. 85) is blue above with wide, black borders.

Resident

Jan. Feb. Mar. Apr. May June July Aug. Sept. Oct. Nov. Dec.

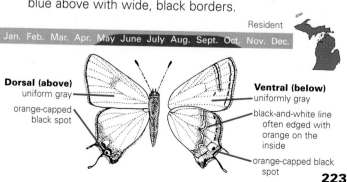

Dorsal (above)
uniform gray
orange-capped black spot

Ventral (below)
uniformly gray
black-and-white line often edged with orange on the inside
orange-capped black spot

223

Comments: This lovely grayish hairstreak is restricted to wetland habitats or other moist areas that support willows. Although widespread across much of the Northeast and Great Lakes, the species tends to occur in relatively small, highly localized colonies but can be rather common when encountered. Adults have a quick, erratic flight and are most often observed at nearby moisture-loving flowers. They are particularly fond of milkweed blossoms.

Acadian Hairstreak
Satyrium acadica

Family/Subfamily: Gossamer Wings (Lycaenidae)/ Hairstreaks (Theclinae)

Wingspan: 1.10–1.45" (2.8–4.0 cm)

Above: brown with a small orange crescent-shaped hindwing spot above a short tail

Below: uniform gray with a postmedian row of round, white-rimmed black spots; hindwing has a submarginal row of orange crescent-shaped spots and a orange-capped blue patch near the tail

Sexes: similar

Egg: white, laid singly on host twigs; eggs overwinter

Larva: green and white lateral stripe, pale white oblique dashes, and a darker green dorsal stripe edged in white

Larval Host Plants: various willows

Habitat: stream margins, pond edges, marshes, swamps, wet roadside ditches, depressions, bogs and moist meadows

Broods: single generation

Abundance: uncommon to occasional; localized

Compare: Edwards's Hairstreak (pg. 121) has graybrown ventral wings and is typically found in more xeric (dry) habitats with oaks.

Resident

Jan. Feb. Mar. Apr. May June July Aug. Sept. Oct. Nov. Dec.

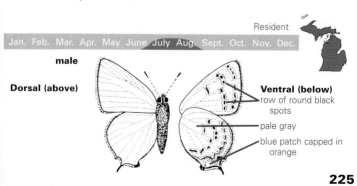

male

Dorsal (above)

Ventral (below)
row of round black spots

pale gray

blue patch capped in orange

Larva

Comments: The Early Hairstreak is a denizen of mixed hardwood forests where it frequents woodland roads or sunlit trails. Although not necessary a rare butterfly, sightings tend to be scarce and sporadic due to the fact that adults spend much of their time high in the canopy. They venture down from the treetops infrequently in search of nectar or to sip moisture at damp earth. They are seldom encountered in numbers. The butterfly requires stands of mature host trees as the slug-like larvae feed primarily on developing nuts.

Early Hairstreak
Erora laeta

Family/Subfamily: Gossamer Wings (Lycaenidae)/ Hairstreaks (Theclinae)

Wingspan: 0.75–1.00" (1.9–2.5 cm)

Above: slate gray with blue scaling toward wing bases; tailless

Below: pale grayish green with a band of white-rimmed reddish orange spots across the wings; hindwing has a second row of smaller white-rimmed reddish orange spots along the outer margin

Sexes: dissimilar; female has increased iridescent blue scaling above with broad, dark gray borders

Egg: pale green laid singly on host leaves, buds, developing fruits and catkins

Larva: yellow green to rust brown with large reddish brown patches on the thorax and abdomen

Larval Host Plants: American Beech and Beaked Hazelnut

Habitat: hardwood forests and clearings, woodland margins, trails, stream corridors and roadsides

Broods: two generations

Abundance: rare

Compare: unique

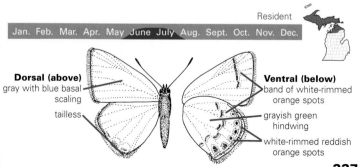

Resident

Jan. Feb. Mar. Apr. May June July Aug. Sept. Oct. Nov. Dec.

Dorsal (above)
gray with blue basal scaling

tailless

Ventral (below)
band of white-rimmed orange spots

grayish green hindwing

white-rimmed reddish orange spots

227

Male

Female

Larva

Comments: The Least Skipper is a tiny, easy-to-identify
butterfly of wet, grassy areas throughout Michigan and
much of eastern North America. Highly adaptable to
human disturbance, it may be encountered in pristine
wetlands or damp drainage ditches, provided suitable
host grasses are present. Although somewhat local in
occurrence, it can at times be exceedingly abundant in
the right location. Adults have a low, weak flight and
flutter slowly through tall grasses pausing frequently to
perch. They regularly visit flowers but prefer low
plants with small blossoms.

Least Skipper
Ancyloxypha numitor

Family/Subfamily: Skippers (Hesperiidae)/
Banded Skippers (Hesperiinae)

Wingspan: 0.7–1.0" (1.8–2.5 cm)

Above: forewing blackish brown with some orange scaling along the costal margin; hindwing orange with dark brownish black border; rounded wings; male has a long, pointed abdomen

Below: forewing dark brown with orange margin; hindwing unmarked golden orange

Sexes: similar, although female has a shorter abdomen

Egg: yellow, laid singly on or near host leaves

Larva: long and slender, light yellow-green with thin dark dorsal stripe and reddish brown head; head has numerous cream stripes

Larval Host Plants: various grasses including Rice Cutgrass, Giant Cutgrass, panic grass and cordgrass

Habitat: moist, grassy areas including roadside ditches, utility easements, wet meadows, pond edges and old fields

Broods: two generations

Abundance: occasional to abundant

Compare: European Skipper (pg. 231) is bright orange above, has more pointed forewings, and is not restricted to moist habitats.

Resident

Jan. Feb. Mar. Apr. May June July Aug. Sept. Oct. Nov. Dec.

male | rounded wings

Dorsal (above)
rounded wings
orange
heavy dark margin

Ventral (below)
dark brown
uniform golden orange

229

Ventral

Larva

Comments: This diminutive electric orange butterfly is a regular sight in open, grassy areas throughout Michigan, where it can be extremely abundant at times. The European Skipper also adapts well to more urban locations, frequently showing up in suburban gardens, parks and vacant lots. As its name implies, the species was accidentally introduced into Ontario, Canada, from Europe in 1910 and continues to expand its range. Although superficially similar to the Least Skipper, it is less restricted to moist habitats. Adults maneuver close to the ground among grassy vegetation with a slow and somewhat erratic flight.

European Skipper
Thymelicus lineola

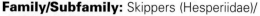

Family/Subfamily: Skippers (Hesperiidae)/
Banded Skippers (Hesperiinae)

Wingspan: 0.9–1.1" (2.3–2.8 cm)

Above: bronzy orange wings with dark brown to black borders; veins are darkened toward outer margins

Below: unmarked orange

Sexes: similar, although female is somewhat darker with veins darkened to base

Egg: white, laid on host stems

Larva: pale green with a darker green dorsal stripe, white lateral stripes and a greenish tan head marked with two vertical cream stripes on the face

Larval Host Plants: various grasses including Timothy Grass, Orchardgrass, Common Velvetgrass and bent-grass

Habitat: open, grassy areas including roadsides, utility easements, old fields, wet meadows, prairies, stream margins, pastures, parks and gardens

Broods: single generation

Abundance: occasional to abundant

Compare: Least Skipper (pg. 229) has more rounded blackish brown wings and produces multiple generations. Delaware Skipper (pg. 247) has more pointed forewings and a black forewing cell-end bar.

Resident

Jan. Feb. Mar. Apr. May June July Aug. Sept. Oct. Nov. Dec.

Dorsal (above)
dark brown borders

veins darker toward outer margins

bronzy orange

Ventral (below)
unmarked orange

231

Dorsal

Larva

Comments: This small species is one of our most distinctive skippers. It has a preference for moist, open grassy sites in or along woodlands or stream corridors. Despite its widespread occurrence throughout much of boreal North America, the Arctic Skipper remains a poorly known butterfly. Many aspects of its biology and behavior need further study. The adults have a relatively weak flight and maneuver low to the ground through grassy vegetation. They regularly perch with their wings held open.

Arctic Skipper
Carterocephalus palaemon

Family/Subfamily: Skippers (Hesperiidae)/
Intermediate Skippers (Heteropterinae)

Wingspan: 0.80–1.25" (2.0–3.2 cm)

Above: dark brown with numerous orange spots;
forewing somewhat elongated

Below: forewing yellow-orange with dark brown spots;
hindwing yellow-orange with dark-brown-rimmed
cream to white spots

Sexes: similar

Egg: pale green, laid singly on host leaves

Larva: pale whitish-green with a darker green dorsal
stripe and a pale yellow or white lateral stripe bordered
beneath by a row of black spots. Larvae construct individual shelters on host by weaving several leaves
together with silk.

Larval Host Plants: various grasses including brome
grass

Habitat: open forest and associated margins and trails,
woodland clearings, adjacent moist grassy sites,
marsh edges and swamp margins

Broods: single generation

Abundance: uncommon to common; local

Compare: unique

Resident Stray

| Jan. | Feb. | Mar. | Apr. | May | June | July | Aug. | Sept. | Oct. | Nov. | Dec. |

Dorsal (above)
attered orange spots

Ventral (below)
dark brown spots

brown-rimmed cream
spots

233

Ventral

Larva

Comments: This dainty orange butterfly is restricted to alkaline wetlands that support its sole larval host. Local and declining throughout much of its range, the species continues to lose available habitat due to urban development, agriculture or other human land use practices. The moth-like adults scurry low to the ground among grassy vegetation and are easily overlooked. Both sexes frequently stop to perch on leaves with their wings held wide open or occasionally visit available flowers. During periods of inclement weather or if disturbed, they often fly quickly and land out of sight on the underside of large, broad leaves.

Swamp Metalmark
Calephelis muticum (listed as *Calephelis mutica* by some authors)

Family/Subfamily: Gossamer Wings (Lycaenidae)/ Metalmarks (Riodininae)

Wingspan: 0.9–1.2" (2.3–3.0 cm)

Above: reddish brown with numerous small dark markings and two narrow, metallic gray bands along the outer edge of the wings

Below: marked similarly to upper surface but brighter orange

Sexes: similar, although female has broader, more rounded wings

Egg: reddish, laid singly on the underside of host leaves

Larva: green with tiny black dots; covered in long whitish hairs

Larval Host Plants: Swamp Thistle

Habitat: moist meadows, alkaline fens, marshes, bogs and other wetland sites

Broods: single generation

Abundance: occasional; locally common

Compare: unique

Resident

Jan. Feb. Mar. Apr. May June July Aug. Sept. Oct. Nov. Dec.

male

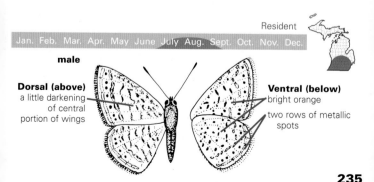

Dorsal (above)
a little darkening of central portion of wings

Ventral (below)
bright orange

two rows of metallic spots

235

Male pg. 115   Larva

Comments: Living up to its name, male Purplish Coppers
have an iridescent purple sheen on the wings above
that is stunning when seen in sunlight. Found in a variety of moist areas, colonies tend to be small and
somewhat localized, but can be relatively abundant
when encountered. While it is not as habitat restricted
as many other coppers, expanding agricultural activities,
urban development and habitat degradation nonetheless
continue to restrict the number of suitable wetland
areas available to the butterfly throughout its eastern
range. Males perch low on grasses or other vegetation
with their wings partially open to await passing females.

Purplish Copper
Lycaena helloides

Family/Subfamily: Gossamer Wings (Lycaenidae)/
Coppers (Lycaeninae)

Wingspan: 1.0–1.2" (2.5–3.0 cm)

Above: male is brown with a strong purplish iridescence
and scattered black; female is primarily orange with
scattered black spots and broad brown borders; hindwing has a broad scalloped orange submarginal band

Below: forewing is orange with scattered black spots
and a purplish brown apex and outer margin; hindwing
purplish brown with small black spots and a narrow,
irregular reddish orange submarginal line

Sexes: dissimilar; female has increased orange scaling
on both wings

Egg: greenish white, laid singly on the host

Larva: green with several yellow stripes

Larval Host Plants: knotweed and dock

Habitat: open, moist habitats including wet meadows,
stream margins, roadside ditches, pond margins, fallow agricultural land and marshes

Broods: two or more generations

Abundance: occasional to common; localized

Compare: Dorcas Copper (pg. 103) is generally smaller
and lacks or has a less extensive orange submarginal
band on the dorsal hindwing. Female has
less orange dorsal scaling.   Resident

Jan. Feb. Mar. Apr. May June July Aug. Sept. Oct. Nov. Dec.

male

Dorsal (above)
iridescent
purple/brown
(both wings)

zig-zag orange
outer margin

Ventral (below)
purplish brown

narrow orange
submarginal line

Comments: The Long Dash is a locally common butterfly of open, moist habitats. Its unusual name makes reference to the narrow dark spot near the tip of the forewing that appears to elongate or extend the black stigma. The energetic adults scurry over the top of wetland vegetation with a rapid, erratic flight. Males perch low to the ground to await passing females. Both sexes may wander into nearby drier habitat sites in search of available nectar sources.

Long Dash
Polites mystic

Family/Subfamily: Skippers (Hesperiidae)/
Banded Skippers (Hesperiinae)

Wingspan: 1.00–1.25" (2.5–3.2 cm)

Above: male yellow-orange with broad, dark brown borders; forewing has a broad, long black stigma below an elongated dark subapical spot; female dark brown with golden orange spot bands

Below: hindwing is reddish brown with a broad yellow postmedian band and small basal spot

Sexes: dissimilar; female is dark brown with golden orange bands; forewing lacks black stigma

Egg: pale green, laid singly on host

Larva: dark brown with fine white mottling and a black dorsal stripe; black head

Larval Host Plants: various gasses including bluegrass

Habitat: swamps, marshes, wet meadows, fens, roadside ditches, woodland margins, other open wetlands

Abundance: occasional to abundant

Broods: single generation

Compare: Peck's Skipper (pg. 127) is smaller and has yellow postmedian band on hindwing below with elongated central spot. Indian Skipper (pg. 257) has a narrower pale postmedian band on the hindwing below and is found in drier habitats.

Resident

Jan. Feb. Mar. Apr. May June July Aug. Sept. Oct. Nov. Dec.

male

Dorsal (above)
long stigma
slightly curved

Ventral (below)
small basal spot

band of equal-sized
yellow spots

Male

Female   Male   Larva

Comments: The Fiery Skipper is a prolific colonizer from the Deep South that regularly expands its range northward each summer to temporarily colonize much of the East before freezing back with the cold. It is an occasional late season vagrant to southern Michigan. Adults have a rapid, darting flight but often stop to perch on low vegetation. They are exceedingly fond of flowers and readily congregate at available blossoms, showing a strong preference for colorful composites. The larvae utilize a variety of grasses including many commonly planted for southern lawns. As a result, the butterfly is often mentioned as a minor turf pest.

Fiery Skipper
Hylephila phyleus

Family/Subfamily: Skippers (Hesperiidae)/
Banded Skippers (Hesperiinae)

Wingspan: 1.00–1.25" (2.5–3.2 cm)

Above: male is golden orange with jagged black border
and black stigma; female is dark brown with orange
bands; both sexes have elongated wings

Below: hindwing golden orange in male or orange brown
in female with scattered, tiny dark brown spots

Sexes: dissimilar; female darker with reduced orange
markings and larger hindwing spots

Egg: whitish green, laid singly on host leaves

Larva: greenish brown with thin, dark brown dorsal
stripe and black head

Larval Host Plants: a variety of weedy grasses including Bermuda Grass, crabgrass and bentgrass

Habitat: open, sunny, grassy areas including old fields,
roadsides, vacant lots, open woodlands, forest edges,
parks, lawns and gardens

Broods: multiple generations where resident; potentially
one or more in Michigan

Abundance: occasional

Compare:

Visitor

Jan. Feb. Mar. Apr. May June July Aug. Sept. Oct. Nov. Dec.

male

Dorsal (above)
orange

jagged black
margins

Ventral (below)
elongated wings

small scattered dark
spots

Ventral

Larva

Comments: Although called the American Copper, some
suggest that the eastern populations of the butterfly
may actually be the result of historical introductions
from Europe. This argument is fueled by the species'
unique preference for open, disturbed habitats and primary use of a weedy, non-native larval host. It tends to
occur in widespread and localized colonies, but is
often very common when encountered. The adults frequently perch on bare soil or on low vegetation with
the wings held in a characteristic, partially open posture. When first seen in bright sunlight, there remains
little doubt as to why the butterfly is called a copper!

American Copper
Lycaena phlaeas

Family/Subfamily: Gossamer Wings (Lycaenidae)/ Coppers (Lycaeninae)

Wingspan: 0.9–1.4" (2.3–3.6 cm)

Above: bright red orange forewings with black spots and dark borders; hindwing is gray with wide scalloped submarginal orange band subtended by black spots along outer margin

Below: forewing is pale orange with prominent white-rimmed black spots and light gray apex and outer margin; hindwing is silvery gray with small white-rimmed black spots and narrow, irregular reddish orange line along outer margin

Sexes: similar, although female is larger and has more rounded wings

Egg: pale greenish white, laid singly host stems or leaves

Larva: variable; yellow green to rose, often with a narrow lateral stripe

Larval Host Plants: Sheep Sorrel and Curly Dock

Habitat: open, sunny areas including old fields, pastures, roadsides, meadows and alfalfa or clover fields

Broods: three generations

Abundance: occasional to common

Compare: Bronze Copper (pg. 263) is larger and has a broad reddish orange submarginal band on the ventral hindwing.

Resident

Jan. Feb. Mar. Apr. May June July Aug. Sept. Oct. Nov. Dec.

Dorsal (above)
bright red orange forewing

black spots and dark border

gray brown hindwing

orange band

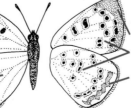

Ventral (below)
light gray

white-rimmed black spots

narrow red orange line

Dorsal

Larva

Comments: Unique in both appearance and behavior, the Harvester is the only North American butterfly with carnivorous larvae. A denizen of woodland habitats, the species tends to be found in small, localized colonies in close association with populations of its host aphids. Males are regularly encountered perching on sunlit leaves or imbibing moisture at damp ground along forest trails, unpaved roads or stream margins. The butterfly has a fast, erratic flight and can be a challenge to follow. Adults feed primarily on sugary aphid honeydew and rarely, if ever, visit flowers.

Harvester
Feniseca tarquinius

Family/Subfamily: Gossamer Wings (Lycaenidae)/ Harvesters (Miletinae)

Wingspan: 1.1–1.3" (2.8–3.3 cm)

Above: orange with brown to black spots, patches and borders

Below: brown; forewing has orange central scaling and several dark patches outlined in white; hindwing has numerous dark spots outlined in white and silver scaling toward base

Sexes: similar

Egg: greenish white, laid singly among aphid colonies

Larva: gray with whitish yellow bumps bordered with brown along top, reddish brown lateral stripes and long gray hairs

Larval Host Plants: does not feed on plant material; carnivorous on woolly aphids

Habitat: forest edges, stream corridors, swamp margins, moist woodlands and associated clearings, trails and roads

Broods: two or more generations

Abundance: occasional; often highly localized

Compare: unique

Resident

| Jan. | Feb. | Mar. | Apr. | May | June | July | Aug. | Sept. | Oct. | Nov. | Dec. |

female

Dorsal (above) orange with black border and spots

Ventral (below) reddish brown with silver scaling and numerous brown spots outlined in white

Female

Ventral

Larva

Comments: The Delaware Skipper is a widespread eastern butterfly of moist, grassy habitats from damp
meadows to marshes, but frequently finds is way into
more human-disturbed locations including suburban
yards. Despite its broad range, the species is seldom
overly abundant and often quite local. Adults have a
quick, darting flight and are fond of flowers. Males
perch on low leaves and grasses and make frequent
exploratory flights.

Delaware Skipper
Anatrytone logan

Family/Subfamily: Skippers (Hesperiidae)/
Banded Skippers (Hesperiinae)

Wingspan: 1.0–1.4" (2.5–3.6 cm)

Above: orange with dark borders and veins; forewings
are elongated and somewhat pointed; male has a
small black cell-end bar on forewing; female has
brown scaling in forewing cell, wider borders, and
larger cell-end bar on forewing

Below: unmarked golden orange

Sexes: similar, although female is darker with reduced
orange coloration

Egg: white, laid singly on host leaves

Larva: bluish white with dark tubercles; black-and-white
head

Larval Host Plants: various grasses including
bluestems, Silver Plumegrass and Switchgrass

Habitat: open woodlands, forest edges, prairies, fens,
roadsides, pastures, wetland edges, retention ponds,
utility easements and old fields

Broods: single generation

Abundance: uncommon to common; local

Compare: European Skipper (pg. 231) is smaller and has
shorter antennae. Ottoe Skipper (pg. 267) is larger.
Both lack the black cell-end bar on the
forewing above.

Resident

Jan.	Feb.	Mar.	Apr.	May	June	July	Aug.	Sept.	Oct.	Nov.	Dec.

male

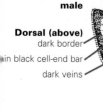

Dorsal (above)
dark border
in black cell-end bar
dark veins

Ventral (below)
unmarked golden
orange

Male

Female pg. 139   Male   Female   Larva

Comments: The Zabulon Skipper is strikingly dimorphic with bright orange males and purplish brown females. A denizen of wooded habitats, the butterfly is most often encountered in dappled sunlit patches along forest trails or clearings. Nonetheless, individuals will wander into nearby, more open landscapes in search of available nectar resources. The pugnacious males perch on branches around head-height to await passing mates and aggressively fly out to engage rival males before returning to the same or nearby perch moments later. Females generally prefer to remain within the confines of shadier locales.

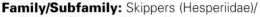

Zabulon Skipper
Poanes zabulon

Family/Subfamily: Skippers (Hesperiidae)/
Banded Skippers (Hesperiinae)

Wingspan: 1.0–1.4" (2.5–3.6 cm)

Above: male is golden orange with dark brown borders
and small brown spot near forewing apex; female is
dark brown with band of cream spots across forewing

Below: male hindwing yellow with a brown base enclosing a yellow spot; female forewing is dark brown with
small light subapical spots; hindwing has lavender scaling on wing margins, and white bar along leading
margin of hindwing

Sexes: dissimilar, female brown with little orange color

Egg: pale green, laid singly on host leaves

Larva: tan with dark dorsal stripe, white lateral stripe and
short, light-colored hairs; reddish brown head

Larval Host Plants: various grasses including
Purpletop Grass, Whitegrass and lovegrass

Habitat: open woodlands, forest margins and roadsides,
stream corridors and adjacent open landscapes

Broods: two generations

Abundance: uncommon to occasional

Compare: Hobomok Skipper (pg. 269) has clear hindwing patch without darker spots.

Stray

Jan. Feb. Mar. Apr. May June July Aug. Sept. Oct. Nov. Dec.

male

Dorsal (above)
dark spot

narrow black cell
end bar

golden orange

clear golden
orange

Ventral (below)
dark base encloses
yellow spot

yellow with darker
spots

249

Ventral

Larva

Comments: The ornately patterned Gorgone Checkerspot occurs throughout much of the central U.S. Although its range historically extended eastward into Michigan, the species has not been reported from the state in many years. Additional surveys are critically needed to determine the current status of the butterfly and identify any relict populations. Adults have a low, erratic flight and frequently stop to nectar at available flowers where their distinctive markings can be closely observed. An excellent colonizer, adults frequently wander far from established populations.

Gorgone Checkerspot
Chlosyne gorgone

Family/Subfamily: Brush-foots (Nymphalidae)/
True Brush-foots (Nymphalinae)

Wingspan: 1.1–1.4" (2.8–3.6 cm)

Above: tawny orange with black bands and spots;
forewing has a postmedian row of solid black spots;
hindwing has a submarginal row of pale crescents

Below: hindwing has a distinct zigzag pattern of white
chevrons between darker bands and a postmedian
band of black spots

Sexes: similar

Egg: pale green, laid in clusters on host leaves

Larva: yellow-orange with black longitudinal stripes and
black branching spines; black head. Young larvae feed
gregariously on host. Late instar larvae overwinter.

Larval Host Plants: various composites (Asteraceae)
including Great Ragweed, sunflowers, asters and
Black-eyed Susan

Habitat: open woodlands, prairie, stream corridors, adjacent dry, open, grassy areas, old fields, utility
easements and previously burned sites

Broods: two generations

Abundance: rare

Compare: Silvery Checkerspot (pg. 287) is larger and
has white-centered black spots on dorsal
hindwing.

Resident

Jan. Feb. Mar. Apr. May June July Aug. Sept. Oct. Nov. Dec.

Dorsal (above)
orange with black
bands and spots

pale orange chevrons
in black border

Ventral (below)
scalloped zig-zag
pattern

251

Dorsal

Larva

Comments: Often called the Inornate Ringlet, this nondescript species is our smallest Satyrine. A butterfly of
open, grassy sites, it is often abundant throughout the
Upper Peninsula. Adults have a quick, bobbing flight
and maneuver close to the ground through grassy vegetation. They frequently alight on low vegetation or
debris. Both sexes readily visit available flowers, an
unusual habit among members of this subfamily.

Common Ringlet
Coenonympha tullia inornata

Family/Subfamily: Brush-foots (Nymphalidae)/
Satyrs and Wood-Nymphs (Satyrinae)

Wingspan: 1.1–1.5" (2.8–3.8 cm)

Above: unmarked orange brown; male's hindwings and
outer forewing margin somewhat darker brown

Below: forewing orange brown toward base; outer margin gray and often with small pale-rimmed black
eyespot; hindwing grayish; both wings bear an irregular white median band (incomplete on hindwing)

Sexes: similar, although female generally has broader,
more rounded wings with increased orange scaling

Egg: yellow-green, laid singly on host leaves

Larva: dark green with pale green lateral stripes and two
short pink tails; larvae overwinter

Larval Host Plants: various grasses including bluegrass

Habitat: a variety of open, grassy landscapes including
sparse woodlands, forest clearings and margins, old
fields, roadsides and meadows

Broods: single generation

Abundance: occasional to common

Compare: unique

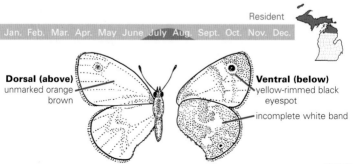

Resident

Jan. Feb. Mar. Apr. May June July Aug. Sept. Oct. Nov. Dec.

Dorsal (above)
unmarked orange
brown

Ventral (below)
yellow-rimmed black
eyespot

incomplete white band

253

Male Female Larva

Comments: The Common Branded Skipper is a widespread and highly variable species found throughout
much of the western U.S. and Canada. Our subspecies laurentina occurs across the Great Lakes and
Northeast. As a result, many authors refer to this butterfly as the Laurentian Skipper. Despite a preference
for open grassy landscapes, it is seldom common and
often relatively local. Adults have a quick, darting flight
and may be encountered feeding on a variety of available blooms.

Common Branded Skipper
Hesperia comma laurentina

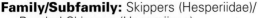

Family/Subfamily: Skippers (Hesperiidae)/
Banded Skippers (Hesperiinae)

Wingspan: 1.1–1.5" (2.8–3.8 cm)

Above: male forewing orange basally with broad, dark
brown margin and a prominent black stigma; hindwing
brown with an irregular orange spot band; female dark
brown with reduced orange markings

Below: hindwing orange with white spots

Sexes: dissimilar; female brown with reduced orange
markings and without black forewing stigma

Egg: whitish green, laid singly on host leaves or stems

Larva: dark greenish brown, often with lighter mottling
and a round black head

Larval Host Plants: various grasses including
bluestem, bluegrass, fescue and brome grass

Habitat: grassy clearings, meadows, old fields and roadsides

Abundance: rare to occasional; local

Compare: Leonard's Skipper (pg. 187) is larger, has a
reddish brown ventral hindwing with a less angled pale
postmedian spot band.

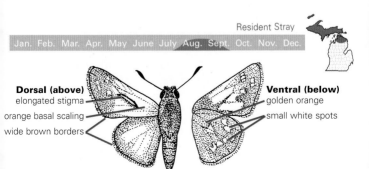

Resident Stray

Jan. Feb. Mar. Apr. May June July Aug. Sept. Oct. Nov. Dec.

Dorsal (above)
elongated stigma
orange basal scaling
wide brown borders

Ventral (below)
golden orange
small white spots

255

Ventral

Female

Larva

Comments: This early season skipper is widespread
throughout the Great Lakes and Northeast.
Nonetheless, it never appears to be overly common.
Colonies are generally spotty and often relatively local
in occurrence. A highly active butterfly, adults have a
very rapid flight and nervously pause for a moment to
nectar at an available flowers before darting off again.

Indian Skipper
Hesperia sassacus

Family/Subfamily: Skippers (Hesperiidae)/
Banded Skippers (Hesperiinae)

Wingspan: 1.2–1.4" (3.0–3.6 cm)

Above: bright orange with wide, somewhat jagged, dark brown borders; male has an elongated black forewing stigma

Below: hindwing is tawny orange with a pale golden orange spot band through center; middle spot displaced outward toward margin

Sexes: similar, although female has broader dark borders, larger, paler yellow orange spot bands and lacks stigma

Egg: whitish green, laid singly on host leaves or stems

Larva: dark greenish brown, often with lighter mottling and a round black head

Larval Host Plants: various grasses including Little Bluestem, panic grasses, Poverty Oatgrass, bluegrass and Red Fescue

Habitat: woodland clearings and margins, pastures, old brushy fields, prairie, meadows and roadsides

Broods: single generation

Abundance: occasional to common; localized

Compare: Leonard's Skipper (pg. 187) has reddish brown ventral hindwings with a bold white postmedian spot band and flies in late summer.

Resident

Jan. Feb. Mar. Apr. May June July Aug. Sept. Oct. Nov. Dec.

male

Dorsal (above)
dark, sharply defined borders

Ventral (below)
pale spot band with center spot offset toward outer margin

257

Male

Male ventral

Female

Female ventral

Larva

Comments: This is one of our most abundant and readily encountered crescents. At home in most open, sunny landscapes with available hosts, it frequents old fields and rural pastures as well as gardens and urban parks. It is seasonally variable; spring and fall (short-day or cool-season form) individuals are darker and more heavily patterned on the ventral hindwings. It is an opportunistic breeder, producing new generations as long as favorable conditions allow. Adults have a rapid, erratic flight. Males perch on low vegetation with wings outstretched and frequently patrol for females. Freshly emerged males may sip moisture at damp ground.

Pearl Crescent
Phyciodes tharos

Family/Subfamily: Brush-foots (Nymphalidae)/
True Brush-foots (Nymphalinae)

Wingspan: 1.25–1.60" (3.2–4.1 cm)

Above: orange with dark bands, spots and wing borders;
postmedian row of small solid black spots on hindwing

Below: male yellow-tan with fine brown reticulations and
a dark marginal patch enclosing a pale crescent;
female has increased brown mottling and heavier reticulations; seasonally variable; cool-season forms have
increased dark coloration and pattern elements

Sexes: similar, although female is paler orange with
increased black markings

Egg: green, laid in clusters on underside of host leaves

Larva: dark brown to charcoal with lateral cream stripes
and numerous short, branched spines

Larval Host Plants: various asters including Frost
Aster, Smooth Blue Aster and Bushy Aster

Habitat: virtually any open, sunny habitat including roadsides, old fields, utility easements, forest edges,
prairies, meadows, pastures and gardens

Broods: two or more generations

Abundance: occasional to abundant

Compare: Northern Crescent (pg. 289) has larger, more
open orange areas on the hindwing above
and orange antennal clubs.   Resident

Jan. Feb. Mar. Apr. May June July Aug. Sept. Oct. Nov. Dec.

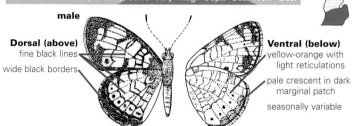

male

Dorsal (above)
fine black lines
wide black borders

Ventral (below)
yellow-orange with
light reticulations

pale crescent in dark
marginal patch

seasonally variable

259

Male   Female   Larva

Comments: Generally an uncommon butterfly throughout its limited Midwestern range, the Black Dash is
restricted to marshes, wet meadows and other open
wetlands with abundant sedge. As a result, populations tend to be small and highly localized to suitable
habitat areas. The adults are swift on the wing but are
easily observed when feeding at nearby wetland wildflowers. Males perch like sentinels on tall grasses
watching keenly for passing females and readily fly out
to engage intruders.

Black Dash
Euphyes conspicua

Family/Subfamily: Skippers (Hesperiidae)/ Banded Skippers (Hesperiinae)

Wingspan: 1.25–1.60" (3.2–4.1 cm)

Above: male golden-orange with broad, dark brown borders and broad black stigma on forewing; female dark brown with cream-yellow spot band through both wings

Below: hindwing orange-brown with a broad yellow postmedian patch

Sexes: dissimilar; female is primarily dark brown above with pale yellow forewing spots

Egg: laid singly on host

Larva: green with fine white mottling; brown head marked with cream lines around the margin and a black oval on the forehead

Larval Host Plants: various sedges including Upright Sedge and Eastern Narrowleaf Sedge

Habitat: marshes, wet grassy meadows, fens, roadside ditches, bogs, woodland margins, other open wetlands

Abundance: uncommon to occasional; localized

Broods: single generation

Compare: Peck's Skipper (pg. 127) is smaller and has yellow basal spots on the hindwing below. Dion Skipper (pg. 273) is larger and has a long pale ray through the hindwing without adjacent postmedian spots.

Resident

Jan. Feb. Mar. Apr. May June July Aug. Sept. Oct. Nov. Dec.

male

Dorsal (above)
broad stigma
dark brown borders
orange

Ventral (below)
red-brown hindwing
curved yellow patch

261

Female

Male pg. 167   Ventral   Larva

Comments: This sexually dimorphic species is our largest copper. Although primarily restricted to moist areas where its weedy larval hosts occur, it frequently wanders into nearby drier habitats in search of nectar. The Bronze Copper tends to occur in small, highly localized colonies but can be rather numerous when encountered. Like many other wetland species, it has suffered from the loss or degradation of available habitat. Males perch low on grasses or other vegetation with their wings partially open to await passing females.

Bronze Copper
Lycaena hyllus

Family/Subfamily: Gossamer Wings (Lycaenidae)/ Coppers (Lycaeninae)

Wingspan: 1.25–1.65" (3.2–4.2 cm)

Above: male is brown with a purplish iridescence and a broad orange submarginal band containing black spots on the hindwing; female has light orange forewings with scattered black spots and a broad brown border; hindwing is purplish brown with a broad orange submarginal band containing black spots

Below: scattered white-rimmed black spots on both wings; forewing is orange with silvery gray apex and margin; hindwing is silvery gray with broad orange submarginal band containing black spots

Sexes: dissimilar; female is larger with rounder wings and increased orange scaling on the dorsal forewing

Egg: whitish, laid singly on host leaves or stems

Larva: yellow-green with a darker green dorsal stripe

Larval Host Plants: knotweed, Curly Dock, Water Dock

Habitat: open, moist habitats including fens, wet meadows and marshes; also adjacent fields

Broods: two generations

Abundance: uncommon to locally common

Compare: American (pg. 243) and Purplish (pg. 237) Coppers are smaller and have a narrow, reddish orange submarginal line on ventral hindwing.

Resident

Jan. Feb. Mar. Apr. May June July Aug. Sept. Oct. Nov. Dec.

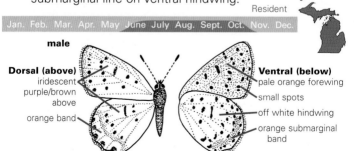

male

Dorsal (above)
iridescent purple/brown above
orange band

Ventral (below)
pale orange forewing
small spots
off white hindwing
orange submarginal band

263

Ventral

Comments: This small, wide-ranging fritillary occurs across much of the Northern Hemisphere. It dips southward into the Great Lakes Region and can be found in several counties within the Upper Peninsula of Michigan. Although primarily a butterfly of scrubby bogs, the Freija Fritillary tends to be found along their margins and may occasionally also wander into nearby woodland areas. Adults maneuver low to the ground with a quick, erratic flight.

Freija Fritillary
Boloria freija

Family/Subfamily: Brush-foots (Nymphalidae)/ Longwing Butterflies (Heliconiinae)

Wingspan: 1.25–1.65" (3.2–4.2 cm)

Above: orange with black bands and spots; wing bases brown-black

Below: hindwing reddish brown with a complex pattern including a central white triangular patch and a black zigzag line

Sexes: similar

Egg: laid singly or haphazardly on or near host

Larva: blackish brown with light spots and numerous short black spines

Larval Host Plants: Cranberry and Bog Blueberry; possibly Dwarf Bilberry and Bearberry

Habitat: sphagnum bogs and adjacent forest clearings and margins

Broods: single generation

Abundance: rare to occasional; local

Compare: Meadow Fritillary (pg. 279) and Frigga Fritillary (pg. 277) lack the complex ventral hindwing pattern.

Resident

Jan. Feb. Mar. Apr. May June July Aug. Sept. Oct. Nov. Dec.

Dorsal (above)
orange with black markings

basal area darker

Ventral (below)
zigzag black median band

pale arrowhead spots

Male   Female   Larva

Comments: This is a large orange skipper of native tall-grass prairies. Like many other prairie species, the Ottoe Skipper has continued to disappear from many portions of its former range as a result of habitat loss. Within Michigan, it can be found only in a few scattered southern counties. Remaining colonies tend to be uncommon and highly local in occurrence. As a result, it is currently listed as a threatened species by the state. The adults are strong fliers and often wary of close approach but may regularly be spotted at available flowers.

Ottoe Skipper
Hesperia ottoe

Family/Subfamily: Skippers (Hesperiidae)/
Banded Skippers (Hesperiinae)

Wingspan: 1.3–1.6" (3.3–4.1 cm)

Above: male bright orange with broad, dark brown borders and a black forewing stigma; female forewing brown with reduced orange scaling and a few glassy cream spots

Below: hindwing clear yellow-orange; often with faint postmedian spot band in females

Sexes: dissimilar, female brown with pale forewing spots; lacks black forewing stigma

Egg: whitish, laid singly on host leaves

Larva: light greenish brown with a dark brown head

Larval Host Plants: Fall Witchgrass

Habitat: woodland clearings, tallgrass prairie and adjacent open areas with native grasses

Broods: single generation

Abundance: rare to occasional; localized

Compare: unique

Resident

Jan. Feb. Mar. Apr. May June July Aug. Sept. Oct. Nov. Dec.

Dorsal (above)
orange with dark borders

Ventral (below)
unmarked yellow-orange

Male | Female | Female "Pocahontas" pg. 177 | Larva

Comments: This small woodland skipper has a single
spring flight. Males perch on sunlit leaves and aggressively dart out at other passing butterflies. They may
also frequently be encountered at wet earth along
forested roads or trails. Although preferring shadier
conditions, both sexes will venture into nearby open
areas to nectar at early-season blossoms. Female
Hobomoks produce two distinct forms. The lighter
form resembles the male and the darker form
"Pocahontas" is superficially similar to Zabulon
Skipper females. Larvae construct individual leaf shelters on the host. Larvae overwinter.

Hobomok Skipper
Poanes hobomok

Family/Subfamily: Skippers (Hesperiidae)/
Banded Skippers (Hesperiinae)

Wingspan: 1.4–1.6" (3.6–4.1 cm)

Above: golden orange with irregular dark brown borders
and a narrow black cell-end bar on the forewing

Below: purplish brown with a broad yellow orange patch
through the hindwing

Sexes: dissimilar; female has two forms. Normal form
resembles male but has reduced orange scaling above.
"Pocahontas" form is dark brown above with pale
forewing spots; hindwing is purplish brown below with
faint band and violet gray frosting along outer margin.

Egg: white, laid singly on host leaves

Larva: brown green with numerous short, light-colored
hairs; round, brown head

Larval Host Plants: various grasses including Little
Bluestem, panic grasses, Poverty Oatgrass, bluegrass
and Rice Cutgrass

Habitat: open woodlands, forest edges, clearings and
trails, roadsides and along forested stream margins

Broods: single generation

Abundance: occasional to common

Compare: Zabulon (pg. 249) and Peck's (pg. 127)
Skippers have yellow basal scaling on ventral hindwing.

Resident

Jan. Feb. Mar. Apr. May June July Aug. Sept. Oct. Nov. Dec.

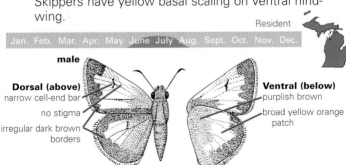

male

Dorsal (above)
narrow cell-end bar
no stigma
irregular dark brown
borders

Ventral (below)
purplish brown
broad yellow orange
patch

Larva

Comments: The Tawny Crescent is an uncommon and highly colonial resident species that has severely declined in recent years over much of its eastern range. In Michigan, it may still be found to be locally common in certain areas, particularly in northern portions of the state. Due to the species' close resemblance to other crescents, many localized populations may be easily overlooked. Adults have a quick, somewhat erratic flight and frequently alight on low vegetation with their wings open. Males occasionally visit mud puddles to sip moisture.

Tawny Crescent
Phyciodes batesii

Family/Subfamily: Brush-foots (Nymphalidae)/
True Brush-foots (Nymphalinae)

Wingspan: 1.30–1.75" (3.3–4.4 cm)

Above: tawny orange with heavy black bands, spots and
broad wing borders

Below: male hindwing golden yellow-brown with very
fine brown markings and a pale crescent along outer
margin; female with darker marginal patch; forewing
with pale outer margin and relatively straight black
median bar extending from costal margin

Sexes: similar, although female typically has more pronounced black markings above

Egg: pale green, laid in clusters on underside of host leaves

Larva: pinkish brown; dark dorsal band and numerous
short, light brown spines. Later instar larvae overwinter.

Larval Host Plants: various asters including Waxyleaf
Aster

Habitat: woodland openings, pastures, dry hillsides and
ridges, stream margins, moist meadows and roadsides

Broods: single generation

Abundance: uncommon to occasional

Compare: Pearl Crescent (pg. 259) and Northern
Crescent (pg. 289) have more extensive open orange
areas on wings above and a distinct dark
marginal patch on ventral hindwing. Resident

Jan. Feb. Mar. Apr. May June July Aug. Sept. Oct. Nov. Dec.

Dorsal (above)

Ventral (below)
lacks dark patch
below apex

broad, straight dark
band

fine brown markings

row of small dark
spots

271

Ventral

Male

Female

Larva

Comments: A large skipper of wetland habitats with sedge, this lovely tawny-orange species has a distinctive but often faint pale ray through the ventral hindwing. Throughout much of its irregular eastern range, the Dion Skipper is quite localized in occurrence and seldom overly numerous. Nonetheless, it can be reliably encountered in most suitable habitat areas. Adults are sluggish fliers through wetland vegetation but can move very quickly if disturbed. Males readily perch on the tops of sedges or grasses but tend to be wary and difficult to closely approach. They do not wander far from their wetland haunts. Larvae overwinter.

Dion Skipper
Euphyes dion

Family/Subfamily: Skippers (Hesperiidae)/
Banded Skippers (Hesperiinae)

Wingspan: 1.4–1.7" (3.6–4.3 cm)

Above: male forewing is orange with broad, dark brown borders and a prominent black forewing stigma; hindwing is faint orange with a dark brown border and distinctly brighter elongated orange spot; female forewing brown with small orange spots; hindwing brown with elongated yellow-orange spot

Below: tawny orange hindwing with two faint light rays

Sexes: dissimilar; female is primarily dark brown dorsally with yellow orange forewing spots and prominent single elongated orange hindwing spot

Egg: light green, laid singly on host leaves

Larva: blue-green with darker green dorsal line; white head marked with a black forehead spot bordered by orange brown vertical lines

Larval Host Plants: various sedges including Hairy Sedge

Habitat: wet meadows, marshes, fens and bogs

Broods: single generation

Abundance: uncommon to occasional; local

Compare: Dukes's Skipper (pg. 281) lacks bright orange scaling above, has rounder wings and prefers shadier habitats.

Resident Stray

Jan. Feb. Mar. Apr. May June July Aug. Sept. Oct. Nov. Dec.

male

Dorsal (above)
prominent stigma
broad, dark borders
elongated orange spot

Ventral (below)
pale ray
tawny orange to reddish brown

273

Ventral

Larva

Comments: This small species is named for its distinctive metallic silver spot bands on the ventral hindwing that quickly distinguish it from the more abundant Meadow Fritillary with which it often flies. Restricted to open moist habitats, the Silver-bordered Fritillary has continued to decline within the state as a result of habitat loss or alteration. As a result, the species is currently listed as threatened in Michigan. Adults have a rapid and somewhat erratic flight typically low to the ground just above the vegetation.

Bog Fritillary
Boloria eunomia

Family/Subfamily: Brush-foots (Nymphalidae)/ Longwing Butterflies (Heliconiinae)

Wingspan: 1.40–1.75" (3.6–4.4 cm)

Above: orange with black lines and spots; both wings have heavy black borders that enclose small orange spots; hindwing often has black overscaling at bases

Below: hindwing reddish brown with postbasal, post-median and marginal bands of black-outlined white spots

Sexes: similar, although female is slightly paler and with more black overscaling

Egg: tiny cream eggs laid singly and somewhat haphazardly near host

Larva: dark gray with black patches, a orange-brown lateral stripe, numerous yellowish spines and two long, black prothoracic spines. Larvae overwinter.

Larval Host Plants: violets

Habitat: wet meadows, bogs, moist prairies, sedge marshes and adjacent fields and roadsides

Broods: three generations

Abundance: rare to occasional; localized

Compare: Meadow Fritillary (pg. 279) lacks the broad, black dorsal wing border and the silver spot bands on the hindwing below.

Resident

Jan. Feb. Mar. Apr. May June July Aug. Sept. Oct. Nov. Dec.

Dorsal (above)
orange with heavy black markings

black basal scaling

Ventral (below)
several rows of black-rimmed white spots

275

Ventral

Larva

Comments: Widespread across Canada from Alaska to Labrador, the range of this dingy Northland butterfly dips down into the northern Great Lakes. Within Michigan, the Frigga Fritillary is restricted entirely to sphagnum bogs in the Upper Peninsula where it is uncommon and quite local in occurrence. The boreal subspecies saga that is found in our area remains relatively poorly studied. There are many aspects of its ecology and behavior that have yet to be determined as well as questions regarding its exact taxonomic status.

Frigga Fritillary
Boloria frigga

Family/Subfamily: Brush-foots (Nymphalidae)/ Longwing Butterflies (Heliconiinae)

Wingspan: 1.4–1.75" (3.6–4.4 cm)

Above: dull orange with black bands and spots; wing bases brown-black; forewing apex rounded

Below: hindwing is mottled brown orange with violet frosting along the margin; hindwing has tan-white basal patch along leading margin

Sexes: similar, although female paler with broader, more rounded wings

Egg: laid singly on host

Larva: black with a purple lateral line and short, black spines. Larvae overwinter.

Larval Host Plants: Bog Rosemary, Cranberry, Bog Laurel; possibly scrub willow and Dwarf Birch

Habitat: sphagnum bogs

Broods: single generation

Abundance: rare to occasional; local

Compare: Meadow Fritillary (pg. 279) has squared-off forewing apex and has less prominent heavy dark scaling at the wing bases. Freija Fritillary's (pg. 265) ventral hindwing has a distinctive central white triangular spot and black zigzag line.

Resident

| Jan. | Feb. | Mar. | Apr. | May | June | July | Aug. | Sept. | Oct. | Nov. | Dec. |

Dorsal (above)
dark basal areas

Ventral (below)
white patch along margin

outer half violet

277

Ventral

Larva

Comments: As its name suggests, the Meadow
Fritillary inhabits a wide variety of open, moist landscapes from stream margins to alkaline fens, and is
quite tolerant of disturbed sites. Because of this
increased habitat flexibility, it is generally the most
abundant member of the genus in Michigan and not
so strongly impacted by the continued loss or degradation of wetlands. Adults have a rapid and somewhat
erratic flight, typically low to the ground just above the
vegetation, but frequently stop to nectar at available
wildflowers.

Meadow Fritillary
Boloria bellona

Family/Subfamily: Brush-foots (Nymphalidae)/
Longwing Butterflies (Heliconiinae)

Wingspan: 1.25–1.90" (3.2–4.8 cm)

Above: orange with black bands and spots; elongated
wings with squared-off forewing apex

Below: hindwing is mottled brown orange with violet
frosting along the hindwing margin

Sexes: similar

Egg: tiny cream eggs laid singly and somewhat haphazardly near host

Larva: purplish black with fine yellow mottling and short
cream-based brown spines

Larval Host Plants: violets

Habitat: old fields, wet meadows, pastures, roadside
ditches, fens, moist prairies and stream corridors

Broods: two generations; possibly a third in some locations

Abundance: occasional to common; local

Compare: Silver-bordered Fritillary (pg. 293) has heavy
black dorsal wing margins and metallic silver spot
bands on the hindwing below.

Resident

Jan. Feb. Mar. Apr. May June July Aug. Sept. Oct. Nov. Dec.

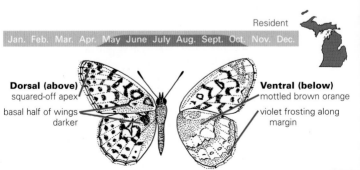

Dorsal (above)
squared-off apex

basal half of wings
darker

Ventral (below)
mottled brown orange

violet frosting along
margin

Ventral

Male · Female · Larva

Comments: This is a reclusive skipper of forested swamps and other scrubby wetlands with sedges. A butterfly of contrasting color, it is a rich tawny-orange below compared to a much darker sooty black dorsal appearance. Primarily restricted to the southeast corner of the state, populations tend to be scattered and often highly localized. Adults maneuver low through sedges and other wetland vegetation with a slow, deliberate flight and can easily be overlooked.

Dukes's Skipper
Euphyes dukesi

Family/Subfamily: Skippers (Hesperiidae)/
Banded Skippers (Hesperiinae)

Wingspan: 1.50–1.75" (3.8–4.4 cm)

Above: male dark sooty brownish black; forewing with
faint tawny orange scaling along base of costal margin
and a black stigma; hindwing has faint orange scaling
in center; wings are somewhat rounded; female
forewing has two small pale central spots

Below: rich brownish orange with two pale rays through
the hindwing; forewing with black base

Sexes: similar, although female has small white forewing
spots

Egg: laid singly on the underside of host leaves

Larva: pale green; reddish brown head with a black spot
on the forehead surrounded by white

Larval Host Plants: various sedges including Hairy
Sedge

Habitat: wooded swamps and marshes

Broods: single generation

Abundance: rare to uncommon; local

Compare: Dion Skipper (pg. 273) has bright orange scaling above with more pointed forewings and prefers
more open, sunlit habitats.

Resident

Jan. Feb. Mar. Apr. May June July Aug. Sept. Oct. Nov. Dec.

male

Dorsal (above)
rounded sooty brown
wings

Ventral (below)
black toward base

pale ray

281

Male

Female | Male | Winter | Larva

Comments: Much debate centers on the origin of the butterfly's common name. One interpretation points to its narrow black forewing spot, which resembles a closed or partially closed eye. Others suggest that behavior is responsible. Individuals in the Deep South overwinter as adults in reproductive diapause. They are highly sedentary during the winter, but often become active on mild days to nectar at available flowers before returning to their apparent slumber. It is a rare and sporadic vagrant or temporary colonist to Michigan. The adults produce distinct seasonal forms that vary dramatically in ventral hindwing coloration.

Sleepy Orange
Eurema nicippe

Family/Subfamily: Whites and Sulphurs (Pieridae)/ Sulphurs (Coliadinae)

Wingspan: 1.3–2.0" (3.3–5.1 cm)

Above: bright orange with broad irregular black wing borders; forewing cell bears small, elongated black spot

Below: hindwings seasonally variable; butter-yellow with brown markings in summer-form and tan to reddish brown with darker pattern elements in winter-form

Sexes: similar, although female is larger and less vibrant with heavier ventral hindwing pattern

Egg: white, laid singly on host leaves

Larva: green with thin, cream lateral stripe and numerous short hairs

Larval Host Plants: various wild and ornamental cassia species including Wild Senna and Maryland Senna

Habitat: open, disturbed sites including roadsides, vacant fields, agricultural land, parks and gardens

Broods: one or more generations

Abundance: rare to uncommon

Compare: Orange Sulphur (pg. 299) has a rounded black forewing cell spot, uniform black wing borders, and a distinct, red-rimmed silver spot on the ventral hindwing.

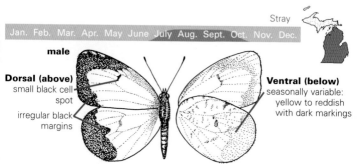

Stray

Jan. Feb. Mar. Apr. May June July Aug. Sept. Oct. Nov. Dec.

male

Dorsal (above)
small black cell spot

irregular black margins

Ventral (below)
seasonally variable: yellow to reddish with dark markings

Male

Larva

Comments: Harris's Checkerspot is closely associated with wetland habitats that support its sole larval host. As a result, populations tend to be rather small and highly localized but nevertheless can be fairly numerous when encountered. Adults have slow, gliding flight and maneuver close to the ground, periodically pausing to perch on low vegetation with their orange and black patterned wings outstretched. Both sexes occasionally seek nectar but are not prolific flower visitors. Males often gather at damp soil or animal dung.

Harris's Checkerspot
Chlosyne harrisii

Family/Subfamily: Brush-foots (Nymphalidae)/ True Brush-foots (Nymphalinae)

Wingspan: 1.4–2.0" (3.6–5.1 cm)

Above: tawny orange with black bands and broad black borders; often appearing extremely dark; hindwing has a row of white-centered, somewhat square black spots that typically touch the broad black border

Below: hindwing is reddish orange with a narrow orange marginal band, and basal, median and submarginal bands of white spots or crescents outlined in black

Sexes: similar, although female is somewhat larger

Egg: yellow, soon turning red, laid in clusters on the underside of host leaves

Larva: reddish orange with black transverse stripes and several rows of branched black spines; black head. Partially grown larvae overwinter and complete development the following spring.

Larval Host Plants: Flat-topped White Aster

Habitat: bogs, wet meadows, marshes, roadside ditches and other wetlands

Broods: single generation

Abundance: rare to occasional; localized

Compare: Silvery Checkerspot (pg. 287) has incomplete row of silvery crescents on the ventral hindwing.

Resident

Jan. Feb. Mar. Apr. May June July Aug. Sept. Oct. Nov. Dec.

Dorsal (above)
primarily orange and black wings

black submarginal spots touching margin

Ventral (below)
white, orange and black checkered pattern

row of white crescents

285

Male

Ventral

Larva

Comments: This is a large checkerspot of moist forest clearings and other semi-open landscapes adjacent to streams or waterways. Populations tend to be highly localized and often fluctuate considerably from year to year, being common in some years or nearly absent in others. Adults maneuver close to the ground in open areas or along woodland roads with a slow flight characterized by alternating quick wing beats and short periods of gliding. Males often gather at damp soil or animal dung.

Silvery Checkerspot
Chlosyne nycteis

Family/Subfamily: Brush-foots (Nymphalidae)/ True Brush-foots (Nymphalinae)

Wingspan: 1.4–2.0" (3.6–5.1 cm)

Above: tawny orange with black bands and wide black borders; hindwing has a submarginal row of white-centered, somewhat square black spots

Below: hindwing is pale yellow brown with submarginal row of black spots, a broad dark marginal patch and an incomplete marginal row of silvery white crescents

Sexes: similar, although female is often much larger

Egg: cream, laid in large clusters on underside of leaves

Larva: dark brownish black; wide yellow orange lateral band and several rows of black spines; black head

Larval Host Plants: various Asteraceae family composites including Wing-stem, Gravelweed, White Crownbeard, asters, sunflowers, Cut-leaf Coneflower and Sneezeweed

Habitat: moist woodland openings, forest margins, stream corridors, wet meadows, marshes or semi-open areas

Broods: two generations

Abundance: uncommon to common; local

Compare: Harris's Checkerspot (pg. 285) has a complete submarginal row of silvery crescents on the hindwing below.

Resident

Jan. Feb. Mar. Apr. May June July Aug. Sept. Oct. Nov. Dec.

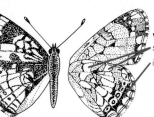

Dorsal (above)
submarginal row of white-centered black spots, not touching border

Ventral (below)
silvery bands

incomplete row of silvery white marginal crescents

287

Male

Male Larva

Comments: This butterfly has only recently been considered a distinct species, and there remains some debate about its true taxonomic position. Living up to its name, the Northern Crescent is one of the commonest species in northern Michigan. It is extremely similar in appearance to the more southern-ranging Pearl Crescent. In many instances, the two cannot be reliably separated in the field, especially across central Michigan where their broad ranges overlap. Adults scurry low to the ground with a quick flight characterized by rapid wing beats followed by short distance glides. Both sexes readily visit available blossoms.

Northern Crescent

Phyciodes selenis (listed as *Phyciodes cocyta* by some authors)

Family/Subfamily: Brush-foots (Nymphalidae)/
True Brush-foots (Nymphalinae)

Wingspan: 1.5–1.9" (3.8–4.8 cm)

Above: tawny-orange with fine black bands, spots and
wing borders; male has a large open area of orange on
the hindwing; antennal clubs orange

Below: male hindwing is golden yellow brown with fine
brown markings and a dark marginal patch with or
without pale crescent; female has increased brown
mottling and heavier dark reticulations

Sexes: similar, although female has more extensive dark
markings above and below

Egg: green, laid in clusters on underside of host leaves

Larva: dark brown with fine white mottling, a dark dorsal
line, a lateral cream stripe and numerous short, pinkish
gray branched spines

Larval Host Plants: various asters although exact
species are unknown

Habitat: moist open woodlands, forest edges, stream
margins and adjacent roadsides and fields

Broods: single generation

Abundance: occasional to abundant

Compare: Pearl Crescent (pg. 259) is slightly smaller and
has more extensive black markings; may not
be reliably separated in the field. Resident

Jan. Feb. Mar. Apr. May June July Aug. Sept. Oct. Nov. Dec.

Dorsal (above)
fine black markings

orange on
hindwing fairly
open

Ventral (below)
orange antennal clubs

dark marginal patch;
often without pale
crescent

289

Male   Larva

Comments: This is a large and distinctive skipper of semi-shaded, moist areas with abundant sedge. Like other wetland species, it has continued to lose habitat from expanding urban development and hydrologic alteration. As a result, populations tend to be widely scattered, highly localized and relatively low-density. Living up to its name, the Broad-winged Skipper has noticeably rounded, somewhat wide wings. Despite their size, adults maneuver through the wetland vegetation with a fairly slow, dancing flight and frequently alight on leaves. Both sexes may be encountered at the blossoms of nearby wetland flowers.

Broad-winged Skipper
Poanes viator

Family/Subfamily: Skippers (Hesperiidae)/ Banded Skippers (Hesperiinae)

Wingspan: 1.3–2.1" (3.3–5.3 cm)

Above: tawny orange with broad, dark brown borders; forewing has rounded apex; hindwing has dark brown scaling along veins; male lacks stigma; female forewing pale orange with broad brown borders and cream spots

Below: hindwing is tawny orange with distinct broad pale ray through pale spot band

Sexes: similar, although female has cream white spots on the forewing above

Egg: grayish, laid singly on the underside of host leaves

Larva: pale brown with an overall velvety appearance; reddish brown head

Larval Host Plants: various sedges and grasses including Annual Wild Rice, Common Reed, Hairy Sedge and Beaked Sedge

Habitat: forested swamps, wet meadows, fens, marshes, roadside ditches and associated clearings

Broods: single generation

Abundance: rare to uncommon; localized

Compare: Dion Skipper (pg. 273) has more pointed forewings and has a less sharply contrasting broad yellow hindwing ray.

Resident

Jan. Feb. Mar. Apr. May June July Aug. Sept. Oct. Nov. Dec.

male

Dorsal (above)
squarish yellow orange spots

lacks stigma

broad dark borders

Ventral (below)
broad pale ray

pale spot band

Ventral

Larva

Comments: This small species is named for its distinctive metallic silver spot bands on the ventral hindwing that quickly distinguish it from the similar Meadow Fritillary with which it often flies. Despite being restricted to moist habitats, the Silver-bordered Fritillary is generally common throughout much of the state. The northern subspecies atrocostalis, found in bogs and adjacent open sites in the Upper Peninsula, has heavier, more pronounced black wing margins. Adults have a rapid and somewhat erratic flight typically low to the ground just above the vegetation.

Silver-bordered Fritillary
Boloria selene

Family/Subfamily: Brush-foots (Nymphalidae)/ Fritillaries (Heliconiinae)

Wingspan: 1.6–2.1" (4.1–5.3 cm)

Above: orange with black lines and spots; both wings have black borders that enclose small orange spots

Below: hindwing mottled orange and reddish brown with bands of iridescent silver spots

Sexes: similar

Egg: tiny cream eggs laid singly and somewhat haphazardly near host

Larva: dark gray with black patches, a orange-brown lateral stripe, numerous yellowish spines and two long, black prothoracic spines. Larvae overwinter.

Larval Host Plants: violets

Habitat: wet meadows, bogs, moist prairies, sedge marshes and adjacent fields and roadsides

Broods: two generations

Abundance: occasional to common; localized

Compare: Meadow Fritillary (pg. 279) lacks the broad, black dorsal wing border and the silver spot bands on the hindwing below. Bog Fritillary (pg. 275) has reddish brown ventral hindwings with a postmedian band of whitish spots.

Resident

Jan. Feb. Mar. Apr. May June July Aug. Sept. Oct. Nov. Dec.

Dorsal (above)
black, chain-like border with orange spots

Ventral (below)
distinctive metallic silver spot bands on hindwing

black submarginal spots

Dorsal

Comments: The Hoary Comma in named for the whitish gray (or hoary) color on the outer portion of the wings beneath that gives the butterfly a distinctive two-toned appearance. It is an uncommon species of boreal forest openings and sun-dappled trails found across a few scattered counties in the Upper Peninsula. The wary adults have an erratic, darting flight and frequently perch on the ground or on fallen logs or rocks. Unlike most other anglewings, both sexes may occasionally be encountered feeding at available blossoms.

Hoary Comma
Polygonia gracilis

Family/Subfamily: Brush-foots (Nymphalidae)/
True Brush-foots (Nymphalinae)

Wingspan: 1.75–2.10" (4.4–5.3 cm)

Above: tawny-orange with bold black spots, heavy dark
brown borders and highly irregular wing margins;
forewing apex extended and squared-off; hindwing
border includes a submarginal row of small yellow-
orange spots and bears a single short, stubby tail

Below: overall bark-like appearance; mottled gray and
brown with dark striations; hindwing has a silver
comma in the center; basal half of wings darker, outer
half silvery gray

Sexes: similar

Egg: green, laid singly on host leaves

Larva: black; anterior portion has reddish brown spines
and spine bases; posterior portion with the white
marks and spines

Larval Host Plants: currant and gooseberry

Habitat: coniferous forest openings, woodland roads,
forest edges and trails, adjacent open brushy areas

Broods: singe generation

Abundance: rare to uncommon

Compare: Gray Comma (pg. 311) lacks the strong two-
toned ventral pattern with the highly
contrasting silvery gray outer portion. Resident

Jan. Feb. Mar. Apr. May June July Aug. Sept. Oct. Nov. Dec.

Dorsal (above)
heavy dark borders
yellow-orange
submarginal spots

Ventral (below)
strong two-toned
appearance
silvery comma

295

Ventral   Larva

Comments: The Variegated Fritillary is another southern
resident that regularly wanders northward to temporarily colonize much of the U.S. each year. Like other
vagrants, its presence is spotty and unpredictable from
year to year. An intermediate of sorts between true
fritillaries and longwings, the butterfly's spiny larvae
are able to utilize both violets and passion flowers as
hosts. It has an affinity for just about any open, sunny
habitat and may occasionally be encountered in home
gardens. Adults have a low, directed flight but regularly
pause to nectar at available flowers.

Variegated Fritillary
Euptoieta claudia

Family/Subfamily: Brush-foots (Nymphalidae)/ Longwings (Heliconiinae)

Wingspan: 1.75–2.25" (4.4–5.7 cm)

Above: pale brownish orange with dark markings, narrow light median band and darker reddish orange base

Below: overall brown; forewing has basal orange scaling; hindwing mottled with tan, cream and dark brown; hindwing lacks silvery spots

Sexes: similar, although female is larger and has broader, more rounded wings

Egg: tiny cream eggs laid singly on host leaves and tendrils

Larva: reddish orange with black-spotted white stripes and black spines

Larval Host Plants: a variety of plants including violets, passion flower and flax

Habitat: open, sunny sites including roadsides, pastures, wet meadows, old fields and utility easements

Broods: one or more generations

Abundance: uncommon to occasional

Compare: Great Spangled Fritillary (pg. 325) and Aphrodite Fritillary (pg. 323) have large, conspicuous silvery spots on the ventral hindwing.

Visitor

| Jan. | Feb. | Mar. | Apr. | May | June | July | Aug. | Sept. | Oct. | Nov. | Dec. |

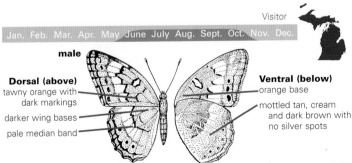

male

Dorsal (above)
tawny orange with dark markings

darker wing bases

pale median band

Ventral (below)
orange base

mottled tan, cream and dark brown with no silver spots

297

Male Female Larva

Comments: This widespread North American species
can be found in virtually any open landscape, but may
be most abundant in commercial clover or alfalfa fields
where it may occasionally become an economic pest.
Because of this strong host preference, it is often
called the Alfalfa Butterfly. It is a prolific colonizer and
readily populates new areas where naturalized or
native leguminous plants abound. Adults have a rapid,
somewhat erratic flight and scurry close to the ground
over low vegetation. Individuals produced in early
spring are generally smaller and less intensely colored
overall than summer adults.

Orange Sulphur
Colias eurytheme

Family/Subfamily: Whites and Sulphurs (Pieridae)/ Sulphurs (Coliadinae)

Wingspan: 1.6–2.4" (4.1–6.1 cm)

Above: bright yellow orange with black wing borders and black forewing cell spot; hindwing has central orange spot

Below: yellow with row of dark submarginal spots; hindwing has one or two central red-rimmed silvery spots

Sexes: similar, although female has yellow spots in broader black wing borders and are less vibrant; female is occasionally white

Egg: white, laid singly on host leaves

Larva: green with thin, cream lateral stripe and numerous short hairs

Larval Host Plants: Alfalfa, White Sweet Clover, White Clover and vetches

Habitat: open, sunny sites including roadsides, meadows, alfalfa or clover fields, parks, utility easements, vacant lots, pastures and home gardens

Broods: two or more generations

Abundance: occasional to abundant

Compare: Clouded Sulphur (pg. 345) lacks orange scaling above. White-form female Clouded and Orange may not be reliably distinguished in the field.

Resident

| Jan. | Feb. | Mar. | Apr. | May | June | July | Aug. | Sept. | Oct. | Nov. | Dec. |

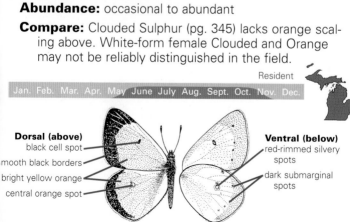

Dorsal (above)
- black cell spot
- smooth black borders
- bright yellow orange
- central orange spot

Ventral (below)
- red-rimmed silvery spots
- dark submarginal spots

299

Ventral

Larva

Comments: Considered a common, weedy butterfly, the American Lady is often overlooked despite its attractiveness. It may be encountered in just about any open, disturbed landscape. A nervous and wary butterfly, it is difficult to approach and closely observe. When disturbed, it takes off in a low, erratic flight but often returns to a nearby location just a few moments later. The larvae construct individual shelters on the host by spinning together leaves and flower heads with silk. They rest inside when not actively feeding. Although generally unable to survive northern winters, it may occasionally overwinter in southern Michigan.

American Lady
Vanessa virginiensis

Family/Subfamily: Brush-foots (Nymphalidae)/
True Brush-foots (Nymphalinae)

Wingspan: 1.75–2.40" (4.4–6.1 cm)

Above: orange with dark marks and borders; forewing
has small white spots near extended and squared-off
apex; hindwing has submarginal row of blue-centered
black spots

Below: brown with ornate, cream cobweb pattern; hindwing has two large eyespots and narrow lavender
submarginal band

Sexes: similar

Egg: small pale green eggs laid singly on upper surface
of host leaves

Larva: variable; greenish yellow with narrow black bands
to black with cream bands and numerous red-based,
branched spines; pair of prominent white spots on
each segment; pupae occasionally overwinter

Larval Host Plants: various herbaceous composites
including cudweeds, Sweet Everlasting and pussy-toes

Habitat: open, disturbed sites including roadsides, old
fields, pastures, utility easements and gardens

Broods: two or more generations

Abundance: occasional to common

Compare: Painted Lady (pg. 303) is pinker and has a row
of four small ventral hindwing eyespots.

Resident

| Jan. | Feb. | Mar. | Apr. | May | June | July | Aug. | Sept. | Oct. | Nov. | Dec. |

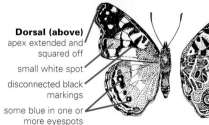

Dorsal (above)
apex extended and
squared off

small white spot

disconnected black
markings

some blue in one or
more eyespots

Ventral (below)
small white spot

ornate cobweb pattern

two large eyespots

301

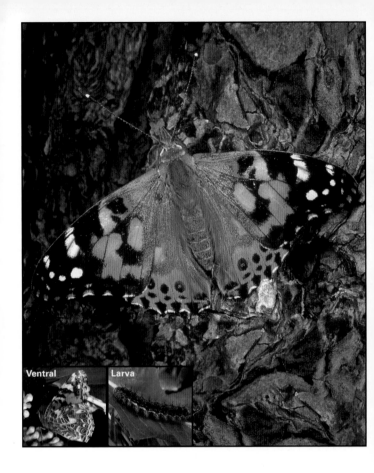

Ventral

Larva

Comments: Unable to survive freezing temperatures, the Painted Lady typically overwinters in Mexico and annually re-colonizes much of the North American continent each summer. Its occurrence in Michigan, as well as many areas in the East, is somewhat sporadic with populations varying considerably in abundance from year to year. They occasionally have huge population outbreaks. It can be found in just about any open, disturbed landscape where its weedy larval hosts abound. The adults have a rapid, erratic flight usually close to the ground but frequently stop to perch or nectar. The larvae construct individual shelters of loose webbing on the host.

Painted Lady
Vanessa cardui

Family/Subfamily: Brush-foots (Nymphalidae)/
True Brush-foots (Nymphalinae)

Wingspan: 1.75–2.40" (4.4–6.1 cm)

Above: pinkish orange with dark markings and small white spots near tip of forewing; hindwing has a submarginal row of black spots

Below: brown with cream patches in ornate cobweb pattern; hindwing has submarginal row of four small eyespots

Sexes: similar

Egg: small pale green eggs laid singly on host leaves

Larva: variable; greenish yellow with black mottling to charcoal with cream mottling and several rows of light-colored, branched spines

Larval Host Plants: wide variety of plants in several families including thistles and mallows; also Hollyhock

Habitat: open, disturbed sites including roadsides, old fields, fallow agricultural land, pastures, utility easements and gardens

Broods: two or more generations

Abundance: uncommon to common

Compare: American Lady (pg. 301) is overall more orange, has a more extended forewing apex and two large ventral hindwing eyespots.

Stray

Jan. Feb. Mar. Apr. May June July Aug. Sept. Oct. Nov. Dec.

male

Dorsal (above)
no small white spot
(as in American
Lady)

connected black
markings

Ventral (below)
ornate cobweb patter

four submarginal
eyespots

303

Ventral

Larva

Comments: This common western species extends eastward across southern Canada and just barely dips down
into the northern Great Lakes. Named for a mythologi-
cal woodland deity, the Satyr Comma is a butterfly of
sunlit boreal forest openings and stream margins where
its hosts commonly grow. It is an uncommon resident
of the Upper Peninsula and is most often encountered
as solitary individuals. The long-lived adults have an
erratic, darting flight and frequently perch on tree trunks
or on overhanging branches. They are often quite wary
and difficult to closely approach. Both sexes feed at rotting fruit, dung, carrion and tree sap. Adults overwinter.

Satyr Comma
Polygonia satyrus

Family/Subfamily: Brush-foots (Nymphalidae)/
True Brush-foots (Nymphalinae)

Wingspan: 1.8–2.4" (4.6–6.1 cm)

Above: orange to golden orange with heavy black spots; highly irregular wing margin; forewing apex is extended and squared off; hindwing has a pale margin, a pronounced submarginal row of yellow spots and bears a single short, stubby tail

Below: pale brown with fine striations, a dark median band and a narrow silver comma in center of hindwing; darker toward base

Sexes: similar

Egg: green, laid singly or in small stacks on host leaves

Larva: black; greenish white dorsal band, pale yellow lateral stripe interspersed with orange, black branched spines on the back becoming whitish along the sides

Larval Host Plants: various nettles including Stinging Nettle

Habitat: woodland clearings, forest edges and trails, and stream margins

Broods: single generation

Abundance: rare to occasional

Compare: Eastern Comma (pg. 309) has a darker hindwing margin with less pronounced golden submarginal spots.

Resident

Jan. Feb. Mar. Apr. May June July Aug. Sept. Oct. Nov. Dec.

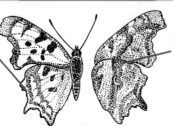

Dorsal (above)
light hindwing margin

Ventral (below)
brown with dark median band

Ventral

Comments: This somewhat reclusive species is named for the distinct row of green spots on the underside of its bark-like wings. Like other members of the genus, the Green Comma overwinters as an adult in log piles, tree hollows or even within manmade structures. As a result, the adults are long-lived and may survive for many months. Once warm weather returns, they become active and reproduce, with the resulting generation flying in early summer. A butterfly of boreal forests, it is typically encountered along sunlit woodland trails or on forested roads. Adults have an erratic, darting flight and frequently perch on the ground.

Green Comma
Polygonia faunus

Family/Subfamily: Brush-foots (Nymphalidae)/
True Brush-foots (Nymphalinae)

Wingspan: 1.9–2.4" (4.8–6.1 cm)

Above: tawny orange with bold black spots, black borders
and highly irregular wing edges; forewing apex extended
and squared off; hindwing bears a stubby tail and border
includes submarginal row of small yellow-orange spots

Below: overall mottled brown bark-like appearance; both
wings have submarginal row of small green spots;
hindwing has silver comma in the center; darker basally

Sexes: similar

Egg: green, laid singly on host leaves

Larva: variable; yellow-brown with transverse black and
yellow bands and spots, two wavy orange lateral lines
and rows of white and orange branched spines

Larval Host Plants: gooseberry, blueberry, alder, willows and birch

Habitat: coniferous and mixed forests, riparian woodlands, wooded roads and adjacent brushy areas

Broods: single generation

Abundance: uncommon to occasional

Compare: Eastern (pg. 309) and Satyr Comma (pg. 305)
have less jagged wing margins and lack the green submarginal spots on the wings below.

Resident

Jan. Feb. Mar. Apr. May June July Aug. Sept. Oct. Nov. Dec.

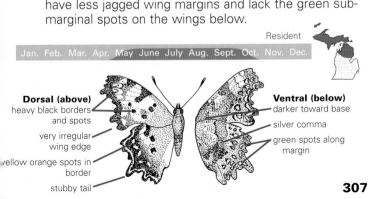

Dorsal (above)
heavy black borders
and spots

very irregular
wing edge

yellow orange spots in
border

stubby tail

Ventral (below)
darker toward base

silver comma

green spots along
margin

307

Summer

Ventral | Winter | Larva

Comments: The Eastern Comma, like its close relative the Question Mark, survives the winter as an adult hibernating in log piles, tree hollows or even within manmade structures. Once warm weather returns in spring, adults become active and reproduce with the resulting generation flying in early summer. A woodland butterfly, it inhabits riparian forests, clearings and adjacent open, brushy areas. Adults have a rapid, erratic flight and frequently perch on overhanging branches or tree trunks. They are often quite wary and difficult to closely approach. Both sexes seldom visit flowers, feeding instead at rotting fruit, dung, carrion and tree sap.

Eastern Comma
Polygonia comma

Family/Subfamily: Brush-foots (Nymphalidae)/
True Brush-foots (Nymphalinae)

Wingspan: 2.0–2.4" (5.1–6.1 cm)

Above: tawny orange with black borders and spots, irregular wing edge; forewing apex is extended and squared off; hindwing has single distinct tail; summer-form hindwing is primarily black; winter-form has increased orange

Below: seasonally variable; dead leaf appearance; summer-form is heavily mottled light and dark brown; winter-form is uniform brown with fine striations; hindwing has a single distinct curved silvery spot in center

Sexes: similar

Egg: green, laid singly or in small stacks on host leaves

Larva: variable; black to greenish brown with a white lateral band and several rows of white, branched spines

Larval Host Plants: Canadian Wood Nettle, American Elm, False Nettle, Common Hop and nettles

Habitat: deciduous forests, riparian woodlands, forest edges, parks, suburban yards and open brushy areas

Broods: two generations

Abundance: occasional to common

Compare: Question Mark (pg. 319) is larger and has silver spots shaped like a question mark in the center of the hindwing below.

Resident

Jan. Feb. Mar. Apr. May June July Aug. Sept. Oct. Nov. Dec.

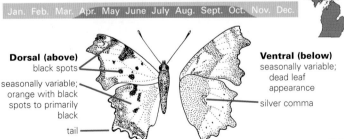

Dorsal (above)
black spots

seasonally variable; orange with black spots to primarily black

tail

Ventral (below)
seasonally variable; dead leaf appearance

silver comma

309

Ventral

Larva

Comments: This woodland butterfly is aptly named for its dull gray, highly striated wings that closely resemble tree bark. Widespread throughout the state, the Gray Comma typically occurs in small, highly localized colonies but is nonetheless a frequently encountered species. Adults have an erratic, darting flight and frequently perch on tree trunks or on overhanging branches. They are often quite wary and difficult to closely approach. Both sexes prefer to feed at rotting fruit, dung, carrion and tree sap.

Gray Comma
Polygonia progne

Family/Subfamily: Brush-foots (Nymphalidae)/
True Brush-foots (Nymphalinae)

Wingspan: 2.1–2.4" (5.3–6.1 cm)

Above: tawny orange with heavy black borders and
spots, highly irregular wing edge; forewing apex is
extended and squared off; hindwing bears a single
short, stubby tail; hindwing border encloses a submarginal row of small yellow orange spots

Below: dull gray with fine striations and anarrow silver
comma in center of hindwing; slightly darker toward
base

Sexes: similar

Egg: green, laid singly on host leaves

Larva: yellow brown with transverse black lines between
segments, dark botches and dashes, and several rows
of pale yellow and black branched spines

Larval Host Plants: gooseberry and currant

Habitat: moist woodlands, forest clearings and trails,
woodland roads, forest edges, swamps and adjacent
open, brushy areas

Broods: two generations

Abundance: occasional to common

Compare: Hoary Comma (pg. 295) has distinctive two-
toned appearance to the wings beneath with
a prominent silvery gray outer half. Resident

Jan. Feb. Mar. Apr. May June July Aug. Sept. Oct. Nov. Dec.

Dorsal (above)
irregular wing edge

yellowish orange
spots in dark
border

Ventral (below)
fine gray brown
striations

two-toned appearance

silver comma

311

Male

Female

Comments: This large and distinctive satyrine is primarily a Canadian butterfly. Its range dips southward into the U.S. from Ontario only in the northern Great Lakes. Within Michigan, Macoun's Arctic is limited only to the extreme northern confines of the state at Isle Royale. It should be looked for on open, rocky forest ridges, hilltops and margins. Adults have a quick, erratic flight and frequently perch on sunlit tree trunks or branches where they can easily be overlooked. They often bask with their wings outstretched. The larvae require two seasons to complete development; adults have synchronous flight in even-numbered years.

Macoun's Arctic
Oeneis macounii

Family/Subfamily: Brush-foots (Nymphalidae)/ Satyrs and Wood-Nymphs (Satyrinae)

Wingspan: 2.1–2.5" (5.3–6.4 cm)

Above: light orange-brown with dark brown margins; forewing has two prominent black submarginal eye-spots with white pupils (often with one or more adjacent smaller black spots); hindwing has a small black spot at the anal angle

Below: mottled brown and gray with fine striations and a darker median band

Sexes: similar, although female is larger with broader, more rounded wings

Egg: whitish, laid singly on host leaves

Larva: green to tan with brown, green and grayish stripes; larva requires two seasons to reach maturity

Larval Host Plants: currently undocumented in Michigan, likely various grasses or sedges

Habitat: woodland clearings, open pine forests, wood-land margins and trails, and adjacent roadsides

Broods: biennial; the larvae require two seasons to complete development

Abundance: rare to uncommon; local

Compare: Chryxus Arctic (pg. 197) is smaller, more golden brown above and has a mottled gray brown ventral hindwing.

Resident

Jan. Feb. Mar. Apr. May June July Aug. Sept. Oct. Nov. Dec.

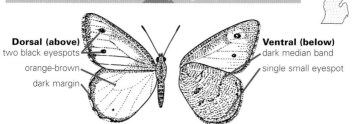

Dorsal (above)
two black eyespots
orange-brown
dark margin

Ventral (below)
dark median band
single small eyespot

313

Ventral

Larva

Comments: The Atlantis Fritillary is primarily a Northland
butterfly of boreal forest openings and adjacent fields
and meadows. Its range dips southward into northern
portions of Michigan where it may regularly be the
most abundant member of the genus. Like other fritillaries, the adults have a swift and rapid flight but
readily pause to feed at available flowers. Males patrol
forest margins, firebreaks and woodland roads for
females.

Atlantis Fritillary
Speyeria atlantis

Family/ Subfamily: Brush-foots (Nymphalidae)/ Longwings and Fritillaries (Heliconiinae)

Wingspan: 2.40–2.75" (6.1–7.0 cm)

Above: orange with black spots and broad, solid black borders

Below: hindwing is dark purplish brown with metallic silver spots and a narrow yellowish tan submarginal band

Sexes: similar, although female is typically larger and more golden orange

Egg: small cream eggs are laid singly and somewhat haphazardly on or near host

Larva: dark brown with fine yellowish striations, black blotches, a black dorsal stripe outlined in yellow and numerous orange-brown spines

Larval Host Plants: various violets

Habitat: open woodlands, forest clearings, margins and trails, old fields, wet meadows and roadsides

Abundance: occasional to common

Broods: single generation

Compare: Aphrodite Fritillary (pg. 323) is larger and lacks the solid black dorsal wing borders.

Resident

Jan. Feb. Mar. Apr. May June July Aug. Sept. Oct. Nov. Dec.

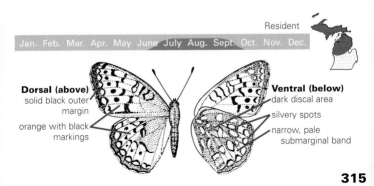

Dorsal (above)
solid black outer margin

orange with black markings

Ventral (below)
dark discal area

silvery spots

narrow, pale submarginal band

315

Male

Ventral   Winter   Larva

Comments: This southern resident is a rare vagrant to Michigan. Its name comes from one of its primary larval hosts. Although brilliant reddish orange dorsally, the leaf-like pattern of its wings below provides superb camouflage. It produces distinct seasonal forms that vary in wing shape and to a lesser extent in ground color. Individuals produced late in the season survive the winter in reproductive diapause. Adults have a strong, darting flight and perch with wings closed on tree trunks, branches or on the ground. They can be quite a challenge to find, let alone closely approach. It does not nectar at flowers but prefers rotting fruit and sap.

Goatweed Leafwing
Anaea andria

Family/Subfamily: Brush-foots (Nymphalidae)/ Leafwings (Charaxinae)

Wingspan: 2.25–3.00" (5.7–7.6 cm)

Above: pointed forewings and hindwing tail; male is bright reddish orange; female is lighter orange with dark markings and pale band along wing margins

Below: seasonally variable; brownish gray resembling a dead leaf; winter-form is more heavily patterned, has longer hindwing tails and a more pronounced hooked forewing apex

Sexes: similar, although female is lighter with more extensive dorsal markings

Egg: gray-green, laid singly on host leaves

Larva: gray-green with light head and numerous tiny light spots

Larval Host Plants: Goatweed

Habitat: forest clearings, woodland edges and adjacent open areas

Broods: one or more generations are possible

Abundance: rare

Compare: Question Mark (pg. 319) has irregular wing edges, an extended and squared-off forewing apex and black dorsal forewing spots.

Stray

Jan. Feb. Mar. Apr. May June July Aug. Sept. Oct. Nov. Dec.

male

Dorsal (above)
hooked apex

tail

Ventral (below)
dead leaf appearance

Summer

Ventral

Winter

Larva

Comments: This large anglewing gets its name from the small silvery hindwing marks that resemble (with some imagination) a rudimentary question mark. In sharp contrast to its bright orange dorsal surface, the wings below are cryptically mottled with brown to help the butterfly resemble a dead leaf when at rest. Found primarily in woodlands, adults have a strong, rapid flight but frequently alight on overhanging branches, tree trunks or leaf litter. Wary and nervous, they are often difficult to closely approach. Males are inquisitive and aggressively investigate virtually any passing insects. Both sexes visit rotting fruit, dung, carrion and sap.

Question Mark
Polygonia interrogationis

Family/Subfamily: Brush-foots (Nymphalidae)/
True Brush-foots (Nymphalinae)

Wingspan: 2.25–3.00" (5.7–7.6 cm)

Above: orange with black spots, narrow lavender borders and irregular, jagged edges; forewing apex is extended and squared off; seasonally variable; summer-form hindwing is primarily black; winter-form has increased orange on hindwing and a longer tail

Below: brown to pinkish brown dead leaf appearance; hindwing has two small median silvery spots that form a question mark; summer-form is darker and heavily pattered below; winter-form plain violet brown

Sexes: similar

Egg: green, laid singly or in small piles on host leaves

Larva: gray to black with orange and cream stripes and spots and several rows of branched spines

Larval Host Plants: Common Hackberry, American Elm, False Nettle, Common Hop and Stinging Nettle

Habitat: deciduous forests, moist woodlands, woodland roads, forest edges and adjacent open areas

Broods: two generations

Abundance: occasional to common

Compare: Eastern Comma (pg. 309) has a comma-shaped silver spot in the center of the hindwing below.

Resident

Jan. Feb. Mar. Apr. May June July Aug. Sept. Oct. Nov. Dec.

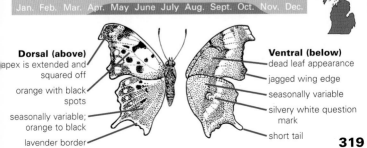

Dorsal (above)
apex is extended and squared off

orange with black spots

seasonally variable; orange to black

lavender border

Ventral (below)
dead leaf appearance

jagged wing edge

seasonally variable

silvery white question mark

short tail

319

Male

Ventral

Larva

Comments: The colorful Viceroy is usually found in or near wetland areas in close proximity to its larval hosts. Males perch on overhanging branches and occasionally dart out to investigate passing objects or to take periodic exploratory flights. Both sexes tend to be somewhat wary and difficult to closely approach. Although once thought to be a palatable mimic of the distasteful Monarch, studies have shown that both species are actually distasteful to certain predators. Adults are often encountered at a variety of flowers but will also feed at dung, carrion, fermenting fruit and tree sap.

Viceroy
Limenitis archippus

Family/Subfamily: Brush-foots (Nymphalidae)/ Admirals and Relatives (Limenitidinae)

Wingspan: 2.6–3.2" (6.6–8.1 cm)

Above: orange with black markings, veins and broad wing borders; borders contain central row of small, white spots; forewing has black postmedian band and white spots; hindwing has distinct thin, black post- median line

Below: as above with lighter orange coloration and increased white markings

Sexes: similar

Egg: gray-green, laid singly on tip of host leaves

Larva: mottled green, brown and cream with two long, knobby horns on thorax

Larval Host Plants: various willows; also Cottonwood

Habitat: pond edges, wetlands, roadside ditches and moist areas supporting willows

Broods: two generations

Abundance: occasional to common; localized

Compare: Monarch (pg. 329) is larger and lacks black postmedian hindwing line.

Resident

| Jan. | Feb. | Mar. | Apr. | May | June | July | Aug. | Sept. | Oct. | Nov. | Dec. |

Dorsal (above)
white spots
thin black line
white spots in black border

Ventral (below)
orange with black bands containing white spots

Ventral   Larva

Comments: This widespread northern species displays
a stronger preference for prairie habitats than its more
abundant relative the Great Spangled Fritillary with
which it is easily confused. As a result, the Aphrodite
Fritillary tends occur in smaller, more highly localized
populations across Michigan, but may still be quite
common when encountered. Individuals are also less
likely to wander far from suitable habitat areas. Adults
have a swift, directed flight and are best observed at
flowers. A patrolling species, males actively search for
females, often following long, circular routes.

Aphrodite Fritillary
Speyeria aphrodite

Family/Subfamily: Brush-foots (Nymphalidae)/ Longwing Butterflies (Heliconiinae)

Wingspan: 2.7–3.3" (6.9–8.4 cm)

Above: bright orange with heavy black lines and spots

Below: hindwing is dark orange brown to reddish brown with numerous large metallic silver spots and a narrow (sometimes almost nonexistent) yellowish submarginal band

Sexes: similar, although female is larger with darker brown wing bases, more pronounced black markings and paler golden orange wings

Egg: tiny cream eggs laid singly and somewhat haphazardly near host leaves

Larva: velvety black with several rows of black spines; lateral two rows of spines reddish brown with black tips

Larval Host Plants: various violets

Habitat: open woodlands, old fields, moist meadows, prairies, pastures, forest edges and roadsides

Broods: single generation

Abundance: occasional to common

Compare: Great Spangled Fritillary (pg. 325) is slightly larger and has wider, more prominent yellowish submarginal band on the ventral hindwing.

Resident

Jan. Feb. Mar. Apr. May June July Aug. Sept. Oct. Nov. Dec.

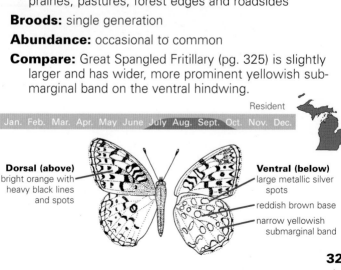

Dorsal (above)
bright orange with heavy black lines and spots

Ventral (below)
large metallic silver spots

reddish brown base

narrow yellowish submarginal band

323

Female

Female   Larva

Comments: The Great Spangled Fritillary is easily the most conspicuous and widespread fritillary in Michigan. It is not nearly as localized and habitat-restricted as other members of the genus. Adults have a strong, directed flight but avidly visit flowers, being particularly fond of milkweed, Bergamot and thistles. Males typically emerge several weeks before females. Females may be on the wing as early as the beginning of July, but do not lay eggs until late summer and often fly well into September. Newly hatched larvae overwinter. Subspecies krautwurmi, found primarily in the Upper Peninsula, has distinctively pale females.

Great Spangled Fritillary
Speyeria cybele

Family/Subfamily: Brush-foots (Nymphalidae)/
Longwing Butterflies (Heliconiinae)

Wingspan: 2.9–3.8" (7.1–9.7 cm)

Above: bright orange with heavy black lines and spots

Below: variable; hindwing is dark orange brown to brown
with numerous large metallic silver spots and a broad
yellowish submarginal band

Sexes: similar, although female is larger with darker
brown wing bases, more pronounced black markings
and paler golden orange to pale yellowish wings

Egg: tiny cream eggs laid singly and somewhat haphazardly on host leaves

Larva: velvety black with several rows of reddish orange-
based black spines

Larval Host Plants: various violets

Habitat: open deciduous woodlands, forest margins,
roadsides, pastures, old fields, wet meadows, prairies
and utility easements

Broods: single generation

Abundance: occasional to abundant

Compare: Aphrodite Fritillary (pg. 323) is smaller, less
common and has a narrower yellowish submarginal
band on the ventral hindwing.

Resident

Jan. Feb. Mar. Apr. May June July Aug. Sept. Oct. Nov. Dec.

Dorsal (above)
heavy black lines and
spots

darker base

Ventral (below)
large metallic silver
spots

wide submarginal
yellowish band

325

Female

Ventral

Larva

Comments: The beautiful Regal Fritillary has disappeared
from much of its previous eastern range as a result of
expanding agriculture, urban development and lack of
proper habitat management. It now serves as a charis-
matic icon for prairie conservation. Once relatively
widespread across many southern counties, it is currently listed as endangered by the Michigan Department
of Natural Resources and may be extirpated from the
state. Adults have a fast, steady flight and maneuver
low over open fields. Individuals often wander exten-
sively and may be encountered far from their population
of origin. It is exceedingly fond of flowers.

Regal Fritillary
Speyeria idalia

Family/Subfamily: Brush-foots (Nymphalidae)/
Longwing Butterflies (Heliconiinae)

Wingspan: 3.1–4.0" (7.9–10.2 cm)

Above: forewing is bright reddish orange with black
markings; hindwing is black with a bluish cast; male
has an outer row of orange spots and a inner row of
white spots on hindwing

Below: hindwing is dark brown with numerous black-
edged white (not silvery) spots

Sexes: similar, although female is larger with both rows
of hindwing spots white

Egg: tiny cream eggs laid singly and somewhat haphazardly near host leaves

Larva: gray black; ochre yellow to reddish orange dorsal
band and similar colored lateral mottling; dorsal spines
are silvery white with black tips while those along the
sides have orange bases

Larval Host Plants: Bird's-foot Violet

Habitat: tallgrass prairie, wet meadows, marshes and
adjacent fields, roadsides and pastures

Broods: single generation

Abundance: rare; possibly extirpated; localized

Compare: unique

No longer present

| Jan. | Feb. | Mar. | Apr. | May | June | July | Aug. | Sept. | Oct. | Nov. | Dec. |

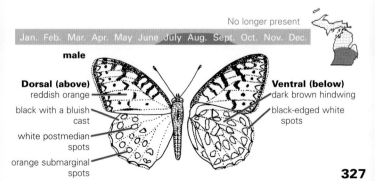

male

Dorsal (above)
reddish orange

black with a bluish
cast

white postmedian
spots

orange submarginal
spots

Ventral (below)
dark brown hindwing

black-edged white
spots

327

Female

Ventral

Larva

Comments: The Monarch is undoubtedly the most familiar and widely recognized butterfly in North America. Its annual fall mass migration is one of the greatest natural events undertaken by any organism on Earth. Adults have a strong, soaring flight and are abundant garden visitors. The striped larvae feed on plants in the Milkweed family from which they sequester toxic chemicals that render them and the resulting adults distasteful to certain predators. The adult butterflies advertise this unpalatability in dramatic fashion with their bold orange and black coloration.

Monarch
Danaus plexippus

Family/Subfamily: Brush-foots (Nymphalidae)/ Milkweed Butterflies (Danainae)

Wingspan: 3.5–4.0" (8.9–10.2 cm)

Above: orange with black veins and wing borders; black borders have two rows of small white spots; male has small black androconial scent patch on center of hindwing

Below: as above with lighter orange coloration

Sexes: similar; female lacks black scent patch

Egg: white, laid singly on host leaves or flowers

Larva: white with transverse black and yellow stripes; there is a pair of long, black filaments on each end

Larval Host Plants: various milkweeds including Swamp Milkweed and Common Milkweed

Habitat: open, sunny locations including old fields, roadsides, utility easements, meadows, prairies, agricultural land, parks and gardens

Broods: two or more generations

Abundance: occasional to common

Compare: Viceroy (pg. 321) is smaller and has a black postmedian line through the hindwing.

Resident

Jan. Feb. Mar. Apr. May June July Aug. Sept. Oct. Nov. Dec.

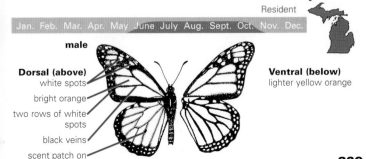

male

Dorsal (above)
white spots
bright orange
two rows of white spots
black veins
scent patch on males only

Ventral (below)
lighter yellow orange

329

Ventral

Larva

Comments: The Common Checkered-Skipper is widespread and generally abundant throughout much of the
central and southern U.S. It regularly expands its range
northward each year to temporarily colonize much of
the Midwest, where it tends to be most frequently
encountered in late summer and early fall. The occurrence of this vagrant within Michigan fluctuates on a
seasonal basis. Look for it in the southernmost counties where it can at times be fairly numerous. Adults
have a fast, erratic flight but alight frequently on low
vegetation. The nervous and combative males seem to
continuously engage one another in a frenzy of activity.

Common Checkered-Skipper
Pyrgus communis

Family/Subfamily: Skippers (Hesperiidae)/
Spread-wing Skippers (Pyrginae)

Wingspan: 0.75–1.25" (1.9–3.2 cm)

Above: male is black with numerous small, white spots
and some bluish white scaling on base of wings and
thorax; female is dark brown with reduced white scaling

Below: white with tan to brown irregular bands and
spots

Sexes: similar, although female has reduced white
markings

Egg: pale green, laid singly on host leaves

Larva: gray-green with dark dorsal stripe, light side
stripes and black head

Larval Host Plants: various mallow family plants
including Common Mallow

Habitat: open, disturbed sites including roadsides, old
fields, utility easements and fallow agricultural land

Broods: one or more generations

Abundance: uncommon to common

Compare: Grizzled Skipper (pg. 45) appears darker overall with less extensive white spotting; dorsal forewing
lacks complete submarginal row of small white spots;
primarily restricted to northern counties of the Lower
Peninsula.

Visitor

| Jan. | Feb. | Mar. | Apr. | May | June | July | Aug. | Sept. | Oct. | Nov. | Dec. |

Dorsal (above)
fringe checkered to
apex

generally black and
white above

marginal spots much
smaller than those
in submarginal row

Ventral (below)
distinct bands

paler below

331

Dorsal

Larva

Comments: The West Virginia White is a small, ghostly white butterfly of early spring. Unlike most other members of the family, it is primarily restricted to rich, moist woodlands. As a result, it tends to be a poor pioneer species that is reluctant to cross large expanses of open habitat to colonize nearby patches of available woodland or second growth forest. Adults have a low, weak flight and maneuver slowly low to the ground along the forest floor, stopping occasionally to nectar. Males frequently puddle at damp ground along woodland trails or roads.

West Virginia White
Pieris virginiensis

Family/Subfamily: Whites and Sulphurs (Pieridae)/ Whites (Pierinae)

Wingspan: 1.2–1.6" (3.0–4.1 cm)

Above: unmarked white to smoky white with black scaling along costal margin and wing bases

Below: hindwings white with brown gray scaling along veins

Sexes: similar, although female typically appears more smoky gray on the wings above

Egg: greenish white, laid singly on underside of leaves

Larva: gray green with longitudinal yellow orange stripes and covered with small black dots

Larval Host Plants: toothworts

Habitat: rich, moist deciduous woodlands, forest edges and occasionally adjacent meadows or open areas

Broods: single generation

Abundance: uncommon to occasional; locally common

Compare: The Cabbage White (pg. 343) has charcoal wingtips, one or two postmedian black spots on the dorsal forewing and inhabits open, disturbed areas. Mustard White (pg. 341) has yellow at the base of the ventral hindwing and a more pointed forewing apex.

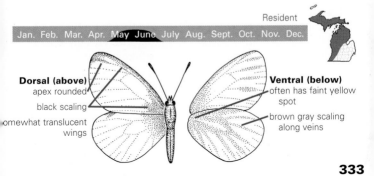

Resident

Jan. Feb. Mar. Apr. May June July Aug. Sept. Oct. Nov. Dec.

Dorsal (above)
apex rounded

black scaling

somewhat translucent wings

Ventral (below)
often has faint yellow spot

brown gray scaling along veins

Ventral   Larva

Comments: This delicate species is one of our earliest
spring butterflies. It tends to be local and uncommon
throughout its Michigan range and is typically encountered in dry habitats. Adults maneuver close to the
ground with a direct and somewhat rapid flight.
Freshly emerged individuals typically have a pinkish or
rosy flush on the ventral hindwing, which fades with
age. Both sexes readily visit a variety of spring flowers.

Olympia Marble
Euchloe olympia

Family/Subfamily: Whites and Sulphurs (Pieridae)/ Whites (Pierinae)

Wingspan: 1.25–1.75" (3.2–4.4 cm)

Above: white with black scaling at bases; forewing has charcoal apex and black cell-end bar; hindwing often has faint black scaling at vein endings

Below: hindwing is white with yellow-green marbling; fresh individuals have a pinkish flush near the base of the hindwing

Sexes: similar

Egg: white, laid singly on host leaves or flower buds

Larva: gray with a yellow stripe, a yellow-white lateral stripe and numerous black dots

Larval Host Plants: various rockcresses

Habitat: dry, sandy habitats such as semi-open oak woodlands, pine-oak barrens and lakeshore dunes

Broods: single generation

Abundance: rare to occasional

Compare: unlikely to be confused with any other Michigan butterfly

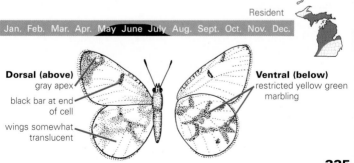

Resident

Jan. Feb. Mar. Apr. May June July Aug. Sept. Oct. Nov. Dec.

Dorsal (above)
gray apex
black bar at end of cell
wings somewhat translucent

Ventral (below)
restricted yellow green marbling

335

Male

Female

Larva

Comments: The Checkered White is an infrequent and
sporadic temporary seasonal colonist of Michigan, being
much more abundant in the southern and western U.S.
As a result, populations often fluctuate from year to
year and tend to be most numerous late in the season.
Adults have a quick, erratic flight and can often be a
challenge to closely approach. The sexes differ dramatically in the amount of dark scaling on the wings and can
generally be told apart even from a distance. Individuals
produced in early spring or late fall (under cooler conditions and shorter daylengths) are typically smaller and
have more heavily patterned ventral hindwings.

Checkered White
Pontia protodice

Family/Subfamily: Whites and Sulphurs (Pieridae)/
Whites (Pierinae)

Wingspan: 1.25–2.00" (3.2–5.1 cm)

Above: male is white with charcoal markings on
forewing and immaculate hindwing; female is grayish
white with extensive black or grayish brown checkered
markings on both wings

Below: hindwings white with grayish markings and yellow-green scaling along the veins; seasonally variable;
cool season individuals are more heavily patterned

Sexes: similar, although female has more black markings

Egg: yellow, laid singly on host leaves or flowers

Larva: gray; longitudinal yellow-orange stripe, black dots

Larval Host Plants: various mustard family plants
including Virginia Peppergrass and Shepherd's Purse

Habitat: open, disturbed sites including roadsides, pastures, utility easements, railroad rights-of-way, vacant
fields and fallow agricultural land

Broods: two or more generations

Abundance: rare to occasional

Compare: Cabbage White (pg. 343) has charcoal
wingtips and distinctive single or double dorsal
forewing spots. Western White (*Pontia occidentalis*)
has a continuous black postmedian spot
band on the dorsal forewing.

Visitor

| Jan. | Feb. | Mar. | Apr. | May | June | July | Aug. | Sept. | Oct. | Nov. | Dec. |

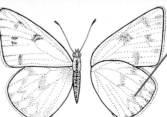

male

Dorsal (above)
white with black
checkered pattern

Ventral (below)
seasonally variable;
cool season forms
are more heavily
patterned

Dorsal **Larva**

Comments: The Large Marble and other members of
the genus Euchloe are named for their distinctive retic-
ulate ventral hindwing pattern. Although widespread
and often common throughout the mountain West, it
extends across eastern North America in a narrow
band along southern Canada and the Upper Great
Lakes to south-central Ontario. Michigan records are
limited solely to Isle Royale, although it is possible that
other Upper Peninsula populations exist. Adults
maneuver close to the ground with a somewhat lazy,
zigzag flight.

Large Marble
Euchloe ausonides

Family/Subfamily: Whites and Sulphurs (Pieridae)/ Whites (Pierinae)

Wingspan: 1.4–2.0" (3.6–5.1 cm)

Above: white with black scaling at bases; forewing has charcoal patterned apex and black cell-end bar; the hindwing in females often has somewhat yellow cast

Below: forewing apex has greenish scaling; hindwing has extensive greenish marbling and yellow lined-veins

Sexes: similar, although the dorsal hindwing has a yellow cast in females

Egg: greenish white, laid singly on host flower buds

Larva: bluish gray with numerous black dots and longitudinal yellow and white stripes

Larval Host Plants: Drummond's Rockcress and possibly Tall Tumblemustard

Habitat: open pine woodlands, rocky outcrops, ridgetops and along forest trails

Broods: single generation

Abundance: rare and localized

Compare: Due to limited range, it is unlikely to be confused with any other Michigan butterfly.

Resident

Jan. Feb. Mar. Apr. May June July Aug. Sept. Oct. Nov. Dec.

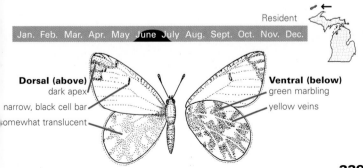

Dorsal (above)
dark apex
narrow, black cell bar
somewhat translucent

Ventral (below)
green marbling
yellow veins

339

Spring form

Dorsal

Larva

Comments: As its name suggests, the Mustard White
utilizes a variety of plants in the mustard family
(Brassicaceae) as larval hosts. It may be found
throughout the state in moist forests, brushy wetlands
and adjacent open areas. Unlike the spring-flying West
Virginia White with which it is easily confused, the
Mustard White produces two generations and may be
encountered on the wing into early September. Adults
have a somewhat low and erratic flight. They are
strongly attracted to a variety of available flowers
including those of their larval hosts.

Mustard White
Pieris oleracea (listed as Pieris napi oleracea by some authors)

Family/Subfamily: Whites and Sulphurs (Pieridae)/ Whites (Pierinae)

Wingspan: 1.20–2.25" (3.0–5.7 cm)

Above: spring form white with charcoal scaling along wing bases and at forewing apex; summer form immaculate white or white with a dusting of gray scaling along costal margin

Below: spring form white with hindwing veins crisply outlined in gray-green; summer form immaculate white; both forms have yellow at the base of the ventral hindwing

Sexes: similar

Egg: greenish white, laid singly on host leaves or stems

Larva: green with yellow longitudinal stripes and covered with small black dots

Larval Host Plants: various mustard family plants including toothwort, watercress, rockcress, mustards

Habitat: rich hardwood forests, woodland edges, bogs, brushy wetlands and adjacent moist meadows

Broods: two generations

Abundance: occasional to locally common

Compare: The Cabbage White (pg. 343) has charcoal wingtips. West Virginia White (pg. 333) has a more rounded forewing apex and has a single spring flight.

Resident

| Jan. | Feb. | Mar. | Apr. | May | June | July | Aug. | Sept. | Oct. | Nov. | Dec. |

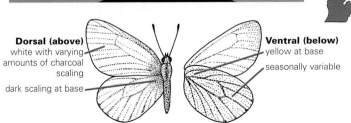

Dorsal (above)
white with varying amounts of charcoal scaling

dark scaling at base

Ventral (below)
yellow at base

seasonally variable

Male

Larva

Comments: Accidentally introduced from Europe around
1860, the Cabbage White (or European Cabbage
Butterfly) quickly radiated across much of North
America. It is generally abundant throughout Michigan.
Readily encountered in almost any open, disturbed
area, it may be particularly noticeable in home veg-
etable gardens or farmers' fields where it utilizes a
variety of cultivated plants as larval hosts. As a result,
it is one of the few butterfly species considered to be
a serious agricultural and garden pest. Adults have a
slow, awkward flight and are easy to observe. The
wings beneath are delicately shaded with yellow.

Cabbage White
Pieris rapae

Family/Subfamily: Whites and Sulphurs (Pieridae)/ Whites (Pierinae)

Wingspan: 1.5–2.0" (3.8–5.1 cm)

Above: male is white with single black postmedian forewing spot and wing tips; female is white with two black postmedian forewing spots

Below: forewing white with two black spots and yellow tips; hindwing immaculate whitish yellow

Sexes: similar, female has two black spots on forewing

Egg: white, laid singly on host leaves and flowers

Larva: green with small lateral yellow dashes and numerous short hairs

Larval Host Plants: cultivated and wild members of the mustard family including Virginia Peppergrass, Wild Mustard, Wild Radish, broccoli, cabbage and turnip

Habitat: open, disturbed sites including vacant lots, roadsides, old fields, utility easements, agricultural land and gardens; occasionally open woodland

Broods: multiple generations

Abundance: occasional to abundant

Compare: Checkered White (pg. 337) has more extensive checkered black markings. Mustard White (pg. 341) and West Virginia White (pg. 333) lack black forewing apex, black forewing spots, and prefer more wooded habitats.

Resident

Jan. Feb. Mar. Apr. May June July Aug. Sept. Oct. Nov. Dec.

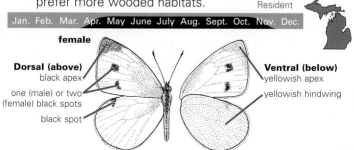

female

Dorsal (above)
black apex
one (male) or two (female) black spots
black spot

Ventral (below)
yellowish apex
yellowish hindwing

343

White-form female

Male pg. 357

Larva

Comments: Like its close relative the Orange Sulphur with which it is often flies, this aggressive colonizer has likely benefitted from the spread of agriculture and human land use practices. Although it may be encountered in just about any open habitat, it is generally most abundant in commercial clover or alfalfa fields where it may occasionally become a pest. It is sexually dimorphic and seasonably variable. Both yellow and white-form females are common. Cool season adults tend to be smaller and darker below than those of the summer generations. Adults have a quick, erratic flight. Males often puddle at moist ground or gravel.

Clouded Sulphur
Colias philodice

Family/Subfamily: Whites and Sulphurs (Pieridae)/ Sulphurs (Coliadinae)

Wingspan: 1.90–2.75" (4.8–7.0 cm)

Above: clear lemon yellow with bold, solid black wing borders and a prominent black forewing cell spot; hindwing has a central orange spot

Below: yellow to greenish yellow; row (often faint or occasionally absent) of dark submarginal spots; pink wing fringes; hindwing has central red-rimmed silvery spot and adjacent smaller satellite spot

Sexes: dissimilar; female is less vibrant, often has more black scaling and broader black borders enclosing yellow spots; also has a common white form

Egg: white, laid singly on host leaves

Larva: blue-green with a lateral cream stripe marked in black below and often containing faint red dashes

Larval Host Plants: Alfalfa, Red Clover, White Clover and White Sweet Clover

Habitat: open, sunny sites including roadsides, meadows, alfalfa fields, parks, pastures and home gardens

Broods: two or more generations

Abundance: occasional to abundant

Compare: White-form female of Orange Sulphur (pg. 299) may not be reliably distinguished in the field.

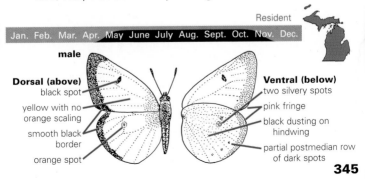

Resident

Jan. Feb. Mar. Apr. May June July Aug. Sept. Oct. Nov. Dec.

male

Dorsal (above)
black spot
yellow with no orange scaling
smooth black border
orange spot

Ventral (below)
two silvery spots
pink fringe
black dusting on hindwing
partial postmedian row of dark spots

Ventral

Larva

Comments: The long-tailed black-and-white-striped Zebra Swallowtail can be confused with no other resident butterfly. It is an uncommon species in Michigan, typically found only in the southernmost counties. Adults have a low, rapid flight and adeptly maneuver through the understory or among shrubby vegetation. Seldom found far from stands of its larval host, it is unlikely to be encountered in highly developed areas but may occasionally wander into nearby home gardens in search of nectar. It has a proportionately short proboscis and cannot feed at many long, tubular flowers. It prefers composites, and is attracted to white flowers.

Zebra Swallowtail
Eurytides marcellus

Family/Subfamily: Swallowtails (Papilionidae)/
Swallowtails (Papilioninae)

Wingspan: 2.5–4.0" (6.4–10.2 cm)

Above: white with black stripes and long, slender tails;
hindwings bear a bright red patch above the eyespot;
spring-forms are smaller, lighter and have shorter tails

Below: as above, but with a red stripe through hindwing

Sexes: similar

Egg: light green, laid singly on host leaves or budding
branches

Larva: several color forms; may be green, green with
light blue and yellow stripes or charcoal with white and
yellow stripes

Larval Host Plants: pawpaw

Habitat: moist deciduous woodlands, forest openings,
stream corridors, forest edges and adjacent clearings
and roadsides; occasionally gardens

Broods: two generations

Abundance: rare to occasional

Compare: unique

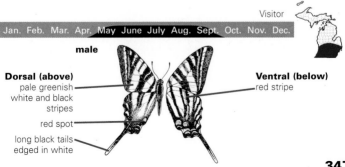

Visitor

Jan. Feb. Mar. Apr. May June July Aug. Sept. Oct. Nov. Dec.

male

Dorsal (above)
pale greenish
white and black
stripes

red spot

long black tails
edged in white

Ventral (below)
red stripe

347

Male

Dorsal Larva

Comments: As its name implies, the Dainty Sulphur is
our smallest sulphur. Although common and widespread throughout much of the Deep South, it is a rare
vagrant or infrequent temporary seasonal colonist to
Michigan and should be considered a "good find"
when encountered. The majority of all state records
are from late summer and fall. Adults have a low,
erratic flight and may be easily overlooked. The butterfly produces distinct seasonal forms that vary
considerably in ventral hindwing coloration. Individuals
produced under cool temperatures and short
daylengths have increased green scaling.

Dainty Sulphur
Nathalis iole

Family/Subfamily: Whites and Sulphurs (Pieridae)/ Sulphurs (Coliadinae)

Wingspan: 0.75–1.25" (1.9–3.2 cm)

Above: lemon yellow with black forewing tip and black bar along trailing edge of forewing; female has orange-yellow hindwings with more extensive black markings

Below: hindwings yellow with greenish markings; seasonally variable; winter-form more heavily pigmented

Sexes: similar, although black markings more extensive on female

Egg: yellow, laid singly on host leaves

Larva: green with thin, lateral yellow and lavender stripes

Larval Host Plants: Spanish Needles, Fetid Marigold and Sneezeweed

Habitat: dry and open disturbed sites including roadsides, pastures, utility easements, vacant fields and fallow agricultural land

Broods: possibly one or more generations

Abundance: rare

Compare: Little Yellow (pg. 351) is larger, has rounder wings, lacks the orange scaling along the costal margin of the ventral forewing and lacks the green scaling on the ventral hindwing.

Stray

Jan. Feb. Mar. Apr. May June July Aug. Sept. Oct. Nov. Dec.

male

Dorsal (above)
black apex
diffuse black bar

Ventral (below)
black spots
orange scaling
seasonally variable; yellow olive to heavily dusted with black

Male

Female   Male   Larva

Comments: The Little Yellow is a small yellow butterfly with a low, scurrying flight and an affinity for disturbed, open habitats. A year-round resident of the Deep South and a highly effective colonizer, it readily moves northward with the onset of warm temperatures to establish temporary breeding populations throughout much of the eastern U.S. It is a frequent but sporadic vagrant or seasonal colonist to Michigan, and may be particularly common in late summer and early fall. Like other members of the genus, it produces different seasonal forms that vary in coloration, behavior and reproductive activity.

Little Yellow
Eurema lisa

Family/Subfamily: Whites and Sulphurs (Pieridae)/ Sulphurs (Coliadinae)

Wingspan: 1.0–1.6" (2.5–4.1 cm)

Above: bright yellow with black forewing tip, narrow black wing borders and often a faint cell spot; female pale yellow to near white with lighter black markings

Below: seasonally variable; hindwings yellow to near white with pinkish red spot on outer margin (often absent on male) and several small, subtle spots or patches; winter-form darker yellow with additional pattern elements and pink wing fringe

Sexes: similar, although female is paler

Egg: white, laid singly on host leaves

Larva: green with thin, lateral cream-white stripe

Larval Host Plants: primarily Partridge Pea

Habitat: open, disturbed sites including roadsides, pastures, utility easements, vacant fields, agricultural land and sparse woodland trails

Broods: one or more generations

Abundance: rare to occasional; sometimes more abundant in southern portions of the state

Compare: Dainty Sulphur (pg. 349) is generally smaller with a prominent black bar along the trailing margin of the dorsal forewing and a distinct black post-median spot on the ventral forewing. Visitor

Jan. Feb. Mar. Apr. May June July Aug. Sept. Oct. Nov. Dec.

Dorsal (above)
black apex
small black cell spot
black border
wing color variable (yellow to whitish)

Ventral (below)
black basal spots
pinkish red spot (often absent in male)
variable dark spots
seasonally variable

351

Larva

Comments: Named for its prominent pink wing fringes, the Pink-edged Sulphur is primarily a Canadian species that enters the U.S. in the Great Lakes and far Northeast. An isolated population occurs in the northern Appalachian Mountains. Within Michigan, the butterfly is more frequently encountered in northern portions of the state and may be locally common in areas that support extensive patches of its larval hosts. Adults have a meandering, weak flight and regularly visit a variety of low-growing flowers. Partially grown larvae overwinter and complete development the following spring.

Pink-edged Sulphur
Colias interior

Family/Subfamily: Whites and Sulphurs (Pieridae)/ Sulphurs (Coliadinae)

Wingspan: 1.8–2.4" (4.6–6.1 cm)

Above: yellow with black wing borders and a small black forewing cell spot; hindwing has central faint orange spot; wing fringes pink

Below: yellow with distinct pink wing fringes; hindwing has single, pink-rimmed silver spot in center

Sexes: similar, although female has reduced black wing borders; white females are rare

Egg: white, laid singly on host leaves

Larva: green with a narrow red lateral stripe outlined in white and numerous short hairs

Larval Host Plants: blueberry

Habitat: roadsides, woodland openings, bogs, pine-oak barrens and recently cleared or burned wooded sites

Broods: single generation

Abundance: rare to occasional; locally common

Compare: Clouded Sulphur (pg. 357) has a submarginal row of dark spots and a double pink-rimmed cell spot on the ventral hindwing. May not be reliably distinguished in flight.

Resident

Jan. Feb. Mar. Apr. May June July Aug. Sept. Oct. Nov. Dec.

Dorsal (above)
yellow with black margin

Ventral (below)
distinct pink fringes

single silver spot

353

Male   Winter   Larva

Comments: The only Michigan sulphur with pointed
forewings, the Dogface is named after the pattern on
the dorsal surface of each forewing that resembles
(with some imagination) the head of a dog in profile.
Its distinctive pattern is visible only during flight; adults
rest and feed with wings tightly closed. Adults have a
strong, rapid flight but frequently stop to nectar. It is
an uncommon vagrant or temporary seasonal colonist
to southern Michigan. Its presence is highly sporadic
and varies considerably from year to year. While the
majority of sightings are of isolated individuals, small
and highly localized colonies may be encountered.

Southern Dogface

Zerene cesonia (listed as Colias cesonia by some authors)

Family/Subfamily: Whites and Sulphurs (Pieridae)/ Sulphurs (Coliadinae)

Wingspan: 1.9–2.5" (4.8–6.4 cm)

Above: yellow; forewing pointed with broad, black margin highly scalloped to form image of dog's head in profile, single back cell spot and increased black scaling on basal area; hindwing has narrow black margin

Below: hindwings seasonally variable; summer-form is yellow with two small silver spots; winter-form has increased rosy pink scaling

Sexes: similar, although black markings duller and less extensive on female

Egg: white, laid singly on host leaves

Larva: variable; plain green to green with orange lateral stripe and transverse black and yellow stripes

Larval Host Plants: False Indigo, Leadplant, White Prairie Clover, Alfalfa and clovers

Habitat: open, sunny sites including prairies, pastures, meadows, sparse woodlands, alfalfa or clover fields, roadsides and overgrown fields

Broods: one or more generations are possible

Abundance: rare; localized

Compare: All other sulphurs in Michigan lack the pointed forewing apex.

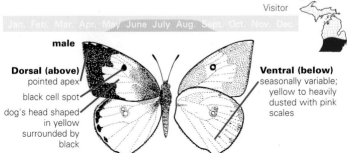

Visitor

Jan. Feb. Mar. Apr. May June July Aug. Sept. Oct. Nov. Dec.

male

Dorsal (above)
pointed apex

black cell spot

dog's head shaped in yellow surrounded by black

Ventral (below)
seasonally variable; yellow to heavily dusted with pink scales

Male

White-form female
pg. 345   Larva

Comments: Like its close relative the Orange Sulphur
with which it is often flies, this aggressive colonizer
has likely benefitted from the spread of agriculture and
human land use practices. Although it may be encountered in just about any open habitat, it is generally
most abundant in commercial clover or alfalfa fields
where it may occasionally become a pest. It is sexually
dimorphic and seasonably variable. Both yellow and
white-form females are common. Cool season adults
tend to be smaller and darker below than those of the
summer generations. Adults have a quick, erratic
flight. Males often puddle at moist ground or gravel.

Clouded Sulphur
Colias philodice

Family/Subfamily: Whites and Sulphurs (Pieridae)/ Sulphurs (Coliadinae)

Wingspan: 1.90–2.75" (4.8–7.0 cm)

Above: clear lemon yellow with bold, solid black wing borders and a prominent black forewing cell spot; hindwing has a central orange spot

Below: yellow to greenish yellow; row (often faint or occasionally absent) of dark submarginal spots; pink wing fringes; hindwing has central red-rimmed silvery spot and adjacent smaller satellite spot

Sexes: dissimilar; female is less vibrant, often has more black scaling and broader black borders enclosing yellow spots; also has a common white form

Egg: white, laid singly on host leaves

Larva: blue-green with a lateral cream stripe marked in black below and often containing faint red dashes

Larval Host Plants: Alfalfa, Red Clover, White Clover and White Sweet Clover

Habitat: open, sunny sites including roadsides, meadows, alfalfa fields, parks, pastures and home gardens

Broods: two or more generations

Abundance: occasional to abundant

Compare: Orange Sulphur (pg. 299) has at least some orange scaling above.

Resident

Jan. Feb. Mar. Apr. May June July Aug. Sept. Oct. Nov. Dec.

male

Dorsal (above)
black spot

yellow with no orange scaling

smooth black border

orange spot

Ventral (below)
two silvery spots

pink fringe

black dusting on hindwing

partial postmedian row of dark spots

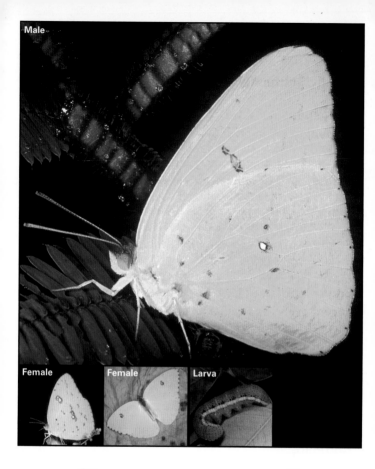

Male

Female

Female

Larva

Comments: The Cloudless Sulphur has a fast, powerful flight. Abundant in the Deep South, it regularly disperses northward to temporarily colonize much of the eastern U.S. each year, but is a rare and sporadic vagrant to Michigan. As a result, it could theoretically turn up in any county. Its presence often depends on past favorable winter weather. As fall approaches, populations throughout the East undergo a massive migration to the Florida peninsula. The annual event is one of the Southeast's most impressive natural phenomena. Adults have a very long proboscis and can feed at many tubular flowers inaccessible to other butterflies.

Cloudless Sulphur
Phoebis sennae

Family/Subfamily: Whites and Sulphurs (Pieridae)/ Sulphurs (Coliadinae)

Wingspan: 2.2–2.8" (5.6–7.1 cm)

Above: unmarked bright lemon yellow; female has broken black wing borders and black forewing spot

Below: male is greenish yellow with virtually no markings; female is yellow with pinkish brown markings and several small silver spots in center of each wing; seasonally variable; winter-form adults more heavily marked

Sexes: similar, although female is more heavily marked

Egg: white, laid singly on host leaves or flower buds

Larva: green or yellow with broad lateral yellow stripe marked with blue spots or transverse bands

Larval Host Plants: various wild and ornamental senna species including Partridge Pea, Wild Senna and Maryland Senna

Habitat: open, disturbed sites including roadsides, vacant fields, agricultural land, parks and gardens

Broods: one or more generations are possible

Abundance: rare

Compare: Clouded Sulphur (pg. 357) and Orange Sulphur (pg. 299) are smaller, have a solid black cell spot on the forewing and broad, solid black wing margins. Southern Dogface (pg. 355) has pointed forewings.

Stray

Jan. Feb. Mar. Apr. May June July Aug. Sept. Oct. Nov. Dec.

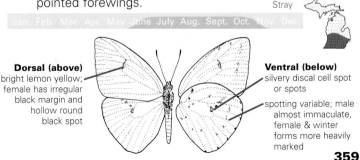

Dorsal (above)
bright lemon yellow; female has irregular black margin and hollow round black spot

Ventral (below)
silvery discal cell spot or spots

spotting variable; male almost immaculate, female & winter forms more heavily marked

359

Male

Female Ventral Larva

Comments: The smaller Canadian Tiger Swallowtail replaces the Eastern Tiger Swallowtail in northern portions of Michigan. The two species are quite similar in appearance and are easily confused, especially in areas where their ranges overlap. Unlike its southern counterpart, the Canadian Tiger Swallowtail produces a single brood and lacks a black female form. Somewhat melanic forms have been recorded but are extremely rare. The adults are swift fliers, best observed at flowers. Males avidly congregate at mud puddles or other damp ground, sometimes in large numbers, to imbibe salts and amino acids.

Canadian Tiger Swallowtail
Papilio canadensis

Family/Subfamily: Swallowtails (Papilionidae)/
   Swallowtails (Papilioninae)

Wingspan: 2.6–3.1" (6.6–7.9 cm)

Above: yellow; black forewing stripes and broad black
   wing margins; single row of yellow spots along outer
   edge of each wing; hindwing has some blue scaling

Below: yellow with black stripes and margins; hindwing
   has broad black band along anal margin, increased blue
   scaling on margins, and submarginal row of yellow to
   orangish crescents; forewing has a continuous yellow
   submarginal band; abdomen yellow with black stripes

Sexes: similar

Egg: green, laid singly on upper surface of host leaves

Larva: green with an enlarged thorax and two small false
   eyespots; early instars are mottled cream and brown
   and resemble bird droppings

Larval Host Plants: birch, Quaking Aspen, poplar, ash
   and Wild Cherry

Habitat: open woodlands, forest margins, stream corridors, gardens, parks and roadsides

Broods: single generation

Abundance: occasional to common

Compare: Eastern Tiger Swallowtail (pg. 363) is larger,
   has a yellow submarginal band broken into
   spots on the ventral forewing.

Resident

Jan. Feb. Mar. Apr. May June July Aug. Sept. Oct. Nov. Dec.

Dorsal (above)
yellow and black
   stripes

broad black border

long tail

Ventral (below)
continuous yellow
   submarginal band

broad black anal
   margin

Male

Female

Dark-form female
pg. 67

Female

Dark-form female

Larva

Comments: Living up to its name, the majestic Eastern
Tiger Swallowtail is easily recognized by its bold, black
stripes and bright yellow wings. Adults have a strong,
agile flight and often soar high in the treetops.
Although fond of woodlands and waterways, it is
equally at home in more urban areas and is a conspicuous garden visitor. Unlike many other swallowtails, the
adults seldom flutter their wings while feeding. They
instead rest on the blossom with their colorful wings
outstretched. Dark-form females mimic the toxic
Pipevine Swallowtail to gain protection from predators.
Males often congregate at moist earth or animal dung.

Eastern Tiger Swallowtail
Papilio glaucus

Family/Subfamily: Swallowtails (Papilionidae)/ Swallowtails (Papilioninae)

Wingspan: 3.5–5.5" (8.9–14.0 cm)

Above: yellow with black forewing stripes and broad black wing margins; single row of yellow spots along outer edge of each wing

Below: yellow with black stripes and black wing margins; abdomen yellow with black stripes; forewing has sub-marginal band broken into spots

Sexes: dissimilar; male always yellow but females have two color forms; yellow female has increased blue scaling in black hindwing border; dark-form female is mostly black with extensive blue hindwing markings

Egg: green, laid singly on upper surface of host leaves

Larva: green; enlarged thorax and two small false eyespots

Larval Host Plants: Wild Cherry, Hop Tree, ash and Tulip Tree

Habitat: deciduous forests, woodland margins, gardens, parks, old fields, pastures and roadsides

Broods: two or more generations

Abundance: occasional to common

Compare: Canadian Tiger Swallowtail (pg. 361) has an unbroken yellow submarginal band on the ventral forewing.

Resident

Jan. Feb. Mar. Apr. May June July Aug. Sept. Oct. Nov. Dec.

male

Dorsal (above)
yellow with black stripes

wide black border

yellow spots

long tail

Ventral (below)
band of yellow spots

yellow-orange spots

blue scaling

363

VERY RARE STRAYS

The following list of nine butterflies includes those that are considered to be very rare strays to Michigan from other areas. They are known only from isolated or very infrequent records. Nonetheless, they have the potential to be found within the state. It is likely that several other species will be added to this list in years to come, especially with the growing interest in butterfly watching.

Blue, Reakirt's . . . . *Hemiargus isola*

Fritillary, Gulf . . . . *Agraulis vanillae*

Queen . . . . *Danaus gilippus*

Sachem . . . . *Atalopedes campestris*

Skipper, Eufala . . . . *Lerodea eufala*

Skipper, Long-tailed . . . . *Urbanus proteus*

Skipper, Ocola . . . . *Panoquina ocola*

Skipper, Swarthy . . . . *Nastra lherminier*

Sulphur, Mexican . . . . *Eurema mexicana*

Sulphur, Orange-barred . . . . *Phoebis philea*

Swallowtail, Old World . . . . *Papilio machaon*

Tortoiseshell, California . . . . *Nymphalis californica*

White, Western . . . . *Pontia occidentalis*

THE BUTTERFLY NAME GAME

As the interest in butterfly watching grows, so does the way that lepidopterists study and name butterflies. As in any discipline, not all lepidopterists agree unanimously on what every species should be called. In many cases, there simply hasn't been enough study to decisively classify a butterfly, and lepidopterists are still making discoveries.

For the purposes of this guide, we are using the common names proposed by the North American Butterfly Association, a private organization of enthusiasts that promotes enjoyment and conservation of butterflies. If you explore other butterfly guides and websites, you may come across some different names. The list below includes the butterflies in Michigan for which you're most likely to encounter different names.

White, Mustard . . . . *Pieris oleracea*
You'll find this butterfly called *Pieris napi oleracea* or *Pieris napi*.

Dogface, Southern . . . . *Zerene cesonia*
Some authors list this butterfly as *Colias cesonia*.

Azure, Summer . . . . *Celastrina neglecta*
Called *Celastrina ladon neglecta* by authors who list the Summer Azure as a subspecies of the Spring Azure. Current research suggests that the Spring Azure may actually represent a complex of as many as seven or more distinct species.

Metalmark, Northern . . . . *Calephelis borealis*
There is debate about whether or not the metalmarks should be listed in their own family, or as a subfamily of Lycaenidae (Gossamer Wings). As a result, you'll often find metalmarks listed as members of the Riodinidae family.

Metalmark, Swamp . . . . *Calephelis muticum*
This butterfly may also be listed as *Calephelis mutica*. Like all other metalmarks, it is sometimes classified as a member of the Riodinidae family.

Crescent, Northern . . . . *Phyciodes selenis*
The Northern Crescent is sometimes listed as *Phyciodes cocyta*.

BUTTERFLY SOCIETIES AND OTHER RESOURCES

Butterfly societies are a great way to learn more about butterflies and moths in Michigan. They also provide resources to make valuable contacts, share your enthusiasm and get out into the field.

The Lepidopterists' Society
http://alpha.furman.edu/~snyder/snyder/lep/

North American Butterfly Association (NABA) www.naba.org

Michigan Butterflies and Skippers: A Field Guide and Reference by Mogens C. Nielsen, Michigan State Extension, Michigan State University, 1999.

PLANTS FOR YOUR BUTTERFLY GARDEN

The following are some recommended adult nectar sources and larval hosts for an Michigan butterfly garden. Most of the species are readily available at most retail garden centers or native plant nurseries. Before purchasing any landscape plant, always inquire with your local nursery personnel as to the specific soil, light, and care requirements needed for optimal growth and maintenance. Additionally, it is also a good idea to understand the plant's growth habit and eventual size at maturity before placing it in the ground. Visit a demonstration garden, a neighbor's yard or a nearby botanical garden to see how the plant looks after it has had a chance to grow a bit. Finally, remember that pesticides are not recommended for any butterfly garden as they can harm the very organisms you wish to attract. Consider using beneficial insects or insecticidal soap first before resorting to more extreme measures. If pesticides are required, always treat pest problems on a local level by applying treatment only to the infested plant and being careful of drift to neighboring vegetation.

Adult Nectar Sources

Herbaceous Perennials

Yarrow *(Achillea millefolium)*

Fragrant Giant Hyssop *(Agastache foeniculum)*

Indian Hemp *(Apocynum cannabinum)*

Swamp Milkweed *(Asclepias incarnata)*

White Swamp Milkweed *(Asclepias perennis)*

Showy Milkweed *(Asclepias speciosa)*

Common Milkweed *(Asclepias syriaca)*

Butterfly Weed *(Asclepias tuberosa)*

New England Aster (Aster novae-angliae)
False Aster (Boltonia asteroides)
Tickseed Coreopsis (Coreopsis lanceolata)
Tall Coreopsis (Coreopsis tripteris)
Purple Prairie Clover (Dalea purpurea)
Pale Purple Coneflower (Echinacea pallida)
Purple coneflower (Echinacea purpurea)
Rattlesnake Master (Eryngium yuccifolium)
Spotted Joe-Pye Weed (Eupatorium maculateum)
Common Boneset (Eupatorium perfoliatum)
Joe-Pye Weed (Eupatorium purpureum)
Blanket Flower (Gaillardia pulchella)
Western Sunflower (Helianthus occidentalis)
Rough Blazing Star (Liatris aspera)
Dotted Blazing Star (Liatris punctata)

Gayfeather (Liatris pycnostachya)
Marsh Blazing Star (Liatris spicata)
Cardinal Flower (Lobelia cardinalis)
Wild Bergamot (Monarda fistulosa)
Horsemint (Monarda punctata)
Summer Phlox (Phlox paniculata)
Gray-headed Coneflower (Ratibida pinnata)
Black-eyed Susan (Rudbeckia hirta)
Brown-eyed Susan (Rudbeckia triloba)
Cup Plant (Silphium perfoliatum)
Prairie Dock (Silphium terebinthinacium)
Stiff Goldenrod (Solidago rigida)
Showy Goldenrod (Solidago speciosa)
Blue Vervain (Verbena hastata)
Common Ironweed (Vernonia fasciculata)
New York Ironweed (Vernonia noveboracensis)
Culver's Root (Veronicastrum virginicum)

Shrubs and Trees
Bottlebrush Buckeye (Aesculus parviflora)
Red Buckeye (Aesculus pavia)
False Indigo (Amorpha fruticosa)
Butterfly Bush (Buddleia davidii)
Bluebeard (Caryopteris x chandonenis)
New Jersey Tea (Ceonothus americanus)
Buttonbush (Cephalanthus occidentalis)
Redbud (Cercis canadensis)

Sweet Pepperbush (Clethra alnifolia)
Dogwood (Cornus spp.)
Virginia Willow (Itea virginica)
Ninebark (Physocarpus opulifolius)
Black Cherry (Prunus serotina)
Chokecherry (Prunus virginiana)
Wild Azalea (Rhododendron canescens)
Viburnum (Viburnum spp.)
Chaste Tree (Vitex agnus-castus)

Annuals
Ageratum (Ageratum houstonianum)
Spider Plant (Cleome hasslerana)
Dianthus (Dianthus chinensis)
Globe Amaranth (Gomphrena globosa)
impatiens (Impatiens spp.)
Sweet Alyssum (Lobularia maritima)

Flowering Tobacco (Nicotiana alata)
Pentas (Pentas lanceolata)
Drummond Phlox (Phlox drummondii)
Tropical Sage (Salvia coccinea)
Mexican sunflower (Tithonia spp.)
Verbena (Verbena X hybrida)
Zinnia (Zinnia elegans)

Larval Host Plants

alder *(Alnus spp.)*
Alfalfa *(Medicago sativa)*
angelica *(Angelica spp.)*
Arbutus, Trailing *(Epigaea repens)*
Arrowwood, Southern *(Viburnum dentatum)*
ash *(Fraxinus spp.)*
Ash, Prickly *(Zanthoxylum americanum)*
Ash, Wafer *(Ptelea trifoliata)*
ashes *(Fraxinus spp.)*
Aspen, Quaking *(Populus tremuloides)*
aspens *(Populus spp.)*
Aster, Bushy *(Aster dumosus)*
Aster, Flat-topped White *(Aster umbellatus)*
Aster, Frost *(Aster pilosus)*
Aster, Smooth Blue *(Aster laevis)*
Aster, Waxyleaf *(Aster undulatus)*
asters *(Aster spp.)*
bean family *(Fabacea)*
Bearberry *(Arctostaphylos uva-ursi)*
Beech, American *(Fagus gandiflora)*
beggarweeds *(Desmodium spp.)*
bentgrass *(Agrostis spp.)*
Bilberry, Dwarf *(Vaccinium caespitosum)*
Birch, Bog *(Betula pumila)*
birches *(Betula spp.)*
Bitternut *(Juglans cinerea)*
Black-eyed Susan *(Rudbeckia hirta)*
blueberries *(Vaccinium spp.)*
Blueberry, Bog *(Vaccinium uliginosum)*
Blueberry, Highbush *(Vaccinium corymbosum)*
bluegrass *(Poa spp.)*
Bluegrass, Kentucky *(Poa pratensis)*
Bluestem, Big *(Andropogon gerardii)*
Bluestem, Little *(Schizachyrium scoparium)*
bluestems *(Andropogon spp.)*
Canarygrass, Reed *(Phalaris arundinacea)*

carrot family *(Apiaceae)* includes dill, fennel and parsley
cassia species *(Cassia spp.)*
Ceanothus, Redstem *(Ceanothus sanguineus)*
Cherry, Black *(Prunus serotina)*
Cherry, Pin *(Prunus pensylvanica)*
Cherry, Wild *(Prunus virginiana)*
Cinquefoil, Shrubby *(Dasiphora floribunda)*
Clover, Alsike *(Trifolium hybridum)*
Clover, Red *(Trifolium pratense)*
Clover, White *(Trifolium repens)*
Clover, White Prairie *(Dalea candida)*
Clover, White Sweet *(Melilotus alba)*
clovers *(Trifolium spp.)*
clovers, bush *(Lespedeza spp.)*
clovers, prairie *(Dalea spp.)*
clovers, sweet *(Melilotus spp.)*
coltsfoot *(Petasites spp.)*
Columbine, Wild *(Aquilegia canadensis)*
composites *(Asteraceae)*
Coneflower, Cut-leaf *(Rudbecia lanciniata)*
cordgrass *(Spartina spp.)*
Cottongrass, Tussock *(Eriophorum vaginatum var. spissum)*
Cottonwood *(Populus deltoides)*
Crabgrass, Hairy *(Digitaria sanguinalis)*
Crabgrass, Slender *(Digitaria filiformis)*
crabgrasses *(Digitaria spp.)*
Cranberry *(Vaccinium macrocarpon)*
Cranberry, Small *(Vaccinium oxycoccos)*
Crownbeard, White *(Verbesina virginica)*
cudweeds *(Gnaphalium spp.)*
currant *(Ribes spp.)*
Cutgrass, Giant *(Zizaniopsis milacea)*
Cutgrass, Rice *(Leersia oryzoides)*
Deertongue *(Dichanthelium clandestinum)*

Dill *(Anethum graveolens)*
Dock, Curly *(Rumex crispus)*
Dock, Water *(Rumex verticillatus)*
docks *(Rumex spp.)*
Dogwood, Flowering *(Cornus florida)*
Dogwood, Gray *(Cornus racemosa)*
dogwoods *(Cornus spp.)*
Elm, American *(Ulmus americana)*
elms *(Ulmus spp.)*
Fabaceae (bean family)
fennel *(Foeniculum vulgare)*
Fescue, Red *(Festuca rubra)*
Fescue, Tall *(Lolium arundinaceum)*
fescue *(Festuca spp.)*
flax *(Linum spp.)*
foxglove, false *(Agalinus spp.)*
Goatweed *(Croton argyranthemus)*
gooseberries *(Ribes spp.)*
Grass, Bermuda *(Cynodon dactylon)*
grass, brome *(Bromus spp.)*
Grass, Indian *(Sorghastrum nutans)*
Grass, Purpletop *(Tridens flavus)*
Grass, Timothy *(Phleum pratense)*
grasses *(Poaceae)*
grasses, panic *(Panicum spp.)*
Gravelweed *(Verbesina helianthoides)*
Hackberry, Common *(Celtis occidentalis)*
Hackberry, Dwarf *(Celtis tenuifolia)*
hackberries *(Celtis spp.)*
hawthorn *(Crataegus spp.)*
Hazelnut, Beaked *(Corylus cornuta)*
heath family *(Ericaceae)* includes blueberries
Hickory, Bitternut *(Carya cordiformis)*
Hickory, Pignut *(Carya glabra)*
Hickory, Shagbark *(Carya ovata)*
hickories *(Carya spp.)*
hollies *(Ilex spp.)*
Hollyhock *(Althaea rosea)*
Hop, Common *(Humulus lupulus)*
Hop Tree *(Ptelea trifoliata)*
huckleberries *(Vaccinium spp.)*

Indigo, Blue Wild *(Baptisia australis)*
Indigo, False *(Amorpha fruticosa)*
Indigo, White Wild *(Baptisia alba)*
Indigo, Wild *(Baptisia tinctoria)*
knotweed *(Polygonum spp.)*
Lamb's Quarters *(Chenopidium album)*
Laurel, Bog *(Kalmia polifolia)*
Laurel, Sheep *(Kalmia angustifolia)*
Leadplant *(Amorpha canescens)*
Leatherleaf *(Chamaedaphne calyculata)*
legumes *(Fabaceae)*
Licorice-root, Scottish *(Ligusticum scoticum)*
Locust, Black *(Robinia pseudoacacia)*
Locust, Honey *(Gleditsia triacanthos)*
Lousewort, Canadian *(Pedicularis canadensis)*
lovegrass *(Eragrostis spp.)*
Lupine, Wild *(Lupinus perennis)*
lupine *(Lupinus spp.)*
mallow family *(Malvaceae spp.)*
Mallow, Common *(Malva neglecta)*
mallows *(Malva spp.)*
mannagrass *(Glyceria spp.)*
Mannagrass, Fowl *(Glyceria striata)*
Marigold, Fetid *(Dyssodia papposa)*
meadowsweet *(Spiraea spp.)*
milk peas *(Galactia spp.)*
milkweed family *(Asclepias spp.)*
Milkweed, Common *(Asclepias syriaca)*
Milkweed, Swamp *(Asclepias incarnata)*
Milkvetch, Canadian *(Astragalus canadensis)*
milkvetch *(Astragalus spp.)*
mustard family *(Brassicaceae)*
Mustard, Wild *(Brassica campestris)*
mustards *(Brassica spp.)*
Nettle, Canadian Wood *(Laportea canadensis)*
Nettle, False *(Boehmeria cylindrica)*
Nettle, Stinging *(Urtica dioica)*

nettles *(Urtica spp.)*
Oak, Black *(Quercus velutina)*
Oak, Bur *(Quercus macrocarpa)*
Oak, Northern Red *(Quercus rubra)*
Oak, Red *(Quercus rubra)*
Oak, Scarlet *(Quercus coccinea)*
Oak, White *(Quercus alba)*
oaks *(Quercus spp.)*
Oatgrass, Poverty *(Danthonia spicata)*
Orchardgrass *(Dactylis glomerata)*
panic grasses *(Panicum spp.)*
parsley *(Petroselinium crispum)*
Parsnip, Wild *(Pastinaca sativa)*
passion flowers *(Passiflora spp.)*
pawpaws *(Asimina spp.)*
pea *(Lathyrus spp.)*
Pea, Cream *(Lathyrus ochroleucus)*
Pea, Partridge *(Cassia fasciculata)*
Peanut, Hog *(Amphicarpa bracteata)*
Pellitory *(Parietaria floridana)*
Peppergrass, Field *(Lepidium campestre)*
Peppergrass, Virginia *(Lepidium virginicum)*
pigweed *(Amaranthus spp.)*
Pine, Eastern White *(Pinus strobus)*
Pine, Jack *(Pinus banksiana)*
pines *(Pinus spp.)*
pipevines *(Aristolochia spp.)*
Plantain, Narrowleaf *(Plantago lanceolata)*
plantains *(Plantago spp.)*
Plum, American *(Prunus americana)*
Plumegrass, Silver *(Erianthus alopecuroidum)*
poplars *(Populus spp.)*
pussy-toes *(Antennaria spp.)*
Queen Anne's Lace *(Daucus carota)*
Radish, Wild *(Raphanus raphanistrum)*
Ragweed, Great *(Ambrosia trifida)*
Ragwort, Round-leaf *(Senecio obovatus)*
Redbud *(Cercis canadensis)*
Reed, Common *(Phragmites australis)*

Rice, Annual Wild *(Zizania aquatica)*
rockcress *(Arabis spp.)*
Rockcress, Drummond's *(Arabis drummondi)*
rose family *(Rosacea)*
Rosemary, Bog *(Andromeda polifolia)*
Sassafras *(Sassafras albidum)*
Sedge, Beaked *(Carex rostrata)*
Sedge, Eastern Narrowleaf *(Carex amphibola)*
Sedge, Hairy *(Carex lacustris)*
Sedge, Pennsylvania *(Carex pensylvanica)*
Sedge, Upright *(Carex stricta)*
sedges *(Carex spp.)*
Senna, Maryland *(Cassia marilandica)*
Senna, Wild *(Cassia hebecarpa)*
senna species *(Cassia spp.)*
serviceberry *(Amelanchier spp.)*
Shepherd's Purse *(Capsella bursa-pastoris)*
Shorthusk, Bearded *(Brachyelytrum erectum)*
Sida *(Sida acuta)*
Snakeroot, Virginia *(Aristolochia serpentaria)*
Sneezeweed *(Helenium autumnale)*
Sorrel, Sheep *(Rumex acetosella)*
Spanish Needles *(Bidens alba)*
Spicebush *(Lindera benzoin)*
Spikerush, Elliptic *(Eleocharis elliptica)*
Strawberry, Virginia *(Fragaria virginiana)*
Sumac, Staghorn *(Rhus typhina)*
Sumac, Winged *(Rhus copallina)*
sumacs *(Rhus spp.)*
sunflowers *(Helianthus spp.)*
Sweet Everlasting *(Gnaphalium obtusifolium)*
Switchgrass *(Panicum virgatum)*
Tea, Bog Labrador *(Ledum groenlandicum)*
Tea, Jersey *(Ceanothus herbaceus)*
Tea, New Jersey *(Ceanothus americana)*

Thistle, Swamp *(Cirsium muticum)*
thistles *(Cirsium spp.)*
toadflax *(Linaria spp.)*
toothworts *(Dentaria spp.)*
Tulip Tree *(Liriodendron tulipifera)*
Tumblemustard, Tall *(Sisymbrium altissimum)*
Turtlehead *(Chelone glabra)*
vegetables (broccoli, cabbage, cauliflower, turnips and others)
Velvetgrass, Common *(Holcus lanatus)*
Vetch, Crown *(Coronilla varia)*
vetches *(Vinca spp.)*
viburnum *(Viburnum spp.)*
Viburnum, Mapleleaf *(Viburnum acerifolium)*
Violet, Bird's-foot *(Viola pedata)*
violets *(Viola spp.)*
Walnut, Black *(Juglans nigra)*
walnuts *(Juglans spp.)*
watercress *(Rorippa nasturtium-aquaticum)*
Whitegrass *(Leersia virginica)*
willows, scrub *(Salix spp.)*
willows *(Salix spp.)*
Wing-stem *(Verbesina alternifolia)*
wisterias *(Wisteria spp.)*
Witchgrass, Fall *(Digitaria cognata)*
Woodoats, Indian *(Chasmanthium latifolium)*

CHECKLIST/INDEX

Use the boxes to check the butterflies you've seen.

ABOUT THE AUTHOR

Jaret C. Daniels, Ph.D., is a professional nature photographer and entomologist at the University of Florida specializing in the ecology and conservation biology of Lepidoptera. He has authored numerous scientific papers, popular articles and books on butterflies, insects, wildlife conservation and butterfly gardening. He currently lives in Gainesville, Florida, with his wife Stephanie.